John Sweney

# Songs of love and praise No. 2

For use in meetings for Christian worship or work

John Sweney

**Songs of love and praise No. 2**
*For use in meetings for Christian worship or work*

ISBN/EAN: 9783337266455

Printed in Europe, USA, Canada, Australia, Japan

Cover: Foto ©Thomas Meinert / pixelio.de

More available books at **www.hansebooks.com**

# SONGS OF LOVE AND PRAISE,

## — No. 2. —

FOR USE IN

MEETINGS FOR CHRISTIAN WORSHIP OR WORK.

EDITORS:

JOHN R. SWENEY, WM. J. KIRKPATRICK

AND H. L. GILMOUR.

"*Love is the golden chain that binds the happy souls above.*"

JOHN J. HOOD,

PHILADELPHIA: 1024 Arch St. | CHICAGO: 910 W. Madison St.

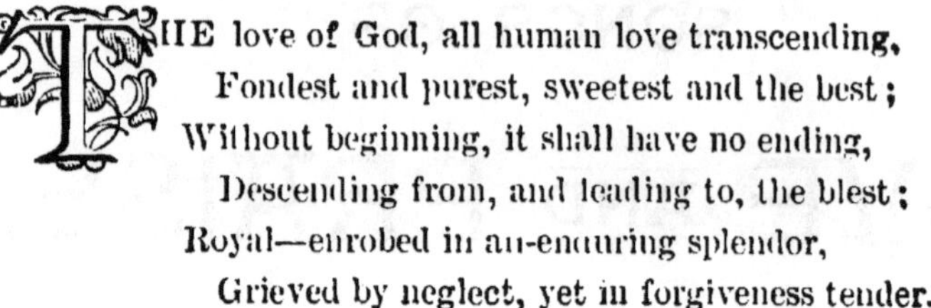

THE love of God, all human love transcending,
Fondest and purest, sweetest and the best;
Without beginning, it shall have no ending,
Descending from, and leading to, the blest;
Royal—enrobed in an-enduring splendor,
Grieved by neglect, yet in forgiveness tender.

Bound, ransomed hearts! High joy excludes the sadness
All tongues enthused, extol eternal love;
Enwreathed with smiles comes tripping sunlit gladness,
Each blessed note an echo from above·
While "Songs of Love and Praise," mingling together,
Increase the bliss of heaven, always, FOREVER!

E. H. STOKES

—No. 2.—

# Songs of Love and Praise.

## In that City.

C. J. B. | Chas. J. Butler.

1. O'er death's sea, in yon blest city, There's a home for ev-'ry one;
2. Here we've no a-bid-ing city, Mansions here will soon de-cay;
3. I have loved ones in that city, Those who left me years a-go;
4. T'ward that pure and ho-ly city Oft my long-ing eyes I cast;
Purchas'd with a price most costly, 'Twas the blood of God's dear Son.
But that cit-y God's built firmly, It can nev-er pass a-way.
They with joy are wait-ing for me, Where no farewell tears e'er flow.
Je-sus whispers sweet-ly to me, Heav'n is yours when earth is past.
CHORUS.
In that cit-y— bright cit-y, Soon with loved ones I shall be;
And with Jesus live for-ev-er, In that cit-y beyond death's sea.

"Look Up! and Praise the Lord!"
As the sainted David B. Updegraff looked at the heads of the penitents at Mt. Lake Park, July 10, 1893, he said, "Look Up! and Praise the Lord."
Fanny J. Crosby.
H. L. Gilmour.
1. Look up, O wea - ry, trembling one, With doubt and fear oppressed,
2. Look up, O weak, de - sponding one, Tho' chrushed thy heart may be,
3. Look up, the clouds are breaking now, The storm is pass- ing o'er,
Lay down thy bur - den at the cross, In Je - sus find thy rest;
Re - mem- ber in thy dark- est hour There's One who cares for thee;
The winds are hushed, the waves are still, The surg - es roll no more;
Be- lieve, and yield with- out re- serve O - bedience to his word,
Hold fast to him, thy dear- est friend, Lean sweetly on his word,
A - bide in him who nev - er fails To keep his promised word,
Fine.
And in the ful- ness of his love "Look up, and praise the Lord!"
And with a sim - ple, trusting faith "Look up, and praise the Lord!"
And with thy last, ex - piring breath "Look up, and praise the Lord!"
D.S.—In joy or grief, in storm or calm, "Look up, and praise the Lord!"
CHORUS.
D.S.
"Look up, . . . . and praise the Lord!" "Look up, and praise the Lord!"
"Look up, look up, and praise the Lord!" "Look up, . . . . . . and praise the Lord!"
Copyright, 1895, by H. L. Gilmour.

# Praise Him in the Heights.

Psalm cxlviii: 1.
E. E. Hewitt.
Wm. J. Kirkpatrick.
1. Praise him, praise him, in the heights of blessing, Soaring skyward on enraptured [wing;
2. ||: Praise him, :|| in the heights of trusting, Rising upward by the steps of prayer;
3. ||: Praise him, :|| in his service holy, Hasting on, his bidding to complete;
4. ||: Praise him, :|| in the heights of glory, Shining angels, spirits bright and fair;
In his favor joy and peace possessing, Light, and love, and vict'ry sing.
Love and wisdom, wondrously adjusting All life's sorrow, all its care.
Still rememb'ring, grace is to the low- ly, Sweetest heights are at his feet.
Harps ce - lestial, swell redemption's story, Till by grace we, too, are there.
CHORUS.
Praise him, praise him, praise him, blessed Giver,
Praise the Lord in whom our song delights;
Praise him, praise him, praise his name forever, Praise, O praise him in the heights.
Copyright, 1896, by Wm. J. Kirkpatrick.

# One is Our Master.

"One is your Master, even Christ: and all ye are brethren."—Matt. xxiii: 8.

E. E. Hewitt. Wm. J. Kirkpatrick.

1. One is our Master, the blessed Redeemer, Strong is the bond that u-
2. One is our Master, with gladness we'll serve him, "Doing the will" of the
3. One is our Master, the highest and noblest. Yet in his tenderness
4. One is our Master, and happy those servants, Watching and ready, when-
nites us in him; O may the love his own Spir- it hath kindled
Lord "from the heart," Knowing his strength is made perfect in weakness,
always "the same;" Be it our hon - or to fol - low his banner,
e'er he may come; Changed in his im- age, "from glory to glo- ry,"
Burn with a light that will nev - er grow dim.
All that is need-ful his grace will im-part.
Bless- ing for - ev - er be un - to his name.
Joy - ful reward in his kingdom and home.
CHORUS.
Brethren in Je - sus,
let us be faithful, Faithful to him who is guiding our ways; His our al-
legiance, our loving obedience, Till in his glo- ry hosan - nas we raise.

# The Blessed Nazarene.

Carrie Ellis Breck.
W. A. Ogden.
1. "Behold an Is-rael-ite indeed" In whom no guile is found, Who
2. O loving, bleeding, dy-ing Lamb, Of sinners I am chief, But
3. O wondrous man, O God of love, A-dor-ing-ly I bow; Thy
came to meet all human need, And make his love abound. The spotless Lamb from
sinful, doubting as I am, "Help thou mine unbelief." In love thou hast re-
praises I shall sing above, And must begin them now. Tho' ev'ry outward
heaven came To make the vilest clean; Tho' blameless, yet he took my blame, The
deemed my soul, And nought shall intervene To take me from thy sweet control, Oh,
joy may cease, Still keep my soul serene; And bring me to thy port of peace, Oh,
CHORUS.
blessed Naz-ar - ene! How "al-together lovely" Art thou on whom I
lean! "The chief among ten thousand," The blessed Naz-ar - ene!
Copyright, 1895, by John J. Hood

# O Blessed Rest.

E. E. Hewitt. "This is my rest for ever."—Ps. cxxxii: 14. Rev. B. C. Lippincott, Jr.

1. O blessed rest in Je- sus! There's no oth - er half so sweet,
2. O blessed rest in Je- sus! Let me lin - ger at his side,
3. O blessed rest in Je- sus, How it cheers me, day by day!
As the peace he free - ly gives me, When I tar - ry at his feet.
While I tell him all my sorrows, And my joys to him con- fide.
For he strengthens me for du - ty, And for ser - vice, by the way;
There I tell the sins that grieve me, And his tones like dewdrops fall,
He will nev - er, nev - er wea- ry, For he waits to an- swer prayer,
And he tells me of the cit- y Where they need no star, no sun;
"Fear ye not, for I've redeemed thee, There is cleansing for them all."
And he whispers that he loves me, That he car- eth for my care.
There he'll give me joy- ful welcome, When my earthly work is done.
Fine.
D. S.—heart to heart with Jesus, What a bless-ed, bless - ed rest!
CHORUS.
O bless- ed, bless - ed rest! Leaning on his loving breast, When I'm
D.S.

# Bring Them to Me.



E. E. Hewitt. "He said, bring them hither to me."—Matt. xiv: 18. Wm. J. Kirkpatrick.

1. Bring them to Je- sus, sweet praises of love, Rising like incense to heav- en a- bove; Let songs of glad- ness for mercies renewed, Bear on bright pinions the heart's grati - tude.

2. Bring them to Je- sus, our needs by the way, Asking in weakness for strength as our day; Bring emp- ty ves- sels, the fountain o'erflows, Bringing the bri- ars, he gives us the rose.

3. Bring them to Je- sus, the puzzles we meet, Casting our doubts at his cru - ci - fied feet; Wait, till the Mas- ter him- self shall ex- plain Every strange link in love's wonder-ful chain.

4. Bring them to Je- sus, our gifts tho' but small, His touch of blessing will hal- low them all; As on the hillside the thousands he fed, With the lad's off'ring of fish - es and bread.

5. Bring them to Je- sus, in con - fi-dent prayer, Longings that others his goodness may share; Sure of such ask- ing he nev- er can tire, Since his own Spir- it cre- ates the de - sire.

CHORUS.

Je- sus is say- ing, "bring them to me, Pleasures or sorrows, what - ev - er they be, Bring them to me, bring them to me, Bring them hither to me."

# Heavenly Sunshine.

Rev. A. D. Kennedy. "Thine eyes shall behold the land."—Isa. xxxiii : 17. A. F. Myers.
1. There's a hap- py land of sunshine, Where the shadow nev- er falls,
2. There no tempests ev - er gath- er To be-cloud the heavenly sky;
3. Death shall nev-er there o'ertake us, While e - ter- nal a - ges roll;
4. Glorious light, thy rays are beaming In our hearts by faith a - new;
Making heav'n with beauty glorious, Gilding all its jas- per walls.
For the Lamb of God for- ev - er Lights the glo- ry - land on high.
Naught a- fraid can ev - er make us; Filled with joy is ev- 'ry soul.
Let it shine up - on our pathway, All our pilgrim journey through.
CHORUS.
Heav'n - ly sunshine, heav'n - ly sunshine, In the
Heav'nly, heav'nly sun - shine, heav'nly, heav'nly sun - shine, In the gold - en
gold - en by and by, Heav'n - ly sun - shine,
sometime, by and by, by and by, Heav'n- ly, heav'n- ly sun - shine,
heav'n - ly sunshine, In the gold - en by and by.
heav'nly, heav'nly sun- shine, In the gold- en sometime, by and by, by and by.
Copyright, 1894, by A. F. Myers, used by per.

# Every One is Sowing.

Chas. H. Gabriel.
1. Ev - 'ry one is sow- ing both by word and deed, All mankind are growing eith - er wheat or weed; Thoughtless ones are throwing an - y kind of seed, Sowing, sowing, sowing.
2. Se- rious ones are seek- ing seed al- read - y sown, Ma- ny eyes are weeping, now the crop is grown; Think up- on the reaping—each one reaps his own, Reaping, reaping, reaping.
3. Ye that would be bringing sheaves of gold- en grain, Mind what you are flinging both from hand and brain; Then with hap- py sing- ing you shall glean great gain, Gleaning, gleaning, gleaning.
CHORUS.
Sure- ly as the sowing shall the har- vest be! See what you are throwing o - ver hill and lea; Words and deeds are growing for eter- ni - ty, Growing, growing, growing.
Copyright, 1895, by John J. Hood.

# Hallelujah! Sing to Jesus.

J. E. H.
J. E. Hall.
1. Praises bring in joy- ful anthem, Voices raise with one ac- cord ;
2. Great is he who hath redeemed us, Great in wisdom, great in love ;
3. Songs of a - dor - a- tion bringing, Worship him the King of kings ;
4. Let the earth ring with the sto - ry Of redemption's theme sublime ;
Honor un - to Christ as - cribing, Christ, Redeemer, Saviour, Lord.
Now to him bring sweet ob - la- tion, Un- to him who reigns a- bove.
Give him glo- ry, homage, blessing, Who to man sal- vation brings.
Herald forth this song of gladness, Un- to ev - 'ry land and clime.
CHORUS.
Hal- le- lu- jah ! sing to Je- sus, Waft his praise in choral song ;
Hal- le- lujah !
Hal- le- lu- jah ! sing to Je- sus, Roll the notes of joy a - long.
Halle- lujah !
Copyright, 1895, by John J. Hood.

# Blest Eden-Land.

Birdie Bell. Wm. J. Kirkpatrick.

1. Blest Eden-land! haven of peace, Country whose joys never shall cease;
2. Dear Eden-land, once thy bright shore Seemed to our souls lost evermore,
3. Glad Eden-land! fadeless thy bloom, O-ver thy walls falleth no gloom;
4. Fair Eden-land! home of the soul! Long we for thee when billows roll;
After the storms on life's rough sea, May we find refuge and shelter in thee!
Till Jesus came, walking the wave, Jesus the loving One, "mighty to save."
Angels of light on heav'nly wing, Rapturous anthems e-ter-nal-ly sing.
May we at last, time's tossing o'er, Meet on thy beautiful, beauti-ful shore.
CHORUS.
Sweet Eden-land! home of the blest, Guide us, O Pilot, to this haven of rest;
Sweet Eden-land! home of the blest, Guide us
Send us a gleam, cheering the night, Beautiful, beautiful land of delight.

# Victory Through Jesus.

"Thanks be unto God who giveth us the victory through our Lord Jesus Christ."—1 Cor xv: 57.

IDA L. REED. Cho. by H. L. G. H. L. GILMOUR.

1. Vict- 'ry shall be ours thro' Je - sus, This our bat - tle cry;
2. Vict- 'ry thro' our Lord and Sav - iour, O - ver ev - 'ry foe;
3. Vict- 'ry shall be ours thro' Je - sus, O - ver ev - 'ry wrong;

We will trust his pow'r so gra - cious, As the days go by.
This the promise of his fa - vor, He will strength bestow.
Thro' his strength and grace we'll glad- ly Sing the vic- tor's song.

Nothing in ourselves a - vail - eth, But the Saviour's arm nev- er
For the conflict he will befriend us, Grace and mercy will e'er at-
Onward then, no e - vil we're fear - ing, Strengthened by his presence so

fail - eth, O- ver ev'ry wrong he prevail - eth, Thro' his might we'll win.
tend us, Overcoming strength he will send us, Thro' his might we'll win.
cheering We will go, his banner still bearing, Thro' his might we'll win.

CHORUS.

Vic- tory thro' Jesus, vic - to- ry, Thanks be unto God, For thus hath he
glad victo- ry,

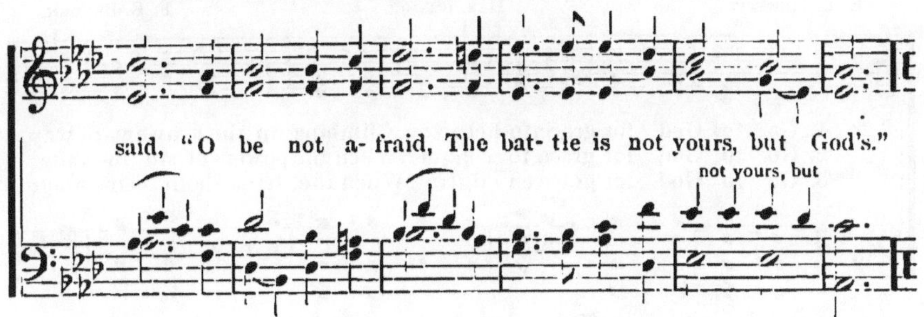
said, "O be not a- fraid, The bat- tle is not yours, but God's."
not yours, but

## O Eden, Dear Eden.

FANNY J. CROSBY. H. S. THOMPSON.

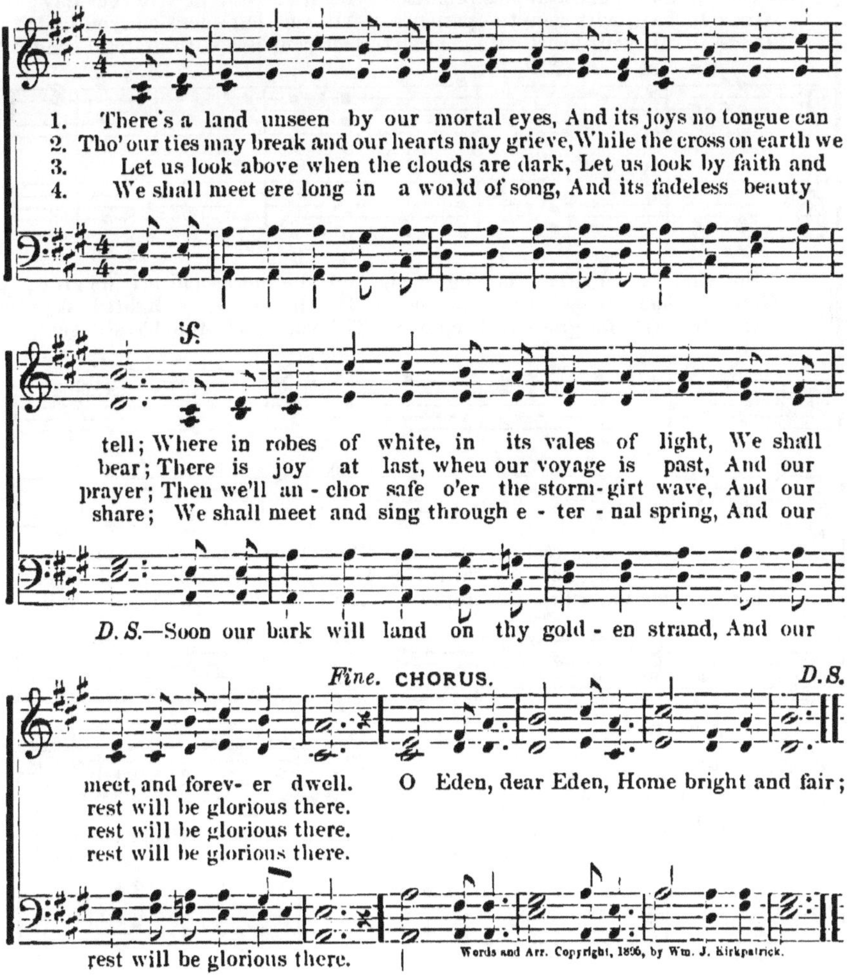

1. There's a land unseen by our mortal eyes, And its joys no tongue can
2. Tho' our ties may break and our hearts may grieve, While the cross on earth we
3. Let us look above when the clouds are dark, Let us look by faith and
4. We shall meet ere long in a world of song, And its fadeless beauty

tell; Where in robes of white, in its vales of light, We shall
bear; There is joy at last, wheu our voyage is past, And our
prayer; Then we'll an - chor safe o'er the storm-girt wave, And our
share; We shall meet and sing through e - ter - nal spring, And our

*D. S.*—Soon our bark will land on thy gold - en strand, And our

*Fine.* CHORUS. *D.S.*

meet, and forev- er dwell. O Eden, dear Eden, Home bright and fair;
rest will be glorious there.
rest will be glorious there.
rest will be glorious there.

rest will be glorious there.

# Go to God for Grace to Help You.

E. E. Hewitt.
Heb. iv: 16.
F. E. Belden.
1. Go to God for grace to help you, Climbing up the heav'nward way,
2. Go to God for grace to conquer, When the powers of sin in- vade;
3. Go to God for grace en - during, When the tri- al-hour seems long;
For we know his word has promised Strength accord- ing to our day;
Grace to bear, with gen- tle patience, All the bur - dens on you laid;
Grace to fill your heart with gladness, And your lips with grateful song.
So, whene'er the road is rug - ged, And the thorns and bri- ars grow,
Grace to look be- yond the tem- pest To the glo - ry- lighted sky,
Go to God for grace to keep you Till you reach the blessed goal,
Let us seek a sweet re - freshing Where the streams of blessing flow.
Where the love of Je - sus shin- ing Meets the meek, up- lift- ed eye.
Where in swelling tides of rapture End- less hal - le - lujahs roll.
REFRAIN.
Go to God . . . for grace to help you In your ev - 'ry time of need;
Go to God for grace to keep you true, Go to him in ev-'ry time of need;
Copyright, 1895, by Wm. J. Kirkpatrick.

You will find .... his throne is mer - cy, When in Jesus' name you plead.
You will find his promise is for you,

# Come to the Fountain To-day.

DELIA T. WHITE. J. WESLEY EWING.

1. Salvation's stream is rolling by, Come to the fountain to-day; A voice is
2. With all your sorrow, all your sin, Come to the fountain to-day; And heav'nly
3. There's blessing in the precious tide, Come to the fountain to-day; And ev- 'ry
4. No drought can touch this living spring, Come to the fountain to-day; E- ternal

CHORUS.

sounding from the sky, Come to the fountain to-day. O come to the fountain,
joys will there begin, Come to the fountain to-day.
need shall be supplied, Come to the fountain to-day.
life its waters bring, Come to the fountain to-day.

Flowing now from Calv'ry's brow; O come to the fountain, Jesus will save you now.

# Accepted I Am.

FRANK R. GRAHAM. JNO. R. SWENEY.

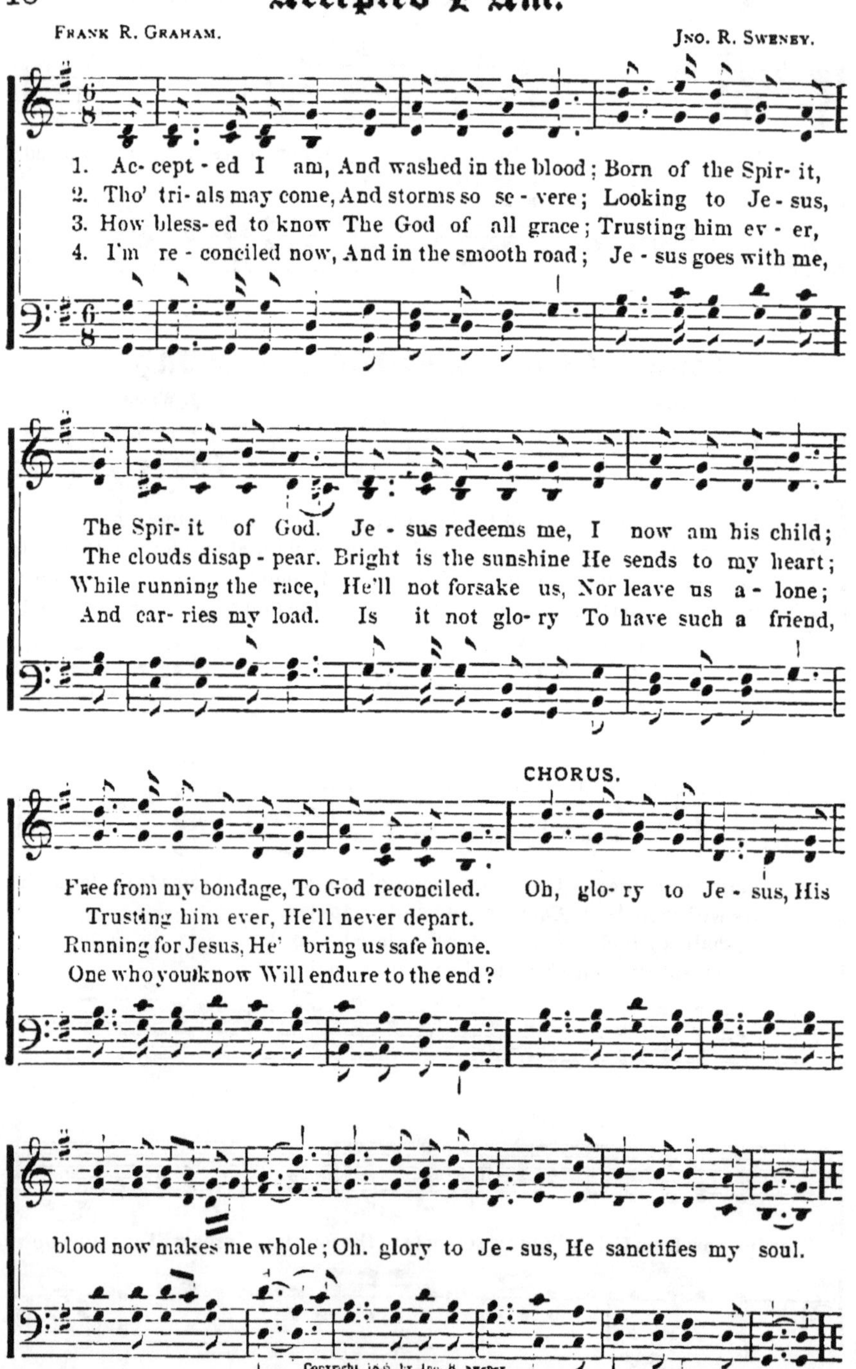
1. Ac- cept - ed I am, And washed in the blood; Born of the Spir- it,
2. Tho' tri- als may come, And storms so se - vere; Looking to Je - sus,
3. How bless- ed to know The God of all grace; Trusting him ev - er,
4. I'm re - conciled now, And in the smooth road; Je - sus goes with me,
The Spir- it of God. Je - sus redeems me, I now am his child;
The clouds disap - pear. Bright is the sunshine He sends to my heart;
While running the race, He'll not forsake us, Nor leave us a - lone;
And car- ries my load. Is it not glo- ry To have such a friend,
Free from my bondage, To God reconciled.
Trusting him ever, He'll never depart.
Running for Jesus, He' bring us safe home.
One who you know Will endure to the end?
CHORUS.
Oh, glo- ry to Je - sus, His
blood now makes me whole; Oh. glory to Je - sus, He sanctifies my soul.
Copyright, 18.6, by Jno. R. Sweney.

# My Choice.

E. E. Hewitt.
Francis Burgette Short.
1. My choice is King Jesus; he's reigning above, His service is gladness, his
2. My choice is King Jesus; I'll trust in his power, He'll help me to follow his
3. My choice is King Jesus; how happy my choice! O would that all others in
4. My choice is King Jesus, my Saviour and Friend, His glorious kingdom shall
banner is love; His soldiers are singing while marching along, I'll
steps ev- 'ry hour; And since in his word he will speak to me still, I'll
him would rejoice; To stand on his side against e - vil and sin, To
nev- ermore end: He's a - ble to keep me to "fight the good fight," Then
learn the sweet music and join in their song.
search for his orders and do his kind will.
gird on his armor and vic - to - ry win.
give me a crown in the mansions of light.
CHORUS.
Halle- lujah, halle- lujah to
Je- sus my King, Halle - lujah, halle - lujah, I'll joy- ful- ly sing; I
choose him, I choose him, with heart glad and free, My Saviour and King he will ev-
[ermore be.

# Faith is the Victory.

John H. Yates. Ira D. Sankey.

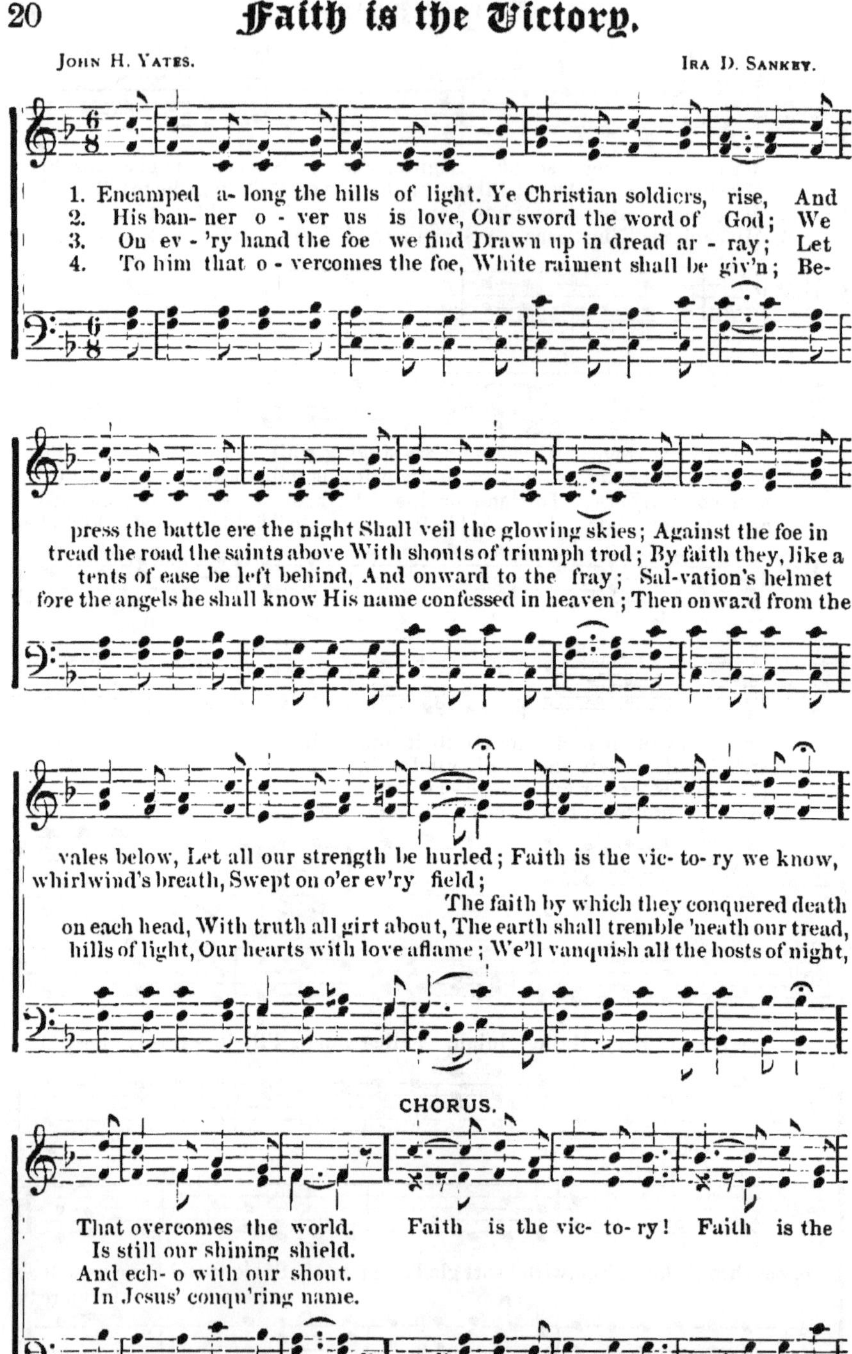
1. Encamped a- long the hills of light. Ye Christian soldiers, rise, And
2. His ban- ner o - ver us is love, Our sword the word of God; We
3. On ev - 'ry hand the foe we find Drawn up in dread ar - ray; Let
4. To him that o - vercomes the foe, White raiment shall be giv'n; Be-
press the battle ere the night Shall veil the glowing skies; Against the foe in
tread the road the saints above With shouts of triumph trod; By faith they, like a
tents of ease be left behind, And onward to the fray; Sal-vation's helmet
fore the angels he shall know His name confessed in heaven; Then onward from the
vales below, Let all our strength be hurled; Faith is the vic- to- ry we know,
whirlwind's breath, Swept on o'er ev'ry field;
The faith by which they conquered death
on each head, With truth all girt about, The earth shall tremble 'neath our tread,
hills of light, Our hearts with love aflame; We'll vanquish all the hosts of night,
CHORUS.
That overcomes the world. Faith is the vic- to- ry! Faith is the
Is still our shining shield.
And ech- o with our shout.
In Jesus' conqu'ring name.

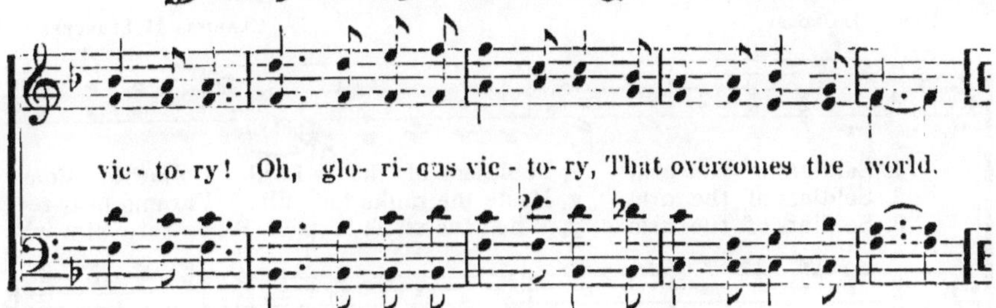
vic - to- ry! Oh, glo- ri- ous vic - to- ry, That overcomes the world.

# Blessed Land of Song.

FANNY J. CROSBY. JNO. R. SWENEY.

1. Oh, the peaceful resting land, Where the saints in glory, Bending at the
2. Where the cloudless beams of day, Banish care and sadness; Lo, the reapers
3. Oh, the tender, loving words, Purest joy re - vealing; Soft and low from
4. Soon to- gether we shall stand, By the crystal riv - er; There to join the

Saviour's feet, Tell the grand old sto- ry.
en-ter now, Bearing sheaves of gladness.
kindred souls, On the twilight stealing.
ho-ly throng, Praising God forev - er.

CHORUS.

Sweetly they are singing, (singing,) *echo.*

Hear the echo ringing, (ringing;) *echo.* In the land of beauty, Blessed land of song. *rit.*

# Soldiers of the Army.

FANNY J. CROSBY.
CLARISSA H. SPENCER.
1. Soldiers of the arm - y, Soldiers of the Lord, Follow our Com-
2. Soldiers of the arm - y, Haste the ranks to fill; Far and near re-
3. Soldiers of the arm - y, When the strife is past, When thro' him who
man - der, Trusting his e - ter- nal word; He the way is lead - ing,
sounding, Hear the trumpet call- ing still; In the midst of dan - ger
loves us, We shall o - vercome at last; Crowned by him triumphant,
D. S.—Wield the sword of conquest,
Fine.
Now his welcome smile we see, Loyal, firm, and steadfast, On to vic- to - ry.
Let our post of du - ty be, On with zeal and courage, On to vic- to - ry.
With the ransom'd host we'll sing, Praise to our Commander, Saviour, Lord, and King.
Shout, rejoicing as we go, Vic-to- ry be - fore us, Death to ev- 'ry foe.
CHORUS.
Soldiers of the arm - y, Wave the roy - al standard high,
poco rit.
D.S.
Lift the cross of Je - sus, Sound a - loud the bat - tle cry;

# Keep Trusting in Jesus.

Rev. H. J Zelley.
H. L. Gilmour.
1. Temptations and trials and doubtings and fears We constantly find in this valley of tears; But you shall have vict'ry if bravely you fight, Keep trusting in
2. If trouble shall come full of sorrow and pain, Hold fast to the promise, "My grace shall sustain;" The day may be dark, but at eve 'twill be light, Keep trusting in
3. When like a dark shadow bereavement shall come, And sadly you part with the light of thy home; The Saviour will help you with his gracious might, Keep trusting in
4. When labors have ended, and death takes your hand To lead you away to the shadowy land; Go fearlessly with him, let nothing affright, Keep trusting in
Jesus, and all will be right.
CHORUS.
Keep trust - - - ing in Jesus, His word . . . . can-not fail; Keep trust - - - ing in Je - sus, And you . . . shall pre-vail.
Keep trust-ing, trust-ing, trust-ing in Je-sus, trust-ing, trust-ing, his word can-not fail; Keep trusting, trusting and you shall prevail.

E. E. Hewitt. Wm. J. Kirkpatrick.

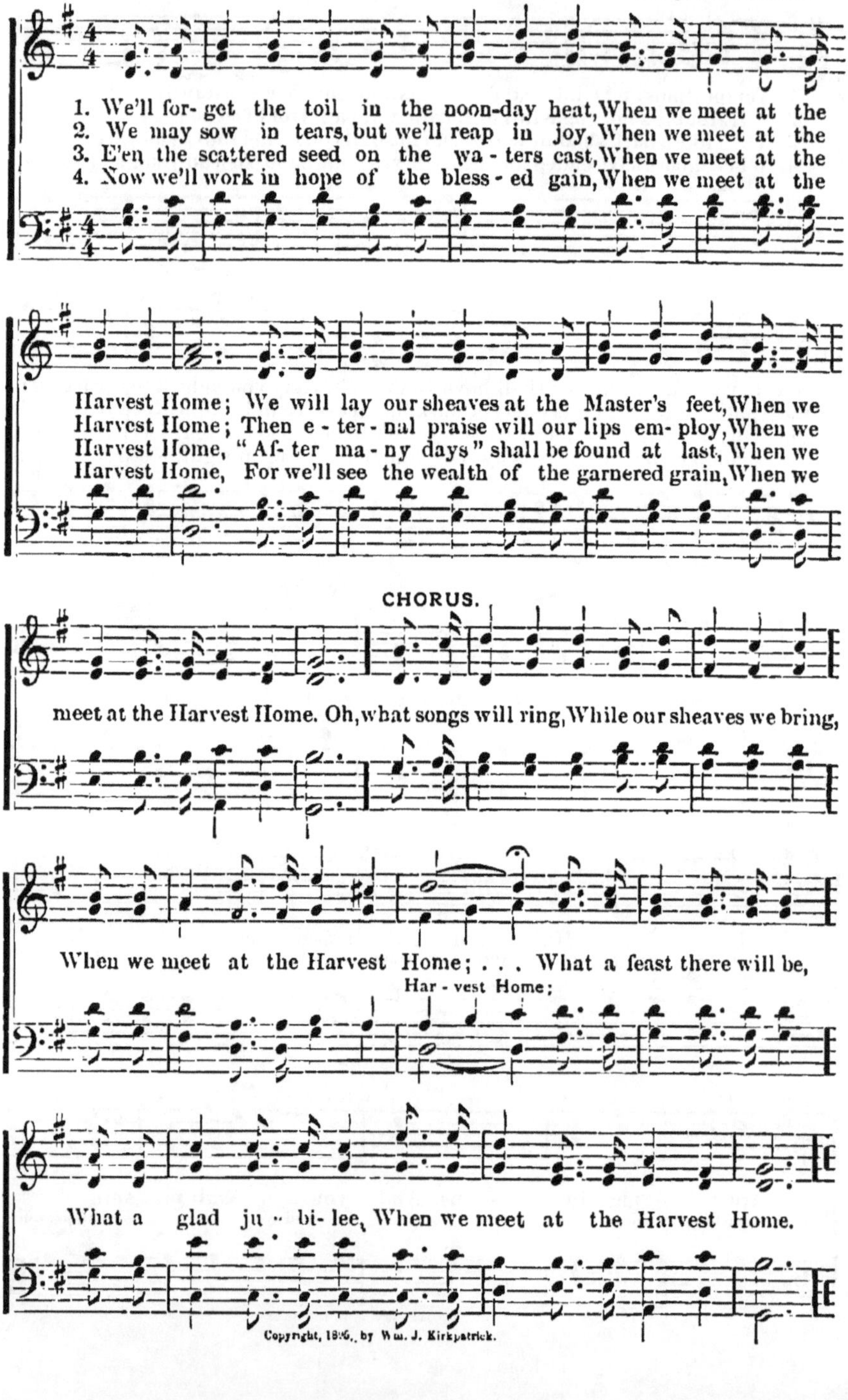

1. We'll for- get the toil in the noon-day heat, When we meet at the
2. We may sow in tears, but we'll reap in joy, When we meet at the
3. E'en the scattered seed on the wa - ters cast, When we meet at the
4. Now we'll work in hope of the bless - ed gain, When we meet at the

Harvest Home; We will lay our sheaves at the Master's feet, When we
Harvest Home; Then e - ter - nal praise will our lips em- ploy, When we
Harvest Home, "Af- ter ma - ny days" shall be found at last, When we
Harvest Home, For we'll see the wealth of the garnered grain, When we

meet at the Harvest Home.

CHORUS.

Oh, what songs will ring, While our sheaves we bring,
When we meet at the Harvest Home; . . . What a feast there will be,
Har - vest Home;
What a glad ju - bi- lee, When we meet at the Harvest Home.

# Will You be There?

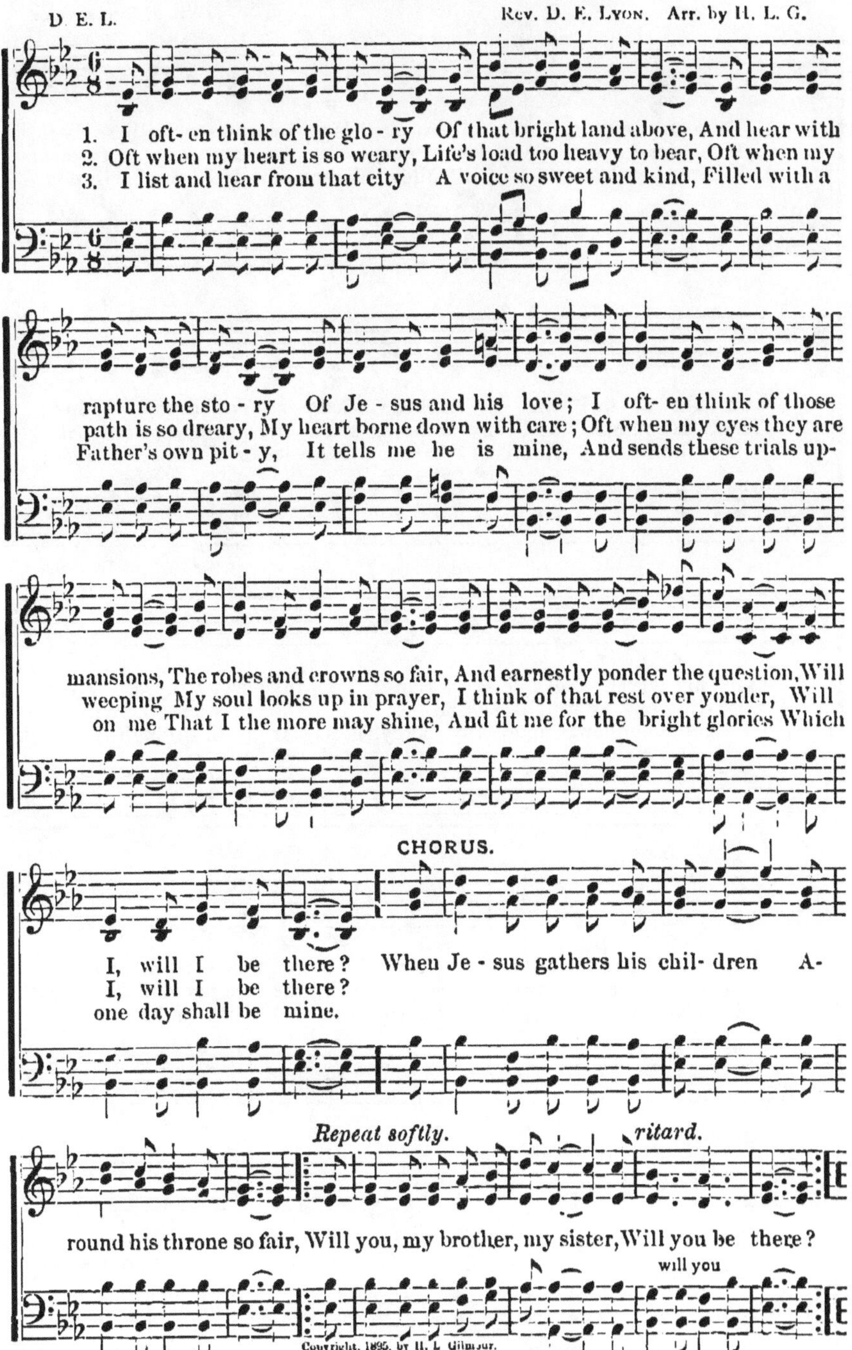
D. E. L.
Rev. D. E. Lyon. Arr. by H. L. G.
1. I oft- en think of the glo - ry Of that bright land above, And hear with
2. Oft when my heart is so weary, Life's load too heavy to bear, Oft when my
3. I list and hear from that city A voice so sweet and kind, Filled with a
rapture the sto - ry Of Je - sus and his love; I oft- en think of those
path is so dreary, My heart borne down with care; Oft when my eyes they are
Father's own pit - y, It tells me he is mine, And sends these trials up-
mansions, The robes and crowns so fair, And earnestly ponder the question, Will
weeping My soul looks up in prayer, I think of that rest over yonder, Will
on me That I the more may shine, And fit me for the bright glories Which
CHORUS.
I, will I be there? When Je - sus gathers his chil- dren A-
I, will I be there?
one day shall be mine.
Repeat softly.
ritard.
round his throne so fair, Will you, my brother, my sister, Will you be there?
will you
Copyright, 1895, by H. L. Gilmour.

# Thine Forever.

Fanny J. Crosby. Wm. J. Kirkpatrick.

1. Thine for-ev-er, thine for-ev-er, My Redeem-er, will I be;
2. Thine for-ev-er, thine for-ev-er,—Oh, the rapture of my heart!
3. Where thou leadest I will follow, Where thou bidst me I will go;
On the al-tar lies my offering, Con-se-crated now to thee;
Thou my refuge and my comfort, Thou my lasting portion art;
In the ve-ry front of battle Fear-less will I meet the foe;
All my fervent soul's de-vo-tion To thy service, Lord, I give;
Cast-ing ev-'ry weight behind me, I the christian race will run,
I shall conquer through thy mercy, I shall triumph through thy might,
For thy honor and thy glo-ry I will la-bor while I live.
Trust-ing thee and taking courage, Till the race my soul has won.
I shall see thee in thy kingdom; There will faith be lost in sight.
CHORUS.
p
Thine forev-er, thine for-ev-er, Saviour, I am resting in thy love;
in thy love;
p

27

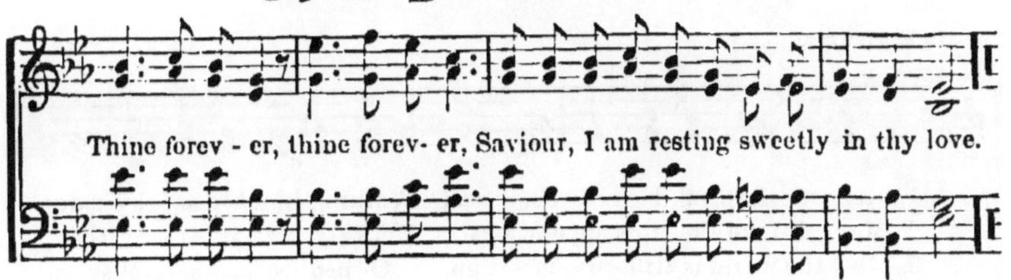
Thine forev - er, thine forev- er, Saviour, I am resting sweetly in thy love.

## He's with Me all the Time.

M. D. K. M. D. KIRKPATRICK.

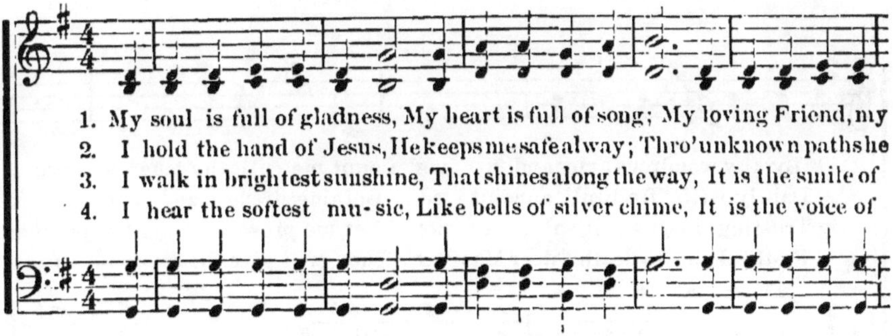

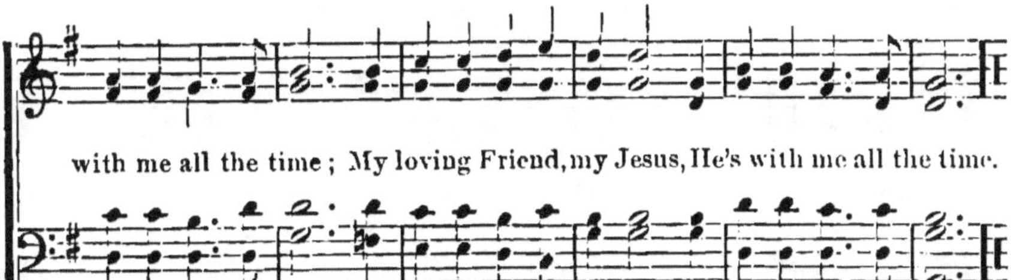

1. My soul is full of gladness, My heart is full of song; My loving Friend, my Je - sus, Is with me all day long.
2. I hold the hand of Jesus, He keeps me safe alway; Thro' unknown paths he guides me, He's with me all the day.
3. I walk in brightest sunshine, That shines along the way, It is the smile of Je - sus, He's with me all the day.
4. I hear the softest mu- sic, Like bells of silver chime, It is the voice of Je - sus, He's with me all the time.

CHORUS.

He's with me all the day, He's with me all the time; My loving Friend, my Jesus, He's with me all the time.

# Keep me Faithful.

E. E. Hewitt. Jno. R. Sweney.

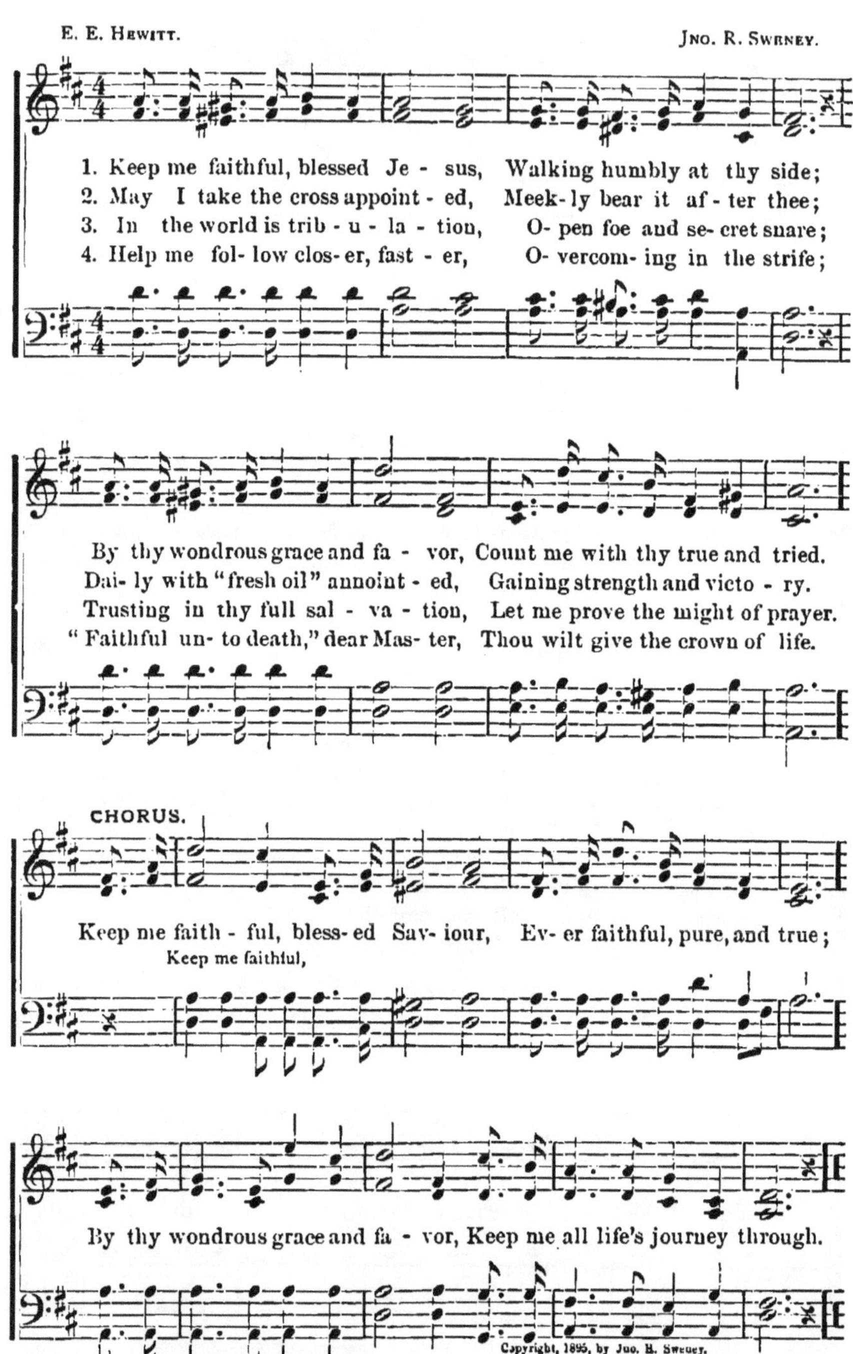
1. Keep me faithful, blessed Je - sus, Walking humbly at thy side;
2. May I take the cross appoint - ed, Meek- ly bear it af - ter thee;
3. In the world is trib - u - la - tion, O- pen foe and se- cret snare;
4. Help me fol- low clos- er, fast - er, O- vercom- ing in the strife;
By thy wondrous grace and fa - vor, Count me with thy true and tried.
Dai- ly with "fresh oil" annoint - ed, Gaining strength and victo - ry.
Trusting in thy full sal - va - tion, Let me prove the might of prayer.
"Faithful un- to death," dear Mas- ter, Thou wilt give the crown of life.
CHORUS.
Keep me faith - ful, bless- ed Sav- iour, Ev- er faithful, pure, and true;
Keep me faithful,
By thy wondrous grace and fa - vor, Keep me all life's journey through.

# Jesus is My Pilot.

Mrs. Carrie Ellis Breck. Wm. J. Kirkpatrick.

*Not too fast.*

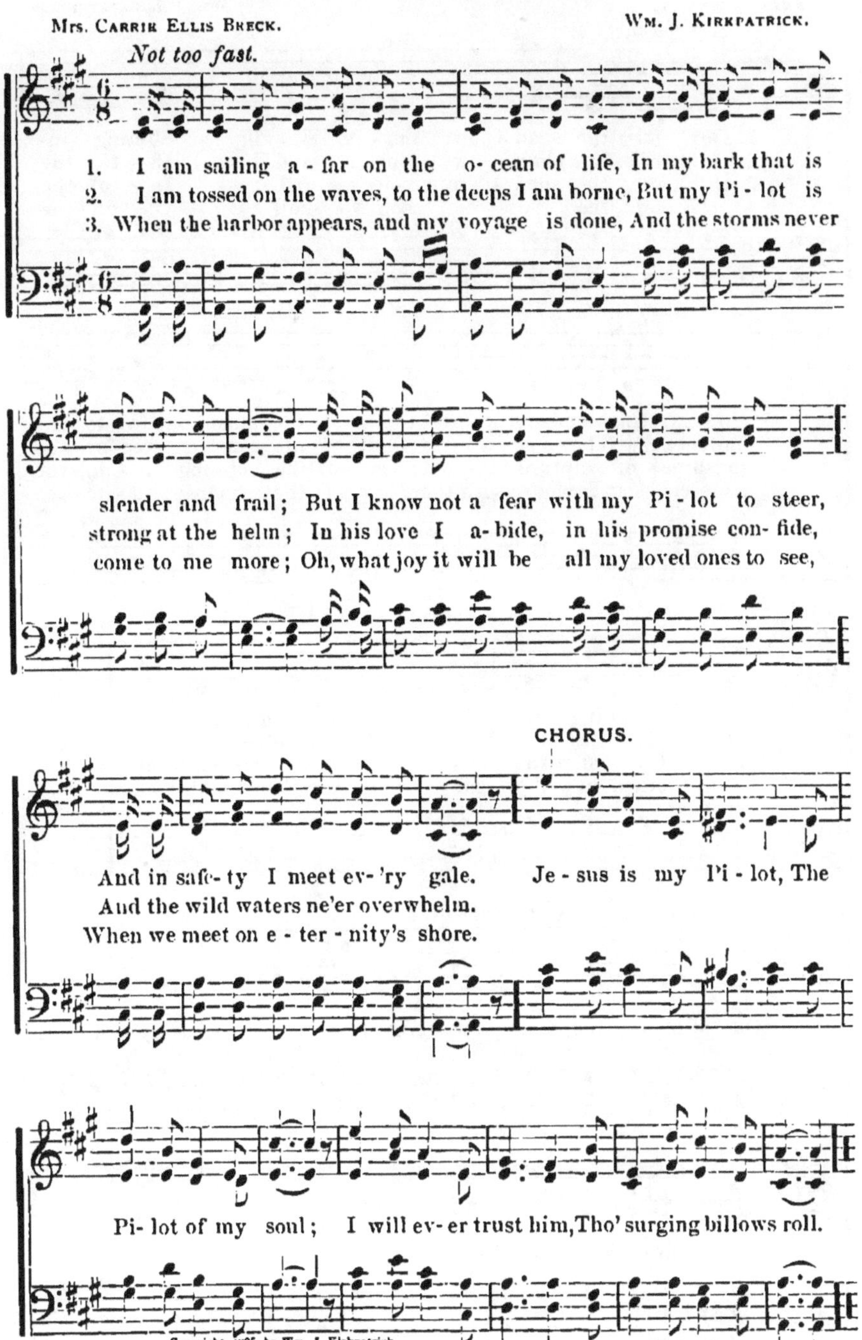
1. I am sailing a - far on the o - cean of life, In my bark that is slender and frail; But I know not a fear with my Pi - lot to steer, And in safe - ty I meet ev - 'ry gale.
2. I am tossed on the waves, to the deeps I am borne, But my Pi - lot is strong at the helm; In his love I a - bide, in his promise con - fide, And the wild waters ne'er overwhelm.
3. When the harbor appears, and my voyage is done, And the storms never come to me more; Oh, what joy it will be all my loved ones to see, When we meet on e - ter - nity's shore.
CHORUS.
Je - sus is my Pi - lot, The Pi - lot of my soul; I will ev - er trust him, Tho' surging billows roll.

# Out of the Shadow.

FANNY J. CROSBY.
WM. J. KIRKPATRICK.
Not too fast.
1. Out of the shad - ow in - to the light, Shining in glo - ry transcendent- ly bright; Out of the gloaming in - to the day, Beaming in splen - dor that fades not a - way.
2. Out of the shad - ow lone- ly and drear, In - to the fu- ture that knows not a fear; Out of the con- flict wea- ry and sore, In - to the home - land of bliss ev - er - more.
3. Out of the shad - ow voiceless and cold, In - to the sunshine of rapture un- told; Out of the hop- ing in - to the blest, Out of the long - ing, with Je - sus at rest.
4. O - ver the riv - er soon we shall be, O - ver the riv - er, dear Saviour, with thee; Out of the shadow in - to the light, Clothed in the gar - ments thy blood hath made white.
CHORUS. With much expression.
p
f
Out of the sighing, fading and dying, Into the perfect, lovely and bright;
Out of the darkness into the dawning, Out of the shadow into the light.
Copyright, 1891, by Wm. J. Kirkpatrick.

# Coming to be Thine Own.

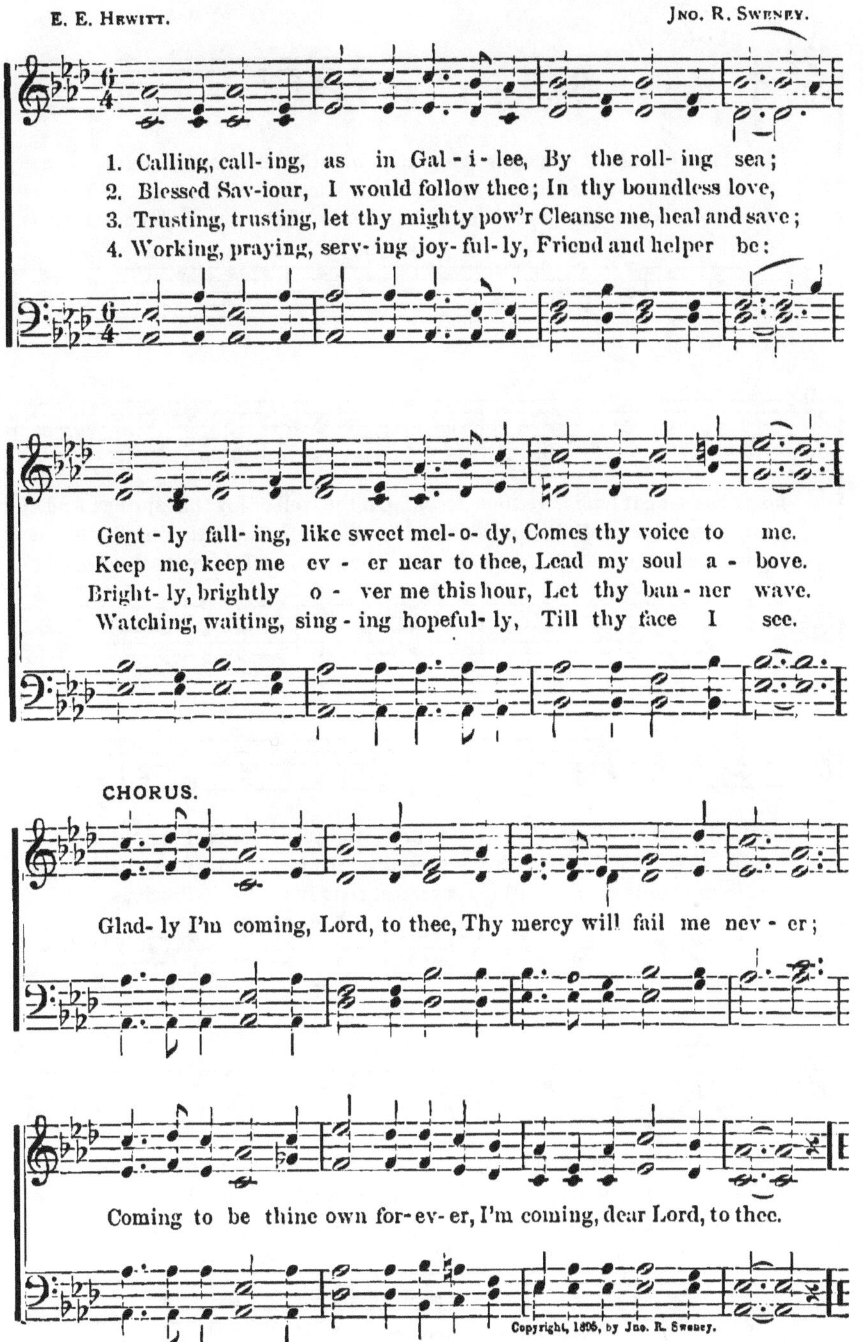
E. E. Hewitt.
Jno. R. Sweney.
1. Calling, call- ing, as in Gal - i - lee, By the roll- ing sea;
2. Blessed Sav-iour, I would follow thee; In thy boundless love,
3. Trusting, trusting, let thy mighty pow'r Cleanse me, heal and save;
4. Working, praying, serv- ing joy- ful- ly, Friend and helper be:
Gent - ly fall- ing, like sweet mel- o- dy, Comes thy voice to me.
Keep me, keep me ev - er near to thee, Lead my soul a - bove.
Bright- ly, brightly o - ver me this hour, Let thy ban - ner wave.
Watching, waiting, sing - ing hopeful- ly, Till thy face I see.
CHORUS.
Glad- ly I'm coming, Lord, to thee, Thy mercy will fail me nev - er;
Coming to be thine own for- ev- er, I'm coming, dear Lord, to thee.

# Precious Jesus.

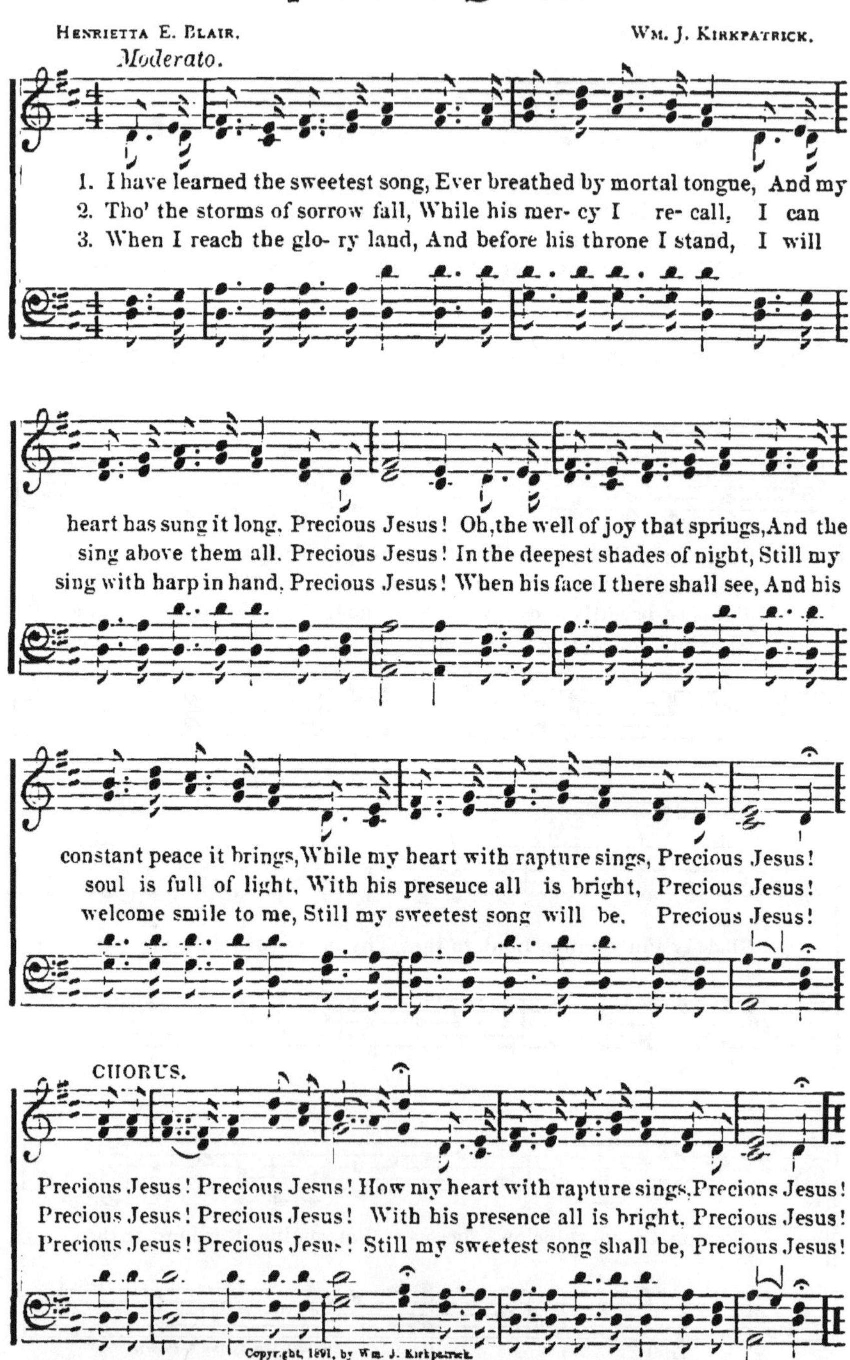
Henrietta E. Blair.
Wm. J. Kirkpatrick.
Moderato.
1. I have learned the sweetest song, Ever breathed by mortal tongue, And my heart has sung it long. Precious Jesus! Oh, the well of joy that springs, And the constant peace it brings, While my heart with rapture sings, Precious Jesus!
2. Tho' the storms of sorrow fall, While his mer- cy I re- call, I can sing above them all. Precious Jesus! In the deepest shades of night, Still my soul is full of light, With his presence all is bright, Precious Jesus!
3. When I reach the glo- ry land, And before his throne I stand, I will sing with harp in hand, Precious Jesus! When his face I there shall see, And his welcome smile to me, Still my sweetest song will be, Precious Jesus!
CHORUS.
Precious Jesus! Precious Jesus! How my heart with rapture sings, Precious Jesus!
Precious Jesus! Precious Jesus! With his presence all is bright, Precious Jesus!
Precious Jesus! Precious Jesus! Still my sweetest song shall be, Precious Jesus!
Copyright, 1891, by Wm. J. Kirkpatrick.

# The Joy of God Makes Glad.

S. H. Bolton. Cho. by H. L. G.
H. L. Gilmour.
1. The joy of God makes glad my heart, Glory, glo - ry, hal - le- lujah!
2. God's perfect peace is mine just now, Glory, glo - ry, hal - le- lujah!
3. "Thy will be done," I always sing, Glory, glo - ry, hal - le- lujah!
4. Oh, come, accept this heav'nly grace, Glory, glo - ry, hal - le- lujah!
I nev - er will from him de - part, Glo- ry, hal - le - lu - jah!
And to his will I glad - ly bow, Glo- ry, hal - le - lu - jah!
All to thy kingdom would I bring, Glo- ry, hal - le - lu - jah!
Yes, let his glo - ry fill the place, Glo- ry, hal - le - lu - jah!
CHORUS.
I'll praise him, I'll praise him; He's my strength and my Redeemer,
I'll praise the Lord, I'll praise the Lord:
My soul he sought, and pardon bought, Glo - ry to his name!
Copyright, 1895, by H. L. Gilmour.

5 Our God does keep in perfect peace,
Glory, glory, hallelujah!
His yoke I wear with joy and ease,
Glory, hallelujah!

6 Oh, let the Holy Ghost come in,
Glory, glory, hallelujah!
He'll fully cleanse from inbred sin,
Glory, hallelujah!

# O Love of Christ.

Fanny J. Crosby — 2 Cor. viii: 9. — Jno. R. Sweney.

1. O love of Christ, who once for us, Tho' rich, yet poor be - came,
That we thro' his pri- va - tion here The soul's true wealth might gain.

2. O love of Christ, who lived for us A life of toil and care,
That we in yon- der world a- bove E - ter - nal joy might share.

3. O love of Christ, the Ho - ly One, Who laid his glo - ry down,
Who bore the cross, endured the pain, That we might wear the crown.

4. O love of Christ, who gives to us The wealth that ne'er de- cays;
While ours the bliss his gift bestows, To him be all the praise.

REFRAIN.

For ye know, for ye know the grace of our Lord Jesus Christ, That, tho' he was rich, that, tho' he was rich. Yet for your sakes, yet for your sakes he be - came poor, he became poor, That ye thro' his

(was rich, ... was rich.)

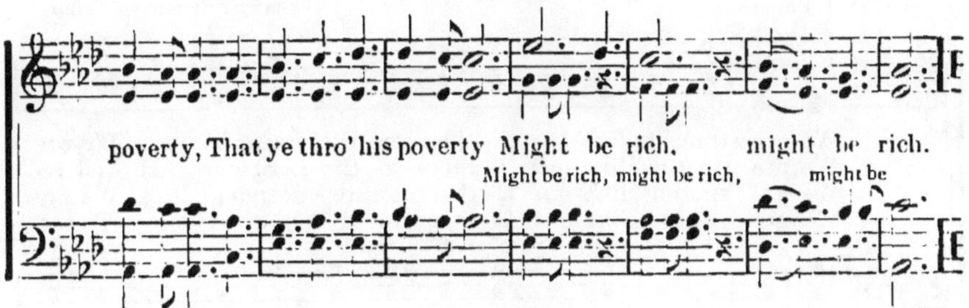
poverty, That ye thro' his poverty Might be rich, might be rich.
Might be rich, might be rich, might be

# Thou Spotless Lamb of God.

MAY MAURICE. WM. J. KIRKPATRICK.

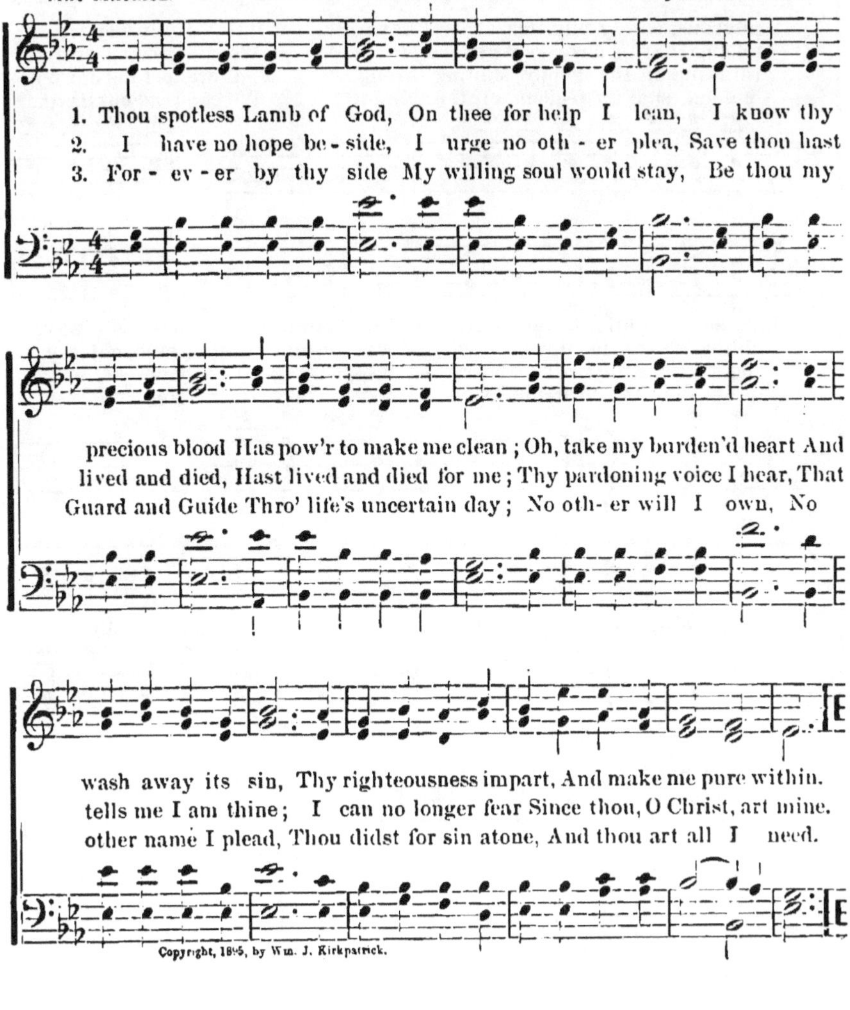

1. Thou spotless Lamb of God, On thee for help I lean, I know thy
2. I have no hope be - side, I urge no oth - er plea, Save thou hast
3. For - ev - er by thy side My willing soul would stay, Be thou my

precious blood Has pow'r to make me clean; Oh, take my burden'd heart And
lived and died, Hast lived and died for me; Thy pardoning voice I hear, That
Guard and Guide Thro' life's uncertain day; No oth- er will I own, No

wash away its sin, Thy righteousness impart, And make me pure within.
tells me I am thine; I can no longer fear Since thou, O Christ, art mine.
other name I plead, Thou didst for sin atone, And thou art all I need.

# The Glory Waiting There.

Fanny J. Crosby — Francis Burgette Short.

1. We are strangers like our fa- thers on the shores of time, We are pilgrims, on - ly pilgrims of a day; But we journey to a kingdom in a bright, bright clime, That will never, nev- er pass a - way.
2. We are trusting like our fa- thers in the Lord our God, And re- joicing that he answers when we pray; We are trying still to follow where the Master trod, As we journey in the grand, old way.
3. We are singing like our fa- thers of re - deeming love, We are thinking of the happy, shining throng That are looking down up- on us from the realms above, As we journey to the land of song.
4. We are go- ing like our fa- thers to a home a - bove, To the golden, sun- ny regions of the blest; We can read our Saviour's promise in the clear, blue sky, As we journey to the land of rest.
CHORUS.
Oh, the glo - ry wait- ing there, in a kingdom bright and fair, Where with Je- sus we shall dwell, and to sorrow bid farewell, When we gather, gather

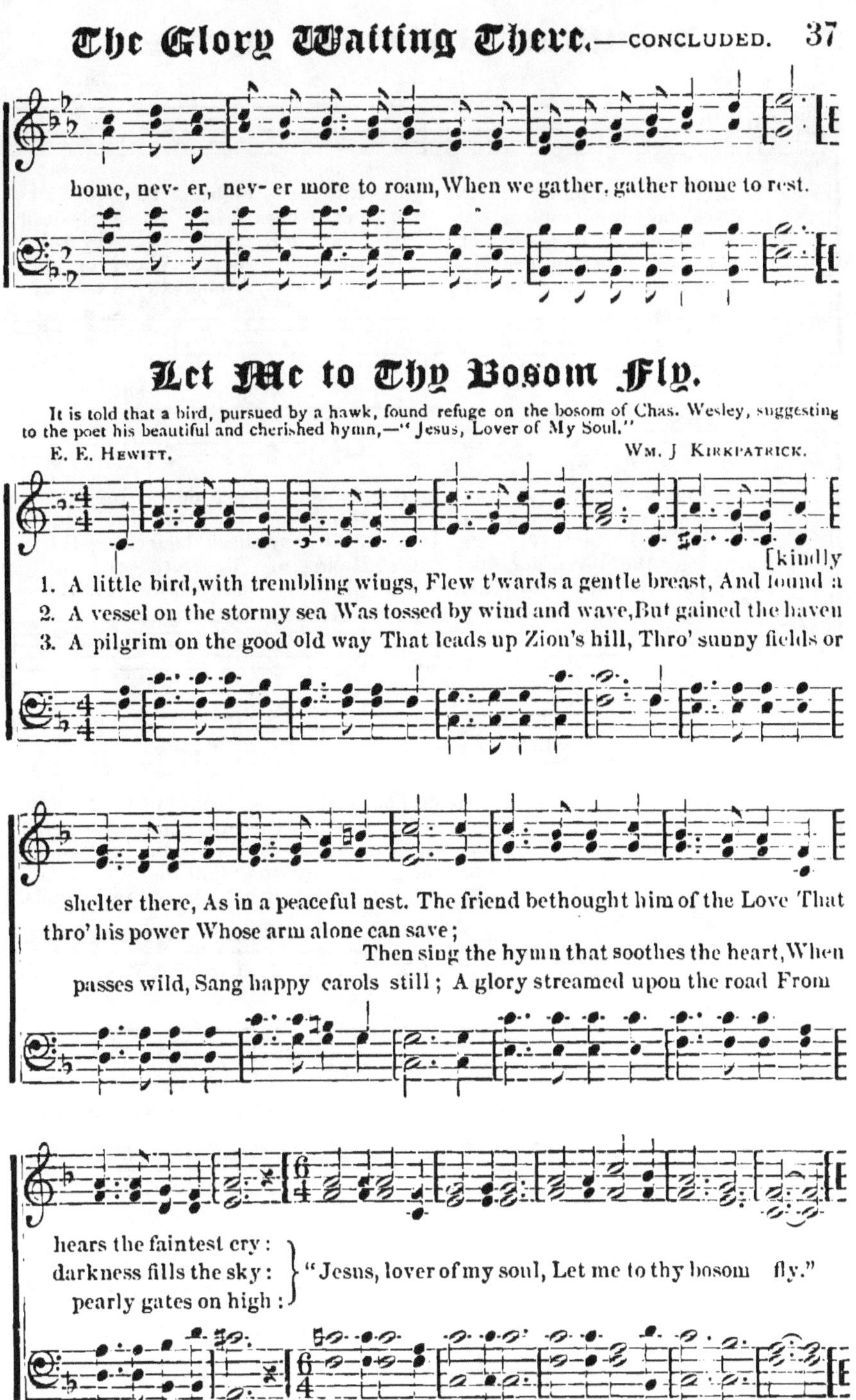
home, nev- er, nev- er more to roam, When we gather, gather home to rest.
Let Me to Thy Bosom Fly.
It is told that a bird, pursued by a hawk, found refuge on the bosom of Chas. Wesley, suggesting to the poet his beautiful and cherished hymn,—"Jesus, Lover of My Soul."
E. E. Hewitt.
Wm. J Kirkpatrick.
1. A little bird, with trembling wings, Flew t'wards a gentle breast, And found a shelter there, As in a peaceful nest. The friend bethought him of the Love That [kindly hears the faintest cry:
2. A vessel on the stormy sea Was tossed by wind and wave, But gained the haven thro' his power Whose arm alone can save; Then sing the hymn that soothes the heart, When darkness fills the sky:
3. A pilgrim on the good old way That leads up Zion's hill, Thro' sunny fields or passes wild, Sang happy carols still; A glory streamed upon the road From pearly gates on high:
"Jesus, lover of my soul, Let me to thy bosom fly."
Copyright, 1895, by Wm J Kirkpatrick.

# Beautiful, Beckoning Hands.

C. C. L.
Heb xii: 1-2.
C. C. Luther.
1. Beck- on - ing hands at the gate- way to - night, Fa - ces all
2. Beck- on - ing hands of a moth - er, whose love Sac - ri- ficed
3. Beck- on - ing hands of a lit - tle one, see! Ba - by voice
4. Beck- on - ing hands of a hus- band, a wife, Watching and
5. Brightest and best of that glo - ri - ous throng, Cen - tre of
shin - ing with ra - di - ant light; Eyes looking down from yon
life its de - vo - tion to prove; Hands of a fa - ther, to
call - ing, O moth-er, for thee; Ro - sy-cheek'd dar-ling, the
wait - ing the loved one of life; Hands of a broth - er, a
all, and the theme of their song, Je - sus our Sav - iour, the
heav- en - ly home, Beau - ti- ful hands, they are beck- on- ing "come."
mem - o - ry dear, Beck - on up high - er the wait- ing ones here.
light of the home, Tak - en so ear - ly, is beck- on- ing "come."
sis - ter, a friend, Out from the gate - way to - night they ex - tend.
Pierc- ed One stands, Lov - ing- ly call - ing with beck- on- ing hands.
REFRAIN.
Beautiful hands, beckoning hands, Calling the dear ones to heaven- ly lands;
Beautiful hands, beckoning hands, Beautiful, beau- ti- ful, beckoning hands.
Copyright, 1880, by C. C. Luther. Used by per.

# Come Home, O Come Home.

JOHNSON OATMAN, JR. JNO. R. SWENEY.

1. O prodigal, wand'ring afar to-day,Come home, O come home; In sin and
2. The world has cheated you o'er and o'er,Come home, O come home; Altho' heart-
3. Your Father is watching you to-day,Come home, O come home; He'll run to
danger no longer stay,Come home, O come home. The world is wicked, the
broken and sick and sore,Come home, O come home. Come back again to your
meet you upon the way,Come home, O come home. While you are out on the
world is cold, Her ma- ny victims cannot be told, Don't stay away from your
vacant chair, A royal welcome awaits you there, For here is bread, and e-
mountains wild, He longs to fold to his breast his child,Come home to-day and be
CHORUS.
Father's fold,Come home,O come home. Come home, O come home,And wander a-
nough to spare,Come home,O come home.
reconciled,Come home,O come home. prodigal,
ritard.
way no more; Come back to your home,no longer roam,Come home,O come home.

Make Glad Haste.

E. E. HEWITT. "The king's business required haste."—1 Sam. xxi: 8. F. E. BELDEN.

1. Make haste, glad haste, in the service of the King, With un-tir - ing
2. Make haste, glad haste, in the service of the King; Sow the seeds of
3. Make haste, glad haste, in the service of the King; Thro' the earth a-
4. Make haste, glad haste, in the service of the King; Let the lit - tle

speed all our days take wing; Let us do our best by his
truth ere the weeds upspring, Scat- ter seeds of love with a
broad let "good tid - ings" ring, Till the whole wide world shall the
ones their ho - san - nas bring, Let the old and young, and the

Spir - it's might, Till our eye - lids close with the last "good-night."
gen - 'rous hand, Work for "God, and home, and our na - tive land."
word re - ceive, Till un- numbered hosts on his name be- lieve.
high and low, Join in bless - ed toil till the har- vest grow.

CHORUS.

Haste, haste, let us make glad haste. Haste, haste, not a moment waste;

We will make glad haste, we will work and sing, In the service of our King.

# Wherever Christ Leads.

E. E. Hewitt.
Wm. J. Kirkpatrick.
1. Wherever Christ leads us he opens the way, Then fear not to listen, fear not to o-bey; To new fields of la-bor, to ser-vice untried, Not a-lone will he send us, he'll walk by our side.
2. Wherever Christ leads us he opens the way, No danger need daunt us, no foe need dismay; When Israel's "high mountains" he calls us to climb, He will take us on safe-ly, one step at a time.
3. Wherever Christ leads us he opens the way, For rich-er revealings we fervent-ly pray; And each blessed promise that shines in his word, Meets a gracious fulfillment; just trust in the Lord.
4. Wherever Christ leads us he opens the way, The clouds will roll backward, dis-closing the day; So sure all our steppings when he goes before, We will fol-low on closely to glory's bright shore.
CHORUS.
Singing on, pressing on, gladly on the way, We are walking in the light, pilgrims of the day; Singing on, pressing on, happy all the way, We are walking in the light, pilgrims of the day.

# We Praise, Adore, and Bless.

FANNY J. CROSBY.
JNO. R. SWENEY.
1. We praise, a- dore, and bless thee, Thou ma-jes - ty sub - lime; Whose
2. We praise, a- dore, and bless thee, Thy wondrous love we sing; Our
3. We praise, a- dore, and bless thee, To whom all praise we owe; We
name the an- gels hallowed Be- fore the birth of time. 'Twas thou whose
Fa - ther and Cre - a - tor, Re-deem- er, Saviour, King. 'Twas thou that
mag - ni - fy thy goodness, From whom all blessings flow. We praise, a-
voice command- ed, And o'er cha- ot - ic night Cre- a - tion's in - fant
in - to be - ing Didst call this world of ours, And cov - er hill and
dore, and bless thee, Whose kingdom hath no end, Be- fore thy roy - al
morning Unveiled its ro - sy light.
valley With spring and summer flow'rs.
scep- tre Shall ev- 'ry creature bend.
CHORUS.
To thee all an- gels cry aloud, And
glo- ri-fy thy name; Whose justice, truth, and mercy Eternal years proclaim.
Copyright, 1895, by Jno. R. Sweney.

# Praise the Lord! Praise Him!

J. R. M.
J. R. Murray.
1. Praise the Lord! praise him! Men and an- gels, u- nite in hap- py song!
2. Praise the Lord! praise him! Praise his name, for his promi - ses are sure;
3. Praise the Lord! praise him! Earth's Redeemer, the blessed Prince of Peace!
Praise the Lord! praise him! Sing Je - hovah's prais- es loud and long!
Praise the Lord! praise him! For his mercies ev - er shall en- dure;
Praise the Lord! praise him! May Je - hovah's prais- es nev - er cease!
DUET or SEMI-CHORUS.
Praise him ye heavens! praise him, ye stars of light! Praise him, ye mountains! oh,
Praise him, ye children! men, maidens, old and young! Kings bow before him from
Sing ye his glo - ry, send forth his name abroad; Tell the glad sto- ry of
CHORUS.
praise him day and night! Praise the Lord! praise him! Men and angels u-
ev - 'ry land and tongue.
this our mighty God.
nite in happy song! Praise the Lord! praise him! Sing Jehovah's praises loud and
[long.

# The Bolted Door.

Rev. John Parker. Wm. J. Kirkpatrick.

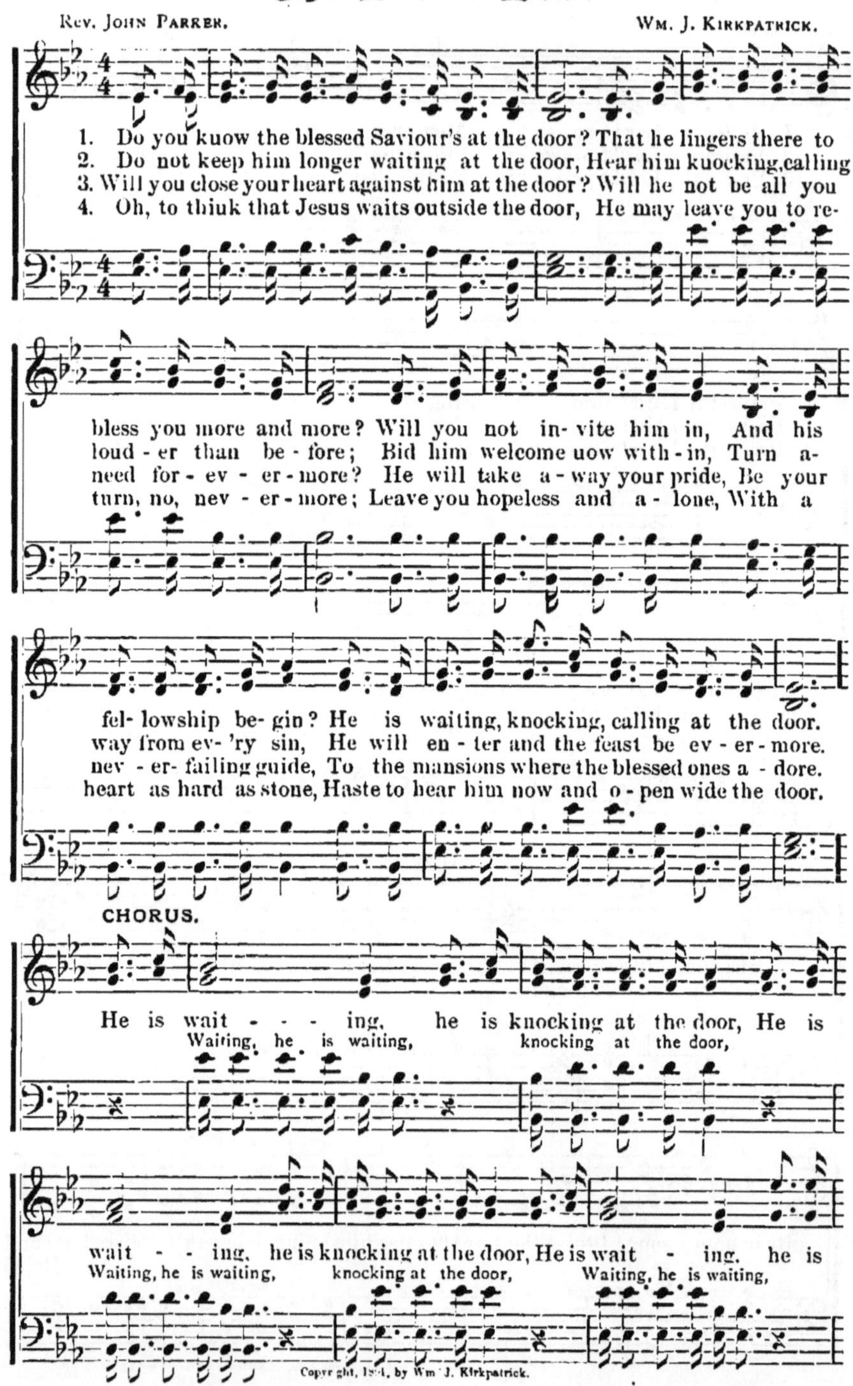
1. Do you know the blessed Saviour's at the door? That he lingers there to
2. Do not keep him longer waiting at the door, Hear him knocking,calling
3. Will you close your heart against him at the door? Will he not be all you
4. Oh, to think that Jesus waits outside the door, He may leave you to re-
bless you more and more? Will you not in- vite him in, And his
loud - er than be - fore; Bid him welcome now with - in, Turn a-
need for - ev - er - more? He will take a - way your pride, Be your
turn, no, nev - er - more; Leave you hopeless and a - lone, With a
fel- lowship be- gin? He is waiting, knocking, calling at the door.
way from ev- 'ry sin, He will en - ter and the feast be ev - er - more.
nev - er- failing guide, To the mansions where the blessed ones a - dore.
heart as hard as stone, Haste to hear him now and o - pen wide the door.
CHORUS.
He is wait - - - ing, he is knocking at the door, He is
Waiting, he is waiting, knocking at the door,
wait - - ing, he is knocking at the door, He is wait - ing, he is
Waiting, he is waiting, knocking at the door, Waiting, he is waiting,

rit.
knocking at the door, He is waiting, he is knocking at the door.
He is knocking at the door.

# Every Little Ray is Needed.

ELTA M. LEWIS. JNO. R. SWENEY.

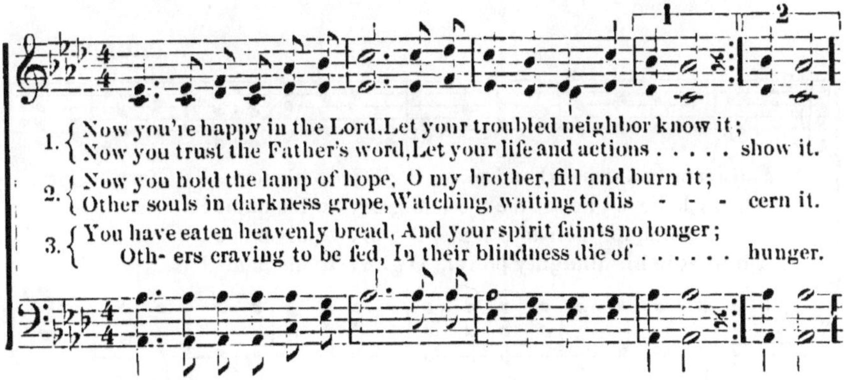

1 2

1. Now you're happy in the Lord, Let your troubled neighbor know it;
Now you trust the Father's word, Let your life and actions . . . . . show it.

2. Now you hold the lamp of hope, O my brother, fill and burn it;
Other souls in darkness grope, Watching, waiting to dis - - - cern it.

3. You have eaten heavenly bread, And your spirit faints no longer;
Oth- ers craving to be fed, In their blindness die of . . . . . . hunger.

CHORUS.

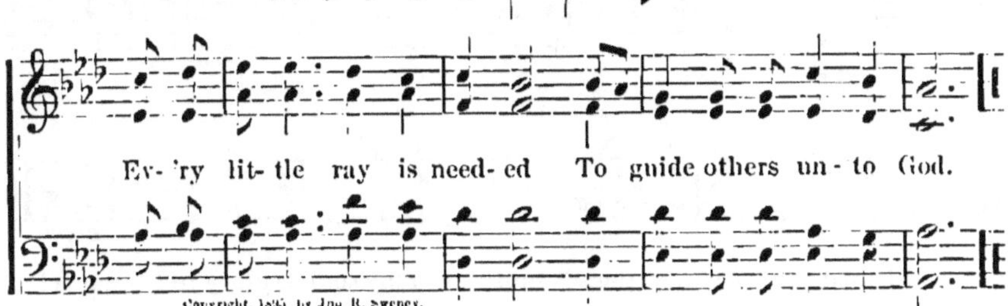

Do not hide . . the light he gives you, Light that ought to shine abroad;
Ev- 'ry lit- tle ray is need- ed To guide others un- to God.

4 If we cannot know the need
Of the groping souls around us,
Yet by shining, word and deed, [us.
We may show them light has found

5 It were sad, indeed, to think
That our neighbor failed of heaven,
Crowded o'er destruction's brink,
Lacking help we might have given.

# O Glory to His Name!

M. E. J. M. Edwin Johnson.

1. I am so hap- py on the way, My night of sin is turned to day,
2. He came to earth, and rescued me By dy- ing on sad Cal- va- ry,
3. The fountain deep by faith I see, The blood of Christ is all my plea;
4. He is my refuge, my high tower, I'll hide in him each day and hour,
And Jesus hears me when I pray, O glory to his name!
When I b lieved he set me free, O glory to his name!
I'll praise him, for it cleanseth me, O glory to his name!
I'll trust in his almighty power, O glory to his name!
CHORUS.
Glory, glory, Glo- ry to his name!
His blood has cleansed and made me whole,
I'm travelling to that blessed goal, And now there's sunshine in my soul, O glory to his name!

# With Me Always.

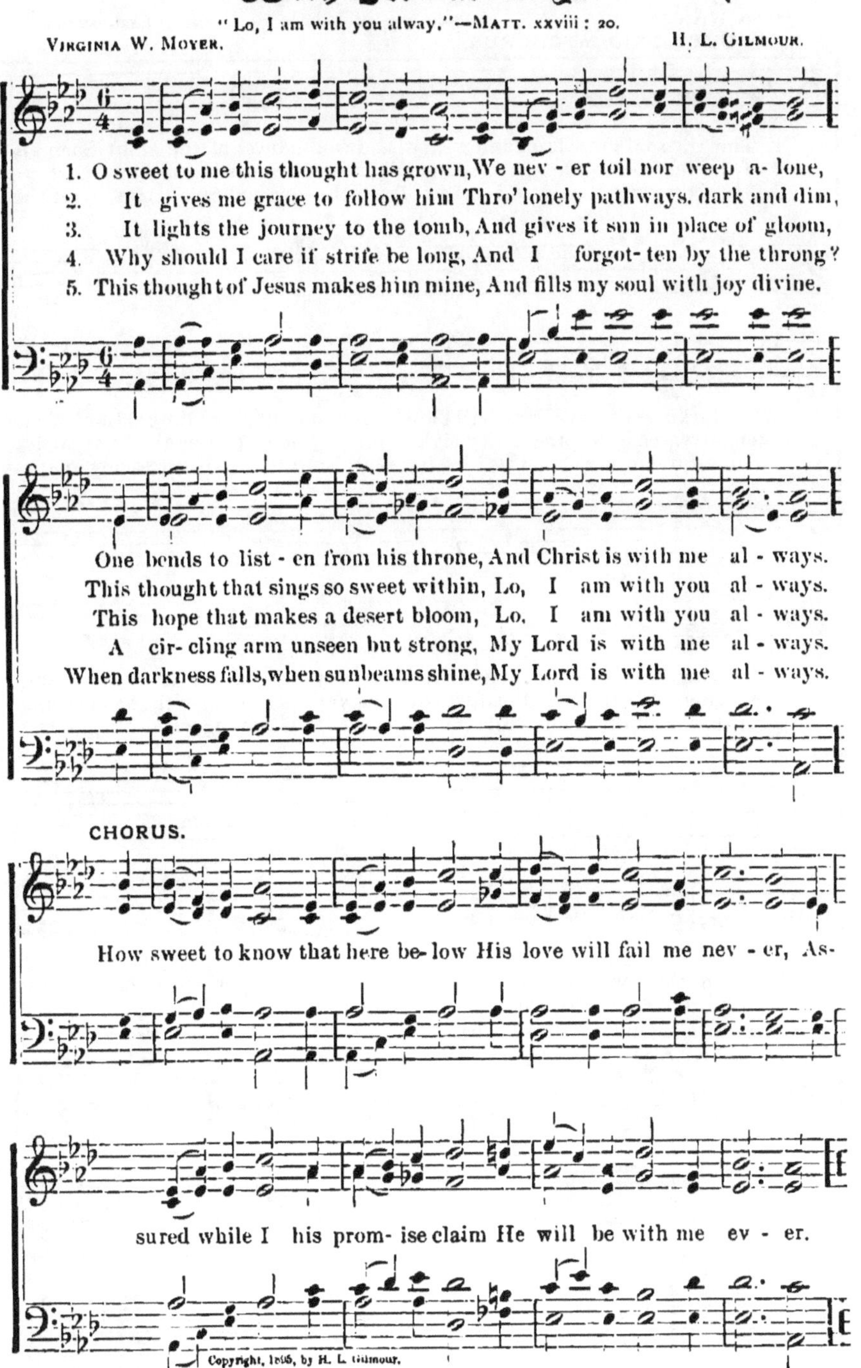
"Lo, I am with you alway."—MATT. xxviii : 20.
VIRGINIA W. MOYER.
H. L. GILMOUR.
1. O sweet to me this thought has grown, We nev - er toil nor weep a- lone,
2. It gives me grace to follow him Thro' lonely pathways, dark and dim,
3. It lights the journey to the tomb, And gives it sun in place of gloom,
4. Why should I care if strife be long, And I forgot- ten by the throng?
5. This thought of Jesus makes him mine, And fills my soul with joy divine.
One bends to list - en from his throne, And Christ is with me al - ways.
This thought that sings so sweet within, Lo, I am with you al - ways.
This hope that makes a desert bloom, Lo, I am with you al - ways.
A cir- cling arm unseen but strong, My Lord is with me al - ways.
When darkness falls, when sunbeams shine, My Lord is with me al - ways.
CHORUS.
How sweet to know that here be- low His love will fail me nev - er, As-
sured while I his prom- ise claim He will be with me ev - er.
Copyright, 1895, by H. L. Gilmour.

Joy is Coming in the Morning.
Jennie Wilson.
Psalm xxx : 5.
Wm. J. Kirkpatrick.
DUET, TRIO and CHORUS.
1. Tho' the soul grow faint and weary 'Mid the sadness of the night, Soon up-
2. Thro' the hours of bitter weeping, When thou seemest all a- lone, God a
3. Thro' the time of pain and sorrow Trust the love and care divine, Wait the
on the darkness dreary There will glow a blessed light; And the gladness of that
tender watch is keeping, Ev'ry sigh to him is known; After all the anxious
radiant to-morrow, Soon its blessing shall be thine; God's unceasing guard is
dawning Will all tears of grief re- pay, Joy is com- ing in the morning,
waking, Af- ter all the fitful dreams, Joy is coming with the breaking
o'er thee, And the gloom will soon be gone, Joy is coming with the glo- ry
CHORUS.
When the shadows flee away. Joy is com - - ing when the morn - ing
Of the morning's golden beams.
Of a holy, cloudless dawn. Joy is coming when the morning Shall in splendor 'round thee shine;
Shall in splen - dor 'round thee shine; Joy is com - - ing in the
Joy is coming when the morning Shall in splendor 'round thee shine; Joy is coming, joy is coming in the
Copyright, 1896, by Wm. J. Kirkpatrick.

ritard.
morn - - - ing, Soul, have faith, no more re - pine. . . . . .
morning, in the morning.
no more repine.

# Taste and See.

Psalm xxxiv: 8.

E. E. Hewitt. H. L. Gilmour.

1. Hear the bless-ed in - vi - ta - tion Of the mighty King of kings!
2. He is wait- ing to be gra- cious, Try his word and find it true;
3. Peace beyond all mor - tal measure, Light that nev- er will grow dim;
4. Taste, but nev - er stop at tasting, Fill your hungry heart with love;

Of - fer of a full sal- va - tion, Ev - 'ry word with blessing rings.
Oth - ers say that he is precious, Don't you want to know it too?
Mer- cy's ev - er - last- ing treasure, Come and find them all in him.
You will nev - er tire of feasting In the ban- quet spread a- bove.

CHORUS.

1 2

Taste and see that the Lord is good, Taste and see, O taste and see;
Feast your soul on the heav'nly food, . . . . . . . . Taste, O taste and see.

# My Saviour.

HENRY A. BOMBERGER. JNO. R. SWENEY.

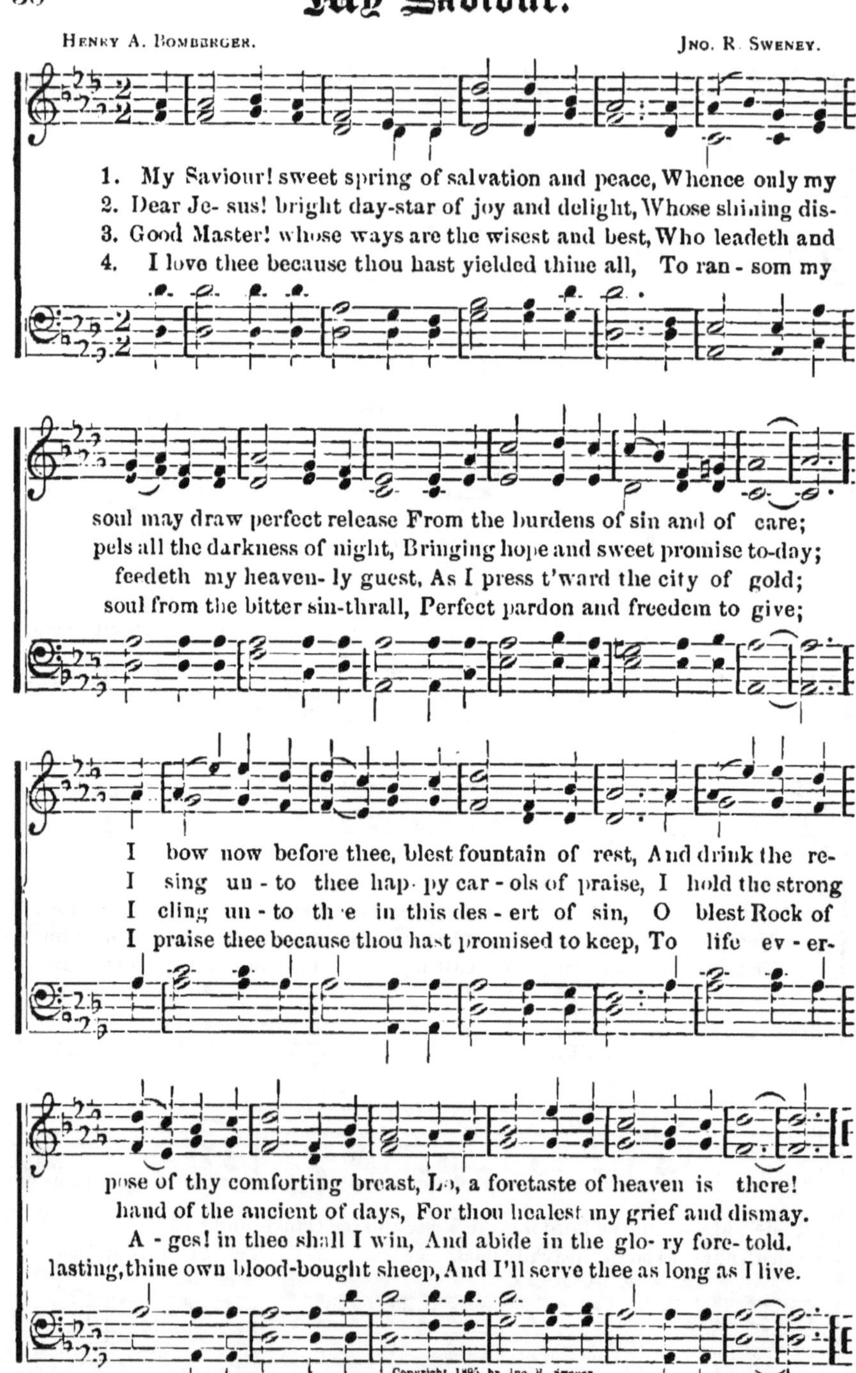
1. My Saviour! sweet spring of salvation and peace, Whence only my
2. Dear Je- sus! bright day-star of joy and delight, Whose shining dis-
3. Good Master! whose ways are the wisest and best, Who leadeth and
4. I love thee because thou hast yielded thine all, To ran - som my
soul may draw perfect release From the burdens of sin and of care;
pels all the darkness of night, Bringing hope and sweet promise to-day;
feedeth my heaven- ly guest, As I press t'ward the city of gold;
soul from the bitter sin-thrall, Perfect pardon and freedom to give;
I bow now before thee, blest fountain of rest, And drink the re-
I sing un - to thee hap- py car - ols of praise, I hold the strong
I cling un - to thee in this des - ert of sin, O blest Rock of
I praise thee because thou hast promised to keep, To life ev - er-
pose of thy comforting breast, Lo, a foretaste of heaven is there!
hand of the ancient of days, For thou healest my grief and dismay.
A - ges! in thee shall I win, And abide in the glo- ry fore- told.
lasting, thine own blood-bought sheep, And I'll serve thee as long as I live.
Copyright, 1895, by Jno. R. Sweney.

# Joy in Service.

S. H. B.
S. H. Bolton. Arr. by H. L. G.
1. Dear Jesus, I am willing to walk, and tell each day Of all the wondrous
2. Just now I am enjoying the love of Christ my Lord, And living in the
3. Dear Je- sus, I am feeding upon the corn and wine, And all the fruits of
beauties, along the King's highway; I've lived in Egypt's bondage, and
sunlight, a- bid - ing in his word; His yoke I find is eas - y, his
Canaan as promised now are mine; I'm praying that the kingdom in-
D. S.—Our God now calls you onward, in
Fine.
in the wilderness, But now enjoy the freedom of Canaan's perfect rest.
bur- den al- so light, He gives me joy in service, upholds me by his might.
to each heart may come, That all may know the fulness of Canaan's perfect home.
perfect love to live, He'll fill you with his Spirit, when all to Christ you give.
CHORUS.
Yes, you can live in Canaan, sur - ren - der to the Lord;
D.S.
Come up up - on the highway, trust ful - ly in his word;

# Let the Saviour Pilot Thee.

F. S. S.
F. S. Shepard.
1. Sailor, is your life-boat driv - en By the sweeping blasts of sin?
2. Sailor, is your vessel drifting From the course of right away?
3. Sailor, is the tempest breaking? Is the sky with clouds o'ercast?
Would you 'scape the shoals and breakers? Take the blessed Pi- lot in.
Would you gain the sheltered ha - ven? Take the Pi - lot in to- day.
Guided by the Lord as Pi - lot You will reach the port at last.
CHORUS.
Sail - ing on . . . . a dang'rous voy - age, O'er a
Sail - ing on
dang'rous voyage,
dark . . . and treach'rous sea, . . . Would you reach . . . the harbor
O'er a dark and treach'rous sea, treach'rous sea,
Would you reach
safe - ly? Let the Sav - iour pi - lot thee.
har - bor safe - ly?
Let the Saviour pi - lot thee, pi - lot thee.

# The Master is Calling.

Rev. E. H. Stokes, D. D. | Jno. R. Sweney

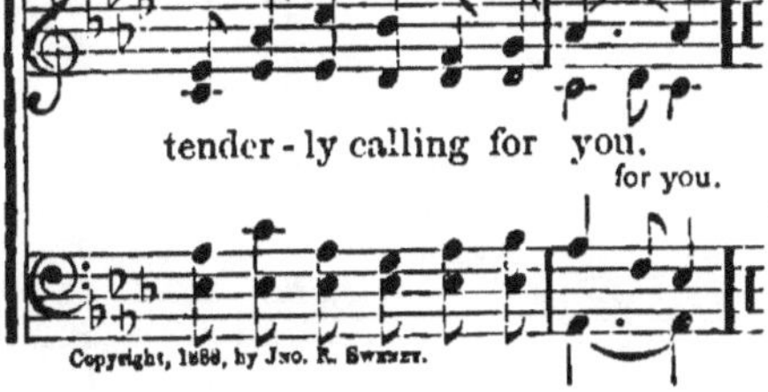

1. The Master is calling for you, dear friend, The Master is calling for you; You have wandered away,—Won't you come back to-day? Come back to the good and the true.
2. He calls by his Word unto you, dear friend, His Word which has come from above, Won't you heed it to-day? Won't you come to him, say? Come back to the heart of his love.
3. He calls by his Spir-it to you, dear friend, His Spirit is moving your heart; Won't you yield to him now? Won't you here make your vow, For heaven at once you will start.

CHORUS.

Come, the dear Master is call - ing, Come, the dear Master is call - ing, Call - ing, (Calling for you,) call - ing, (calling for you,) Is tender - ly calling for you. (for you.)

4 He calls by his providence, too, dear friend,
In ways which have sorrows untold;
Though your spirit may sigh,
Let your fond heart reply,
Dear Lord, I'll return to thy fold.

5 The Master is calling you all, dear friends,
The Master is calling us, too;
We have wandered away,
Let us come back to-day,
Come back to the good and the true.

# Earth has Her Ties.

JOHNSON OATMAN, Jr. Cho. by H. L. G. H. L. GILMOUR.

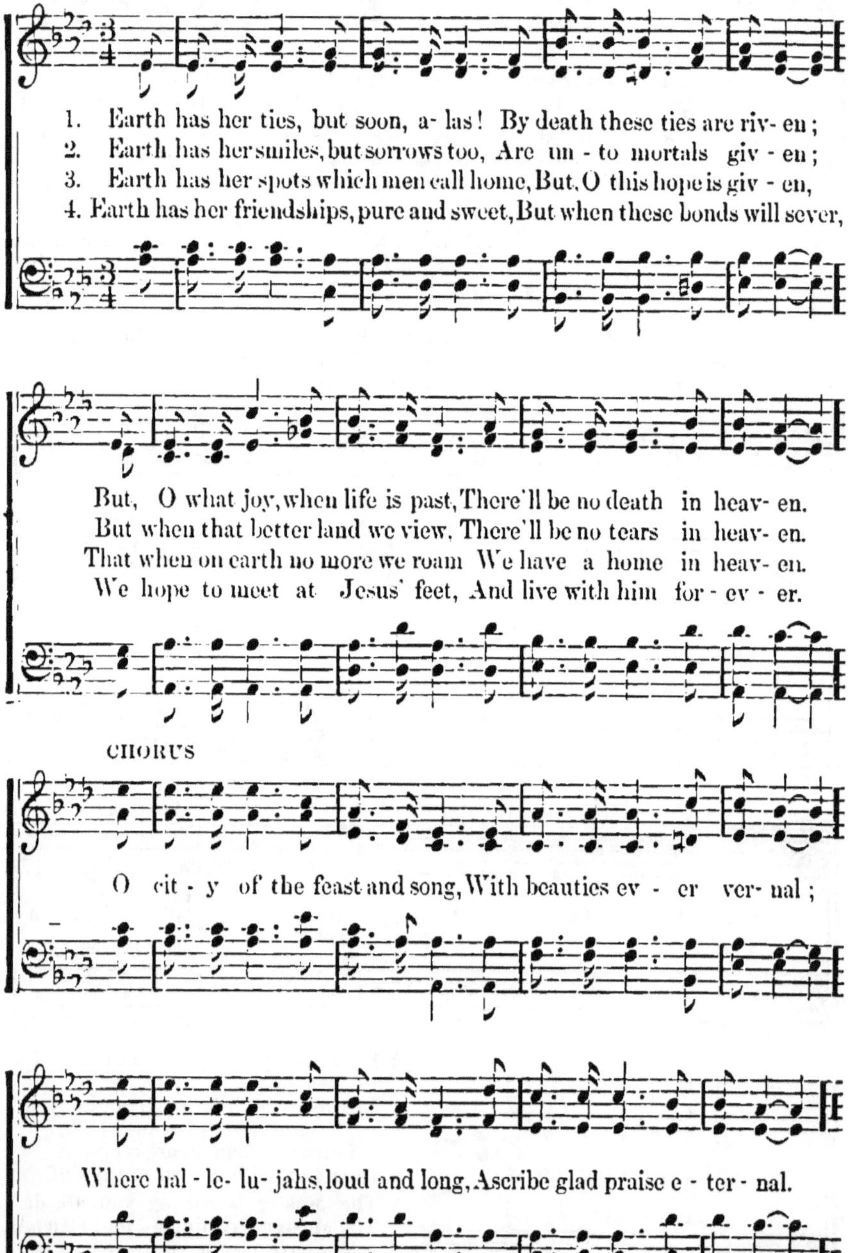

1. Earth has her ties, but soon, a- las! By death these ties are riv- en;
2. Earth has her smiles, but sorrows too, Are un - to mortals giv - en;
3. Earth has her spots which men call home, But, O this hope is giv - en,
4. Earth has her friendships, pure and sweet, But when these bonds will sever,

But, O what joy, when life is past, There'll be no death in heav- en.
But when that better land we view, There'll be no tears in heav- en.
That when on earth no more we roam We have a home in heav- en.
We hope to meet at Jesus' feet, And live with him for - ev - er.

CHORUS

O cit - y of the feast and song, With beauties ev - er ver- nal;
Where hal - le- lu- jahs, loud and long, Ascribe glad praise e - ter - nal.

# The Birth-Place of My Soul.

Johnson Oatman, Jr. Jno. R. Sweney.

1. The stars now shining o'er me Are call - ing me a- way,
2. While here on earth's dominions, As I view the beacon light,
3. No power on earth can hold me, I am press- ing to that land,
For stretching out be - fore me Is that land of end- less day;
My soul doth stretch her pin- ions For her ev - er- last- ing flight;
Where God's arm will en- fold me, As be - fore his throne I stand;
While on the tide I'm drift - ing I can hear the surg- es roll,
There I'll nev - er know a sor - row, There no fun - 'ral bells will toll,
For there no sin can sev - er, Safe with Christ who made me whole,
I can see the shadows lift - ing O'er the birth-place of my soul.
There will come no sad to - morrow In the birth-place of my soul.
I will live with him for - ev - er In the birth-place of my soul.
Fine.
D.S.—Don't you hear the mu - sic ring- ing In the birth-place of my soul?
CHORUS.
Hark, the an - gel choirs are singing, Don't you hear the anthems roll?
D.S.

# The Stately Steppings of Our Lord.

Johnson Oatman, Jr. | Jno. R. Sweney.

1. When the fires are brightly burning on the al - tars here, Then the
2. When we're kneeling with a sinner who is seek - ing rest, And the
3. When a saint of God is dy - ing, when his work is o'er, And his
Lord of hosts doth vis - it, and his people cheer; When our pray'rs and songs are
Mighty God approaches, how we all are blest; When upon the troubled
soul doth stretch her pinions for the heav'nly shore; When he calls for God to
D. S.—sees his child in
blending in a sweet ac - cord, Then we always hear the stately steppings
spir - it oil of love is poured, Then we always hear the stately steppings
help him cross the drear - y ford, Then we always hear the stately steppings
danger, be his name a - dored Oh, 'tis then we hear the stately steppings
Fine.
CHORUS.
of our Lord. Weary saint of God, take courage, when we need him most,
D.S.
Then we always hear the steppings of the Lord of hosts; When he

# Not One Day Without My Saviour.

E. E. HEWITT. F. E. BELDEN.

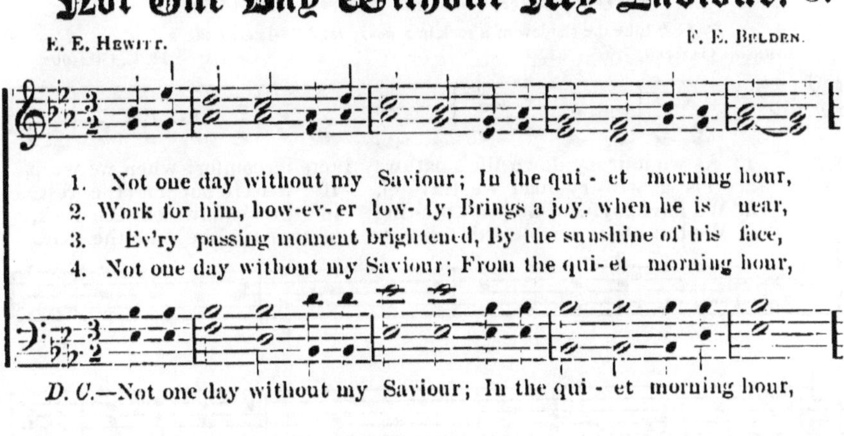
1. Not one day without my Saviour; In the qui - et morning hour,
2. Work for him, how-ev- er low- ly, Brings a joy, when he is near,
3. Ev'ry passing moment brightened, By the sunshine of his face,
4. Not one day without my Saviour; From the qui- et morning hour,
D. C.—Not one day without my Saviour; In the qui - et morning hour,

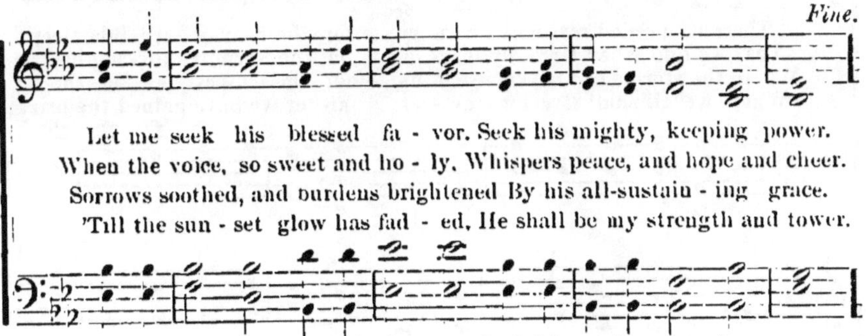
Fine.
Let me seek his blessed fa - vor. Seek his mighty, keeping power.
When the voice, so sweet and ho - ly, Whispers peace, and hope and cheer.
Sorrows soothed, and burdens brightened By his all-sustain - ing grace.
'Till the sun - set glow has fad - ed, He shall be my strength and tower.
Let me seek his blessed fa - vor, Seek his mighty, keeping power.

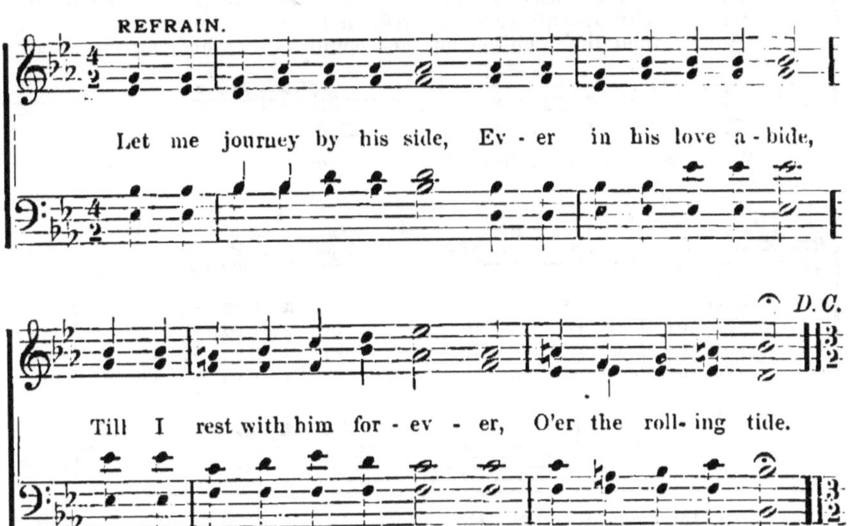
REFRAIN.
Let me journey by his side, Ev - er in his love a - bide,
D. C.
Till I rest with him for - ev - er, O'er the roll- ing tide.

# The Shadow of a Rock.

"Like the shadow of a rock in a weary land."—Isa. xxxii: 2.

JOHNSON OATMAN, Jr. H. L. GILMOUR.

1. As we journey down life's pathway there is comfort when we weep,
2. 'Tis a wea- ry road we trav - el, if it were not for the rest
3. We have joyful times, re - pos- ing in the shadow of the rock,
4. We have here a blessed foretaste of that land beyond the skies,

There is needed rest when wea- ry, for the heav- y eye- lids, sleep;
That we find when tired, by lean- ing on the Saviour's lov- ing breast;
Where the storms can never reach us, nor the tempest ev - er shock;
Where we all shall live for - ev - er, af- ter we have gained the prize;

And the face of our dear Saviour, shows a- bove the heated strand,
But when we are heav- y lad - en, then he leads us by the hand
Here our wills are all sur- rendered, and the Lord takes full command,
But till then, life's guiding an- gel points us with his gold- en wand

*D. S.*—With the breezes fresh from Beu- lah our spir- its will be fanned,

*Fine.*

Like the shad- ow of a rock in a wea - ry land.
To the shad- ow of that rock in a wea - ry land.
In the shad- ow of that rock in a wea - ry land.
To the shad- ow of that rock in a wea - ry land.

wea- ry, wea - ry

In the shad- ow of that rock in a wea - ry land.

## The Shadow of a Rock.—CONCLUDED.

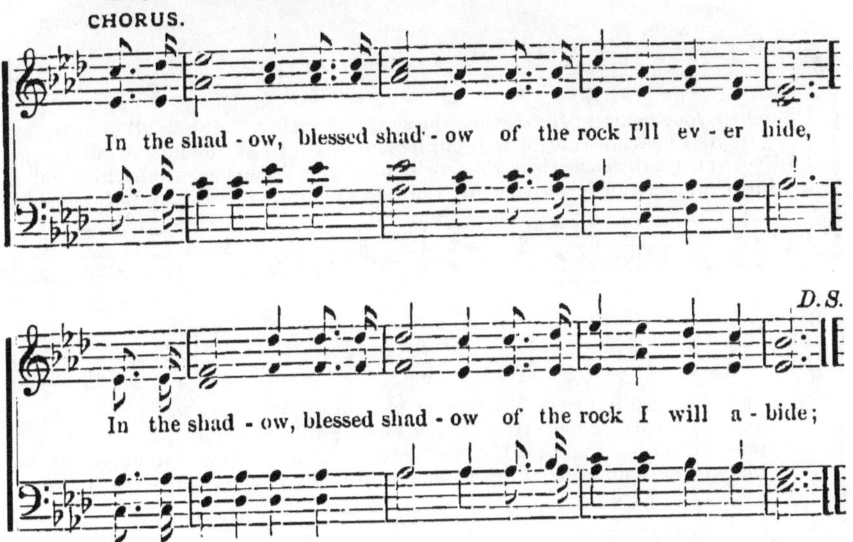
CHORUS.
In the shad - ow, blessed shad - ow of the rock I'll ev - er hide,
D.S.
In the shad - ow, blessed shad - ow of the rock I will a - bide;

## O Thou, Supreme in Might.

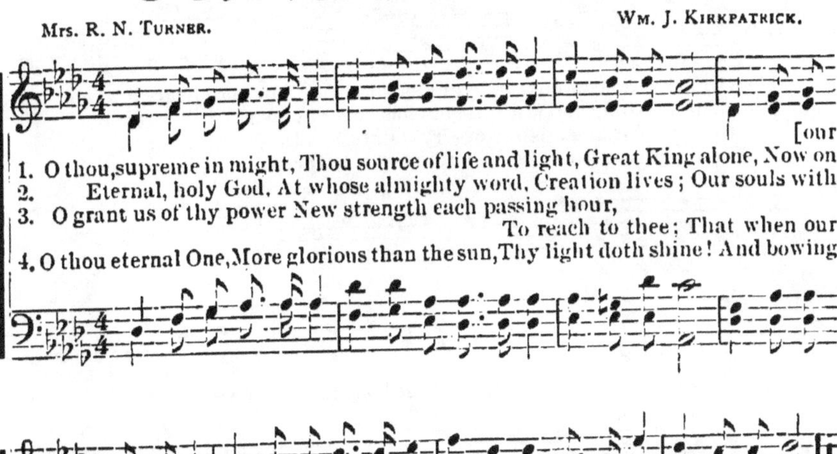
Mrs. R. N. Turner.
Wm. J. Kirkpatrick.
1. O thou, supreme in might, Thou source of life and light, Great King alone, Now on [our
2. Eternal, holy God, At whose almighty word, Creation lives; Our souls with
3. O grant us of thy power New strength each passing hour,
To reach to thee; That when our
4. O thou eternal One, More glorious than the sun, Thy light doth shine! And bowing

[own!
darkness shine. And by thy love divine Lift up these hearts of thine, Thy power to
zeal inspire, And light with sacred fire Each fervent, high desire Thy Spirit gives!
foes assail, Their strength and power may fail,
And we o'er all prevail, In Christ made free!
at thy throne, Thee only would we own, Our Saviour, Lord alone, Great King divine!

# Lift Your Heart to Jesus.

Ida L. Reed. H. L. Gilmour.

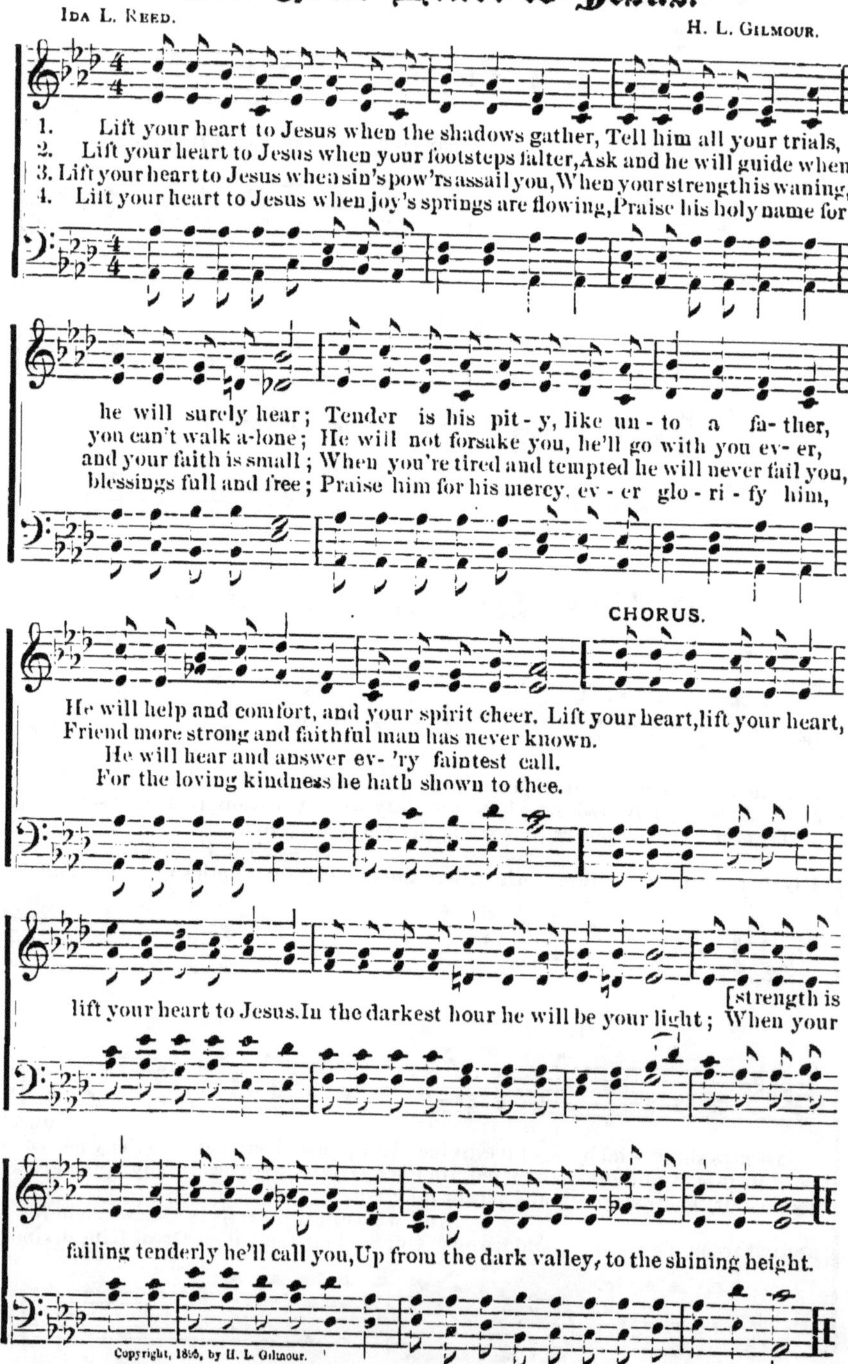
1. Lift your heart to Jesus when the shadows gather, Tell him all your trials,
2. Lift your heart to Jesus when your footsteps falter, Ask and he will guide when
3. Lift your heart to Jesus when sin's pow'rs assail you, When your strength is waning,
4. Lift your heart to Jesus when joy's springs are flowing, Praise his holy name for
he will surely hear; Tender is his pit-y, like un-to a fa-ther,
you can't walk a-lone; He will not forsake you, he'll go with you ev-er,
and your faith is small; When you're tired and tempted he will never fail you,
blessings full and free; Praise him for his mercy, ev-er glo-ri-fy him,
He will help and comfort, and your spirit cheer.
Friend more strong and faithful man has never known.
He will hear and answer ev-'ry faintest call.
For the loving kindness he hath shown to thee.
CHORUS.
Lift your heart, lift your heart, lift your heart to Jesus. In the darkest hour he will be your light; When your strength is failing tenderly he'll call you, Up from the dark valley, to the shining height.

# The Wonderful Story Again.

Fanny J. Crosby. Wm. J. Kirkpatrick.

1. I will tell you the won-der-ful sto - ry a-gain, Of Je - sus, the
2. I will tell you the won-der-ful sto - ry a-gain, Of par-don to
3. I will tell you the won-der-ful sto - ry a-gain, So precious and
4. I will tell you the won-der-ful sto - ry a-gain, The won-der-ful
mighty to save; Who purchased sal-va-tion for all on the cross,
all that be - lieve; And, oh, that the Spir - it will help you just now,
dear to my heart; 'Twil give you a com- fort the world cannot give,
sto - ry so true; O haste to the fountain of mer - cy di - vine,
And triumphed o'er death and the grave.
The mes- sage of grace to re - ceive.
A joy it can nev- er im - part.
Whose wa- ters are flowing for you.
CHORUS.
O hear it a - gain, blessed
sto - ry of love, Redemption thro' Jesus from sin; . . . . He opened the
from sin;
por- tals of life to my soul, And ten- der- ly welcomed me in.

# He will Lead Us.

Fanny J. Crosby

Jno. R. Sweney.

1. Are we walking in the counsel of the Lord? Are we growing, dai- ly
2. Are we walking with the blessed King of kings? Are we resting, sweetly
3. Are we temples where the Holy Spirit dwells? Do we lift our willing
4. Are we liv- ing in the sunshine of his love? Are we looking, are we
growing in the knowledge of his word? Have we felt the precious cleansing of the [soul?
resting in the shadow of his wings? Are we trusting, fully trusting in his power,
voices when the song of rapture swells? Unto Jesus have we left our many cares?
longing for a city built above? Are we faithful to the grace already given,
CHORUS.
Has the blood of our Redeemer made us whole? Then his banner will be ov- er us,
And believing he will keep us ev'ry hour?
Are we feasting at the banquet he prepares?
And our treasures have we laid them up in heav'n.
And his mighty arm from evil will de- liv - er us; He will lead us by his
might - ty arm
hand to a fair and goodly land, With the brightness of his glory he will cover us.

# I'm Resting in Jesus.

Rev. F. Bottome, D. D. By per. Wm. J. Kirkpatrick.

1. The conflict is o- ver, the tempest is past, I'm resting in Je- sus. I'm
2. There's peace in believing, sweet peace to the soul, To know that he maketh me
3. Oh, hinder me not while his love I proclaim, My soul makes her boasts of his
4. There's peace in believing, sweet peace to the soul, To know that he maketh me
rest - ing at last; The billows that filled my poor soul with a- larm Are
per - fectly whole; There's joy ev- er - lasting to feel his blood flow, 'Tis
won - derful name; I stand with my foot on the neck of my foe, Then,
per - fectly whole; Oh, come to the fountain, oh, come at his call! There's
hushed at his word in - to stillness and calm.
life from the dead my Redeem- er to know.
bounding with gladness, triumphant I go.
healing, and cleansing, and welcome for all.
CHORUS.
I'm rest- ing in Je- sus, I'm
resting at last, I'm resting in Jesus, my soul anchored fast; All doubting and
ad lib.
conflict with me now is past, I'm resting in Je- sus, I'm resting at last.

# Jesus is Mine.

E. E. Hewitt. Wm. J. Kirkpatrick.

1. Jesus is mine; on Calv'ry he bought me; Leaving his glory, tenderly sought me; Wonderful Saviour, faithful and kind; All that I need, in him I find.
2. Jesus is mine; for ev'ry to-morrow; Strength in my weakness; joy in my sorrow; Leaning on him, the pilgrimage way Glows with the dawn of perfect day.
3. Jesus is mine; all else shall be given; Pardon and cleansing; meetness for heaven; No good, he tells me, e'er is denied, When in his promise I confide.
4. Jesus is mine; time's pleasures are fleeting; Words of farewell soon follow the greeting; Tho' blossoms wither, sunbeams decline, This joy grows brighter—he is mine.
5. Jesus is mine; oh, marvellous treasure! Love passing knowledge; grace beyond measure; When endless glories 'round me shall shine, Praise him forever, he'll be mine.

CHORUS.

Wonderful Saviour—joy all-di- vine; Jesus has saved me; Jesus is mine;
Wonderful Saviour, faithful and kind; All that I need, in him I find.

# The Hills of Glory.

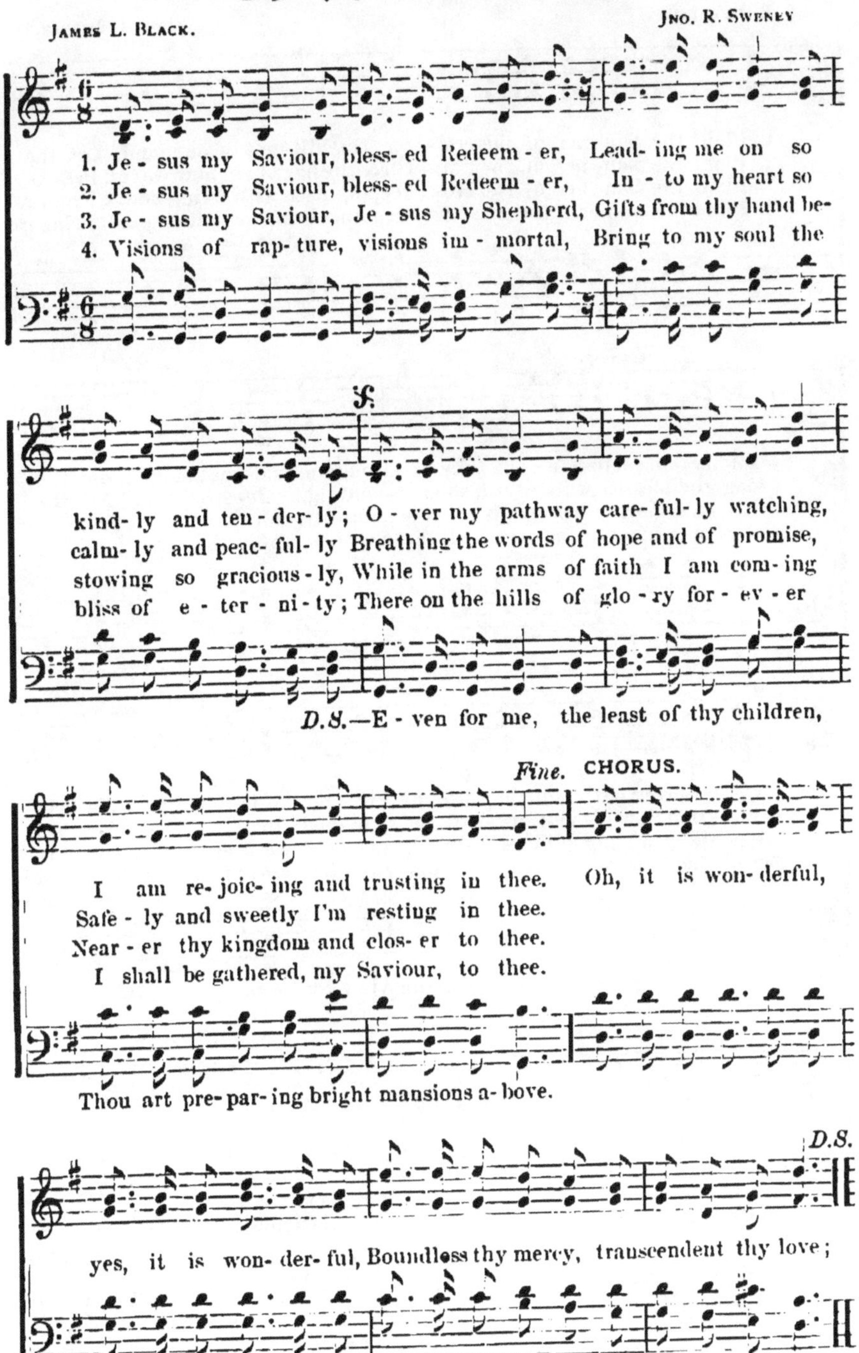
James L. Black.
Jno. R. Sweney
1. Je - sus my Saviour, bless- ed Redeem - er, Lead- ing me on so kind- ly and ten - der- ly; O - ver my pathway care- ful- ly watching, I am re- joic- ing and trusting in thee.
2. Je - sus my Saviour, bless- ed Redeem - er, In - to my heart so calm- ly and peac- ful- ly Breathing the words of hope and of promise, Safe - ly and sweetly I'm resting in thee.
3. Je - sus my Saviour, Je - sus my Shepherd, Gifts from thy hand be- stowing so gracious - ly, While in the arms of faith I am com- ing Near - er thy kingdom and clos- er to thee.
4. Visions of rap- ture, visions im - mortal, Bring to my soul the bliss of e - ter - ni - ty; There on the hills of glo - ry for - ev - er I shall be gathered, my Saviour, to thee.
D.S.—E - ven for me, the least of thy children,
Fine.
CHORUS.
Oh, it is won- derful, yes, it is won- der- ful, Boundless thy mercy, transcendent thy love;
Thou art pre- par- ing bright mansions a- bove.
D.S.
Copyright, 1895, by Jno. R. Sweney.

# Plant the Banner of the Cross.

E. E. Hewitt. Jno. R. Sweney.

1. Plant the ban- ner of the cross on the hill-tops of our land, Let the soldiers of King Je- sus take a strong and val- iant stand; Bid the val- leys ring with mu- sic, while the vic - tor hosts go by, We will set our colors flying where the mountains kiss the sky.
2. Plant the ban- ner of the cross where the flag of sin now waves, Pass a- long the blessed watchword, shout a- loud that "Je- sus saves;" All the wrongs that now di- vide us shall be rightened from a- bove, Ev - 'ry wound shall find sweet healing in the gospel balm of love.
3. Plant the ban- ner of the cross, keeping pace with flying hours, From A- las- ka's snow- y headlands to the sun - ny vale of flow'rs; From At- lan- tic's curl- ing billows to the pla - cid west- ern sea, All our native land for Jesus, and his truth shall make us free.
4. Plant the banner of the cross; let the mines bring forth their gold, Bring the treasures of the for - est and the rich - es of the fold; All to swell the fame of Je - sus, and his sav - ing power proclaim, Sing from hill- top and from valley hal- le- lujahs to his name.
D.S.—val- leys ring with mu- sic, while the vic - tor hosts go by, We will set our colors flying where the mountains kiss the sky.
Fine. CHORUS.
Plant the ban - -
Plant the banner of the

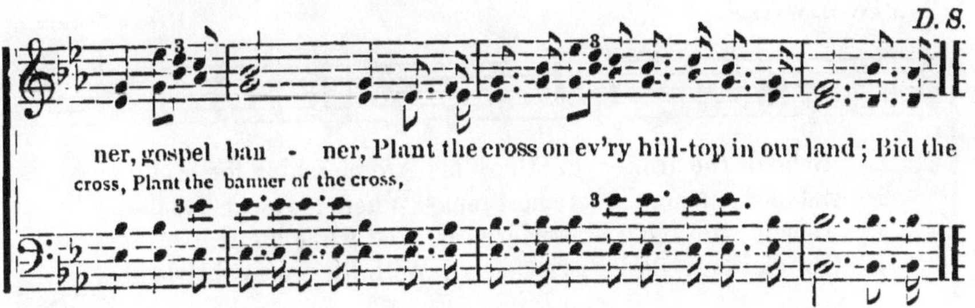
D. S.
ner, gospel ban - ner, Plant the cross on ev'ry hill-top in our land; Bid the
cross, Plant the banner of the cross,

# Take Time to be Holy.

"Be ye holy: for I am the Lord your God."—Lev. xx: 7.

W. D. LONGSTAFF. GEO. C. STEBBINS.

1. Take time to be ho - ly, Speak oft with thy Lord; A - bide in him
2. Take time to be ho - ly, The world rushes on; Spend much time in
3. Take time to be ho - ly, Let him be thy Guide, And run not be-
4. Take time to be ho - ly, Be calm in thy soul, Each thought and each

al - ways, And feed on his Word; Make friends of God's children,
se - cret With Je - sus a - lone; By looking to Je - sus,
fore him, What - ev - er be - tide; In joy or in sor - row,
mo - tive Be- neath his con - trol; Thus led by his Spir - it

Help those who are weak, For- getting in nothing His blessing to seek.
Like him thou shalt be; Thy friends in thy conduct His likeness shall see.
Still follow thy Lord, And, looking to Je- sus, Still trust in his Word.
To fountains of love, Thou soon shalt be fitted For service a - bove.

# The Armies of the King.

MARY G. WALKER. HENRY BURTON.

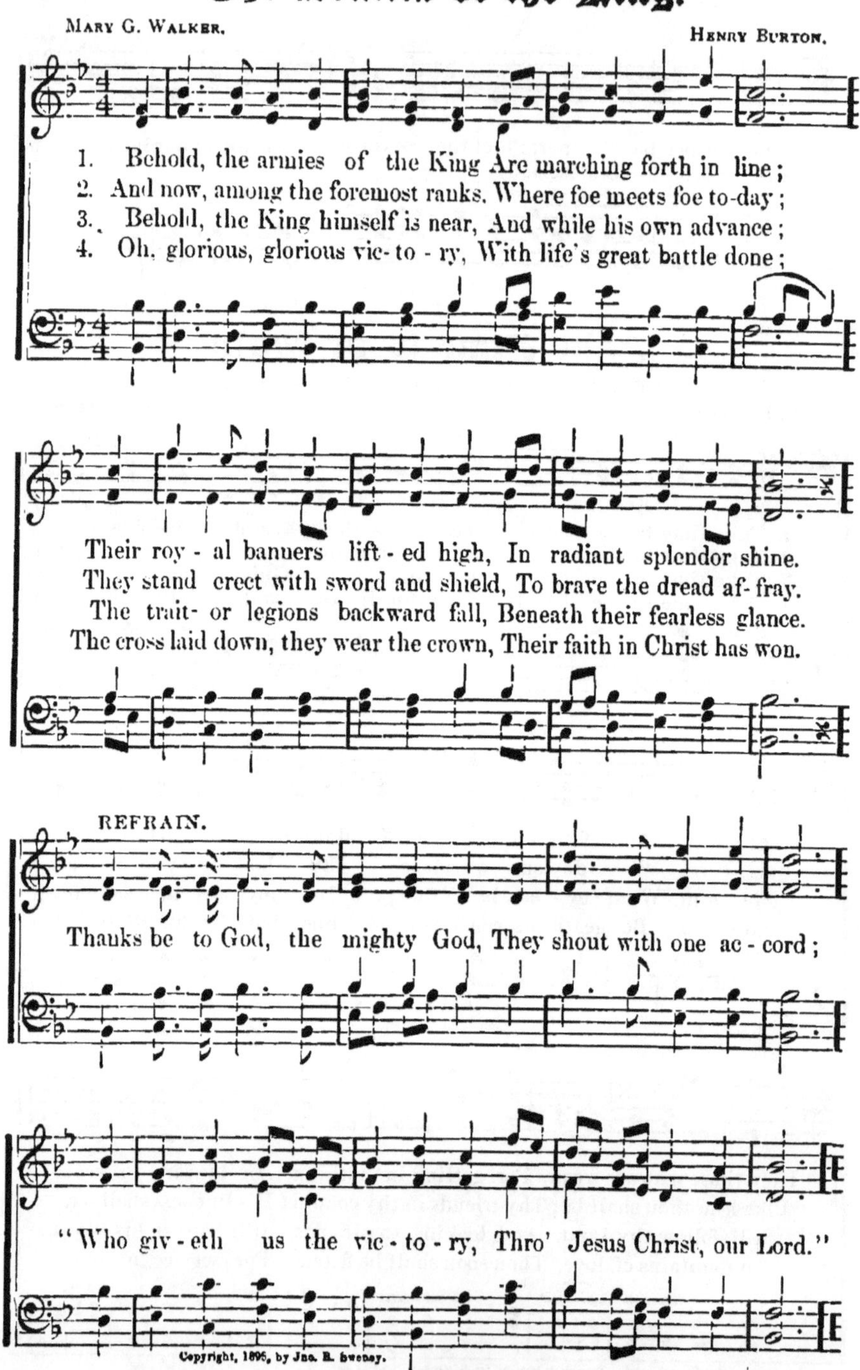
1. Behold, the armies of the King Are marching forth in line;
2. And now, among the foremost ranks, Where foe meets foe to-day;
3. Behold, the King himself is near, And while his own advance;
4. Oh, glorious, glorious vic- to - ry, With life's great battle done;
Their roy - al banners lift - ed high, In radiant splendor shine.
They stand erect with sword and shield, To brave the dread af- fray.
The trait- or legions backward fall, Beneath their fearless glance.
The cross laid down, they wear the crown, Their faith in Christ has won.
REFRAIN.
Thanks be to God, the mighty God, They shout with one ac - cord;
"Who giv - eth us the vic - to - ry, Thro' Jesus Christ, our Lord."

# We Are Soldiers of the Lord.

E. E. Hewitt. Jno. R. Sweney.

1. We are soldiers of the Lord, Pressing onward at his word, We are girding on the armor he provides; With our faces toward the sky, Where his banner floats on high.
2. There are foes on ev'ry hand, Strong temptations to withstand, How we need his arms around us, hour by hour; As his holy steps we trace, Let us seek his saving grace,
3. There are crowns of starry light, There are robes of snowy white, There are sweeter songs than those which angels sing; For his soldiers, good and true, Who have kept his cross in view,
CHORUS.
Let us follow where the mighty Master guides.
And his name shall be our biding-place and tow'r.
Endless glory in the presence of the King.
Marching onward, ever on- ward,
We have heard the gospel's loud, resounding call; We are soldiers of the Lord,
Pressing onward at his word, We will crown him King of kings, and Lord of all.

# Stepping Heavenward.

E. E. Hewitt. Wm. J. Kirkpatrick.

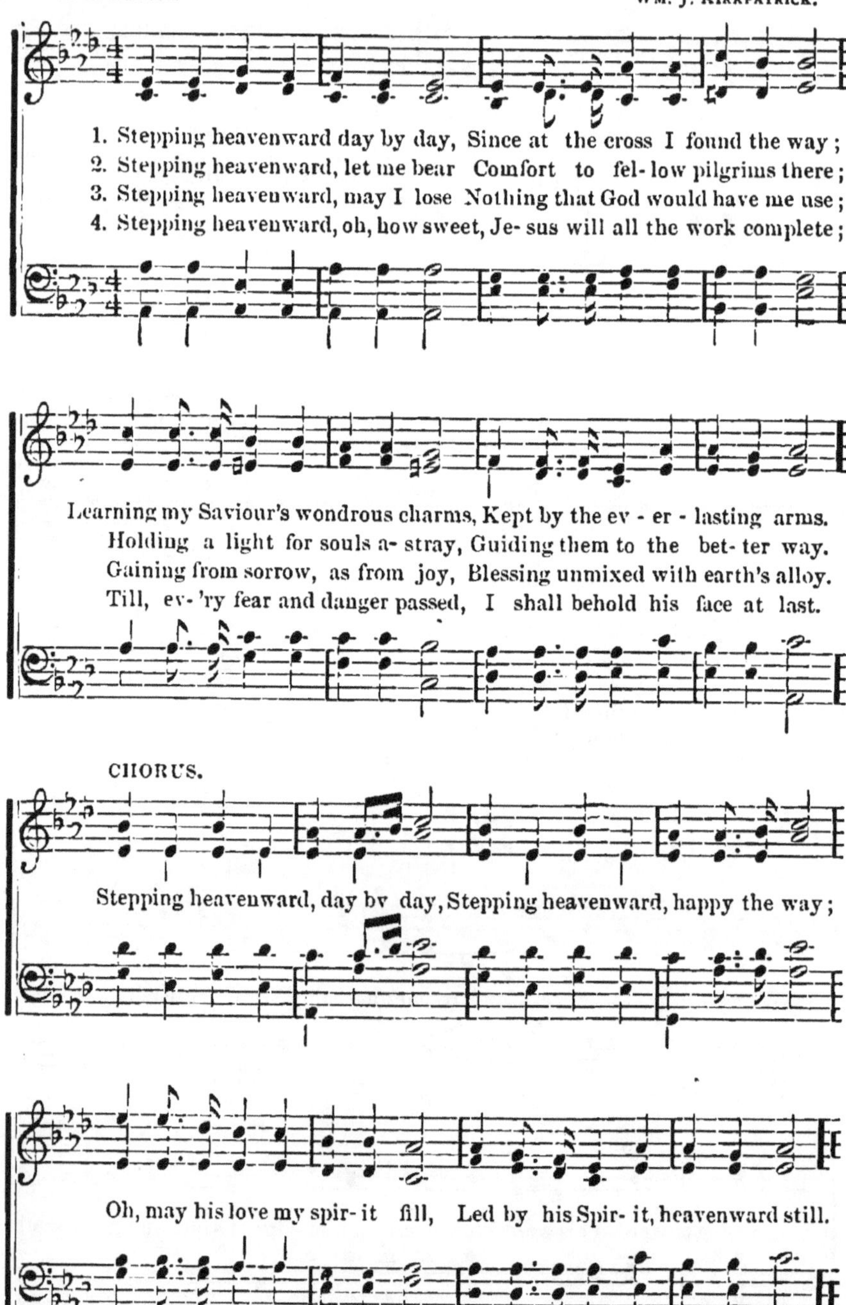
1. Stepping heavenward day by day, Since at the cross I found the way;
2. Stepping heavenward, let me bear Comfort to fel- low pilgrims there;
3. Stepping heavenward, may I lose Nothing that God would have me use;
4. Stepping heavenward, oh, how sweet, Je- sus will all the work complete;
Learning my Saviour's wondrous charms, Kept by the ev - er - lasting arms.
Holding a light for souls a- stray, Guiding them to the bet- ter way.
Gaining from sorrow, as from joy, Blessing unmixed with earth's alloy.
Till, ev- 'ry fear and danger passed, I shall behold his face at last.
CHORUS.
Stepping heavenward, day by day, Stepping heavenward, happy the way;
Oh, may his love my spir- it fill, Led by his Spir- it, heavenward still.

# Jesus, Our Help, is Near.

Rev. W. J. Stuart. Jno. R. Sweney.

1. There's many a heart is break- ing, The world to them is drear; There's
2. Go, car- ry to them the tid - ings, That bring such glad re- lief; Go,
3. He'd car- ry all our sor- rows, Were they but rolled on him; There
ma- ny an eye is weep- ing The sad and bit- ter tear. There's many a
tell them that in his hid- ings God sees them in their grief. There's many a
would be no sad to- morrows, Were not our faith so dim. Then let us
soul re- pin- ing Its sad and lonely sphere, Ne'er for a moment divining
soul awaiting The word of Christly cheer; Go, tell the hearts that are breaking,
trust our Fa- ther To wipe a- way the tear; We will not faint nor murmur,
CHORUS.
Jesus, our Help, is near. Then we will on him our burdens roll, Blessed Saviour
of the soul; There is nothing that we should fear, Jesus, our Help, is near.

# Gladly We will Go.

Fanny J. Crosby.
Clarissa H. Spencer.
1. The Lord is our shepherd, precious friend and guide, We'll trust him ever,
2. Thro' sunshine or tempest, o - ver land or sea, Whate'er befalls us,
3. The Lord is our keep - er, watching ev - er near, In him confid- ing,
trust him ev- er, walking by his side; Be this our en- dea - vor faithful-
where he calls us, quickly we would be; The toils that a- wait us tho' we
firm abiding, wherefore should we fear? We'll cling to the promise left us
ly to show, Where Jesus leads our willing feet beside him still shall go.
cannot know, At his command with heart and hand bes'de him we will go.
here be- low, And wheresoe'er he leadeth us beside him we will go.
CHORUS.
We'll go, we'll go, we'll glad- ly, glad- ly go, Tho' skies are
We'll go, we'll go, Tho' skies
dark and chill- y winds may blow; The lost to find, or
are dark The lost to find,
Copyright, 1895, by Wm. J. Kirkpatrick.

bravely meet the foe, Wherever Jesus calls us we'll gladly, gladly go.
There's a Glorious Saviour.
E. E. Hewitt.
H. L. Gilmour.
1. There's a glorious Saviour for you and for me, He's able and willing to save;
2. O this glorious Saviour is "able to keep," If on - ly we trust in his power;
3. O this glorious Saviour one day we'll behold, His service our lives shall employ;
He walks on the billows of life's tossing sea, To snatch us from sin's dark wave.
He comes as a shepherd to seek his lost sheep, His grace will avail each hour.
Then dwelling with him in the city of gold, We'll praise him in songs of joy.
CHORUS.
There's a glorious Saviour for you, There's a glorious Saviour for me; All who
yield to his love find the cit- y above, In the land by the crystal sea.
Copyright, 1896, by H. L. Gilmour.

# I've Heard of a Saviour.

From "Special Songs."
Jno. R. Sweney.
1. I've heard of a Saviour whose love was so strong, He loved a poor sinner like me;
2. This wonderful Saviour took such a low place, To save a poor sinner like me;
3. This Jesus had nowhere to lay his head, To save a poor sinner like me;
4. This God of all grace is waiting here now, To save a poor sinner like you;
He turned his back on the glo-rified throng, To save a poor sinner like me.
His heart overflowing with wondrous grace, To save a poor sinner like me.
He was a Lamb to the slaugh- ter led, To save a poor sinner like me.
Come as you are, at the mercy-seat bow, He'll save a poor sinner like you.
The angels they sang him from glo- ry, I'm glad that they told me the story;
Was born in a sta- ble and man- ger, In his own world was a stranger,
'Midst darkness my Saviour is dy - ing, "'Tis finished!" I hear Jesus crying,
Your life may be all re- bel- lion, Still you may have this salvation;
He came from on high to suf- fer and die, To save a poor sinner like me.
With all things did part to win my hard heart, And save a poor sinner like me.
My soul may go free, he died on the tree, To save a poor sinner like me.
Back- slid- er as well, I'm so glad to tell, He'll save a poor sinner like you.
Copyright, 1895, by Jno. R. Sweney.

CHORUS.
My sins rose as high as a mountain, They all disappeared in the Fountain;
He put my name down for a palace and crown, O bless his dear name, I am free.
How Sweet to Rest.
Fanny J. Crosby.
Wm. J. Kirkpatrick.
1. How sweet to rest, se- cure and blest, Beneath my Saviour's care;
2. A joy is mine, a peace di- vine, That gent-ly flow to me;
3. He keeps my soul from waves that roll, He keeps me ev - 'ry hour;
4. To him I'll cling, his praise I'll sing, Who seals my heart his own;
Fine.
To watch and wait at mer- cy's gate, And know he answers prayer.
While at the gate of prayer I wait, And there his smile I see.
While still I wait be- side the gate, O'er-shadowed by his power.
I'll watch and wait at mer- cy's gate, And live for him a - lone.
D.S.—No ill can harm, nor fear a- larm, Since Je - sus an- swers prayer.
CHORUS.
D.S.
I call and he hears me, With his promise he cheers me;

# Blood of Jesus.

Rev. E. H. Stokes, D. D.

Jno. R. Sweney.

1. Sal- va - tion! is the bat - tle - cry, Thro' the blood of Je - sus; Sal- vation from sin's deepest dye, Thro' the blood of Je- sus; Lift the crimson ban- ner high, All the hosts of sin de - fy, Vic - to - ry is always nigh,

2. Sal- va - tion from all fears within Thro' the blood of Je - sus, From outward and from inward sin, Thro' the blood of Je- sus; Let the high cru- sade be- gin, For our faith has always been, All the saints of God shall win,

3. Sal- va - tion cometh with a song, Thro' the blood of Je - sus; The victor's shout is loud and long, Thro' the blood of Je- sus; Ho! the cry of saintly throng Like a riv - er flows along, Life to right and death to wrong,

4. Sal- va - tion faith always obtains Thro' the blood of Je - sus; Sal- vation from sin's last remains, Thro' the blood of Je- sus; Saved! the Spirit now exclaims, Saved, a crown forever claims, Saved, a king forev - er reigns,

REFRAIN.

Thro' the blood of Je - sus. Thro' the blood, thro' the blood, Thro' the blood of

Je - sus; Vic - to - ry is always nigh, Thro' the blood of Je - sus.
Je - sus; All the saints of God shall win, Thro' the blood of Je - sus.
Je - sus; Life to right and death to wrong, Thro' the blood of Je - sus.
Je - sus; Saved, a king for - ev - er reigns, Thro' the blood of Je - sus.

# Let me be Something.

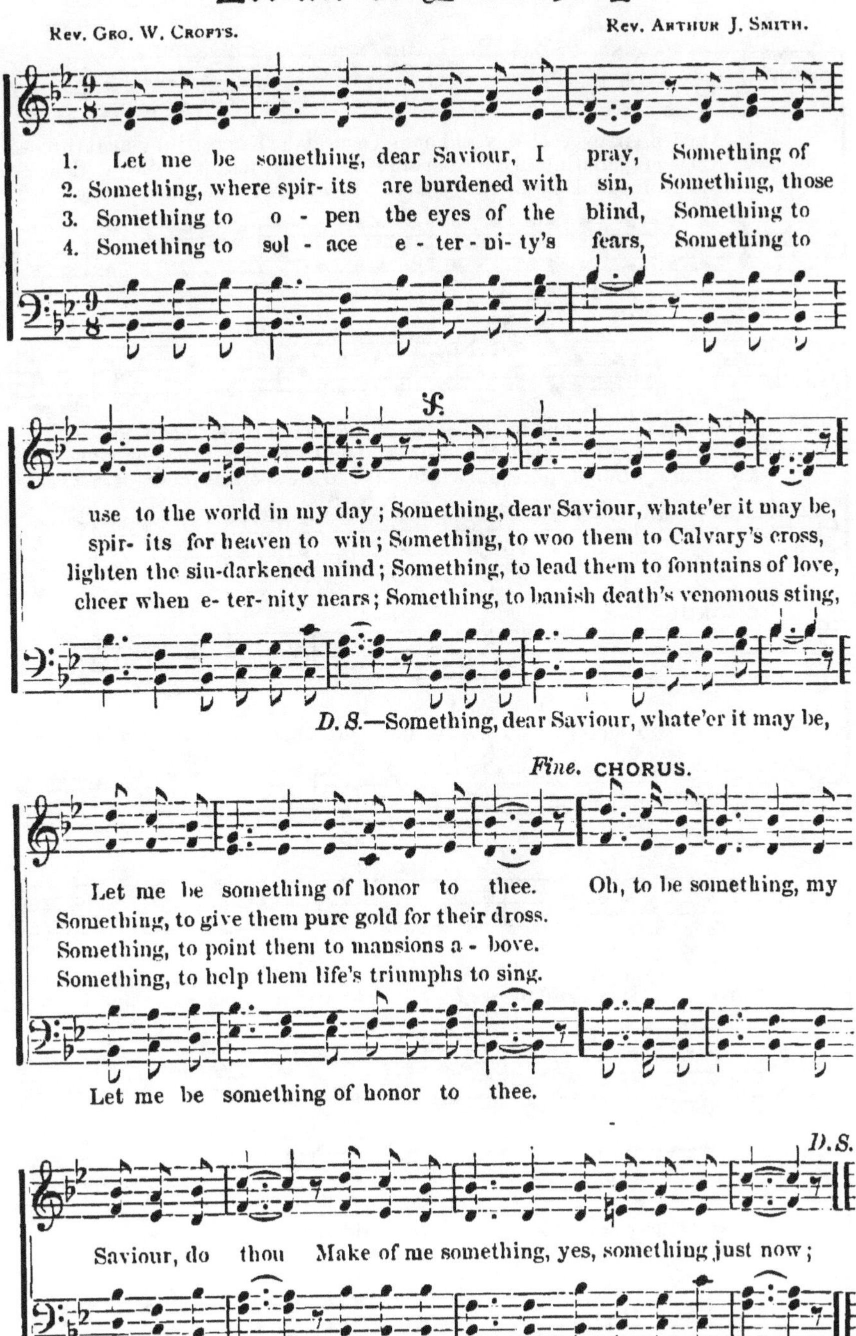
Rev. Geo. W. Crofts.
Rev. Arthur J. Smith.
1. Let me be something, dear Saviour, I pray, Something of use to the world in my day; Something, dear Saviour, whate'er it may be, Let me be something of honor to thee.
2. Something, where spir- its are burdened with sin, Something, those spir- its for heaven to win; Something, to woo them to Calvary's cross, Something, to give them pure gold for their dross.
3. Something to o - pen the eyes of the blind, Something to lighten the sin-darkened mind; Something, to lead them to fountains of love, Something, to point them to mansions a - bove.
4. Something to sol - ace e - ter - ni - ty's fears, Something to cheer when e- ter- nity nears; Something, to banish death's venomous sting, Something, to help them life's triumphs to sing.
D. S.—Something, dear Saviour, whate'er it may be,
Let me be something of honor to thee.
Fine.
CHORUS.
Oh, to be something, my Saviour, do thou Make of me something, yes, something just now;
D.S.

# Am I Prepared?

L. E. J. L. E. Jones.

1. Am I prepared each day and hour To meet the King on judgment throne?
2. Am I prepared, absolved from sin? Is ev- 'ry task and du- ty done?
3. Am I prepared to meet my Lord? To him account for talents given?
Or would I blush and be ashamed If he should come to call his own?
Tho' fierce the fight 'gainst self and sin Have I thro' Christ the vict'ry won?
Are all my garments pure and white, Like to the spotless robes of heaven?
CHORUS.
Am I prepared by day or night?
Am I pre - pared . . . . . by day or night? . . . . . Am I pre-
Am I prepared my Lord to see? The question comes,
pared . . . . my Lord to see? . . . . The question comes, . . . am I pre-
am I prepared To spend with him e - ter - nity?
pared . . . . . to spend with him . . . . . e- ter - ni - ty? . . . . .

# When the Bridegroom Comes.

E. R. Latta. Alt.
Wm. J. Kirkpatrick.
1. Will our lamps be filled and ready, When the Bridegroom comes? And our
2. Shall we hear a welcome sounding, When the Bridegroom comes? And a
3. Don't de- lay our prepar - ation Till the Bridegroom comes; Lest there
4. It may be a time of sorrow, When the Bridegroom comes; If our
5. Oh, there'll be a glorious meeting, When the Bridegroom comes; And a
lights be clear and steady, When the Bridegroom comes? In the night, that solemn
shout of joy resounding, When the Bridegroom comes? In the night, that solemn
be a separation, When the Bridegroom comes. In the night, that solemn
oil we hope to borrow, When the Bridegroom comes. In the night, that solemn
hallelujah greeting, When the Bridegroom comes. In the night, that joyful
night, that solemn night, Will our lamps be burning bright, When the Bridegroom comes?
night, that solemn night, Will our lamps be burning bright, When the Bridegroom comes?
night that solemn night, Will our lamps be burning bright, When the Bridegroom comes?
night, that solemn night, Will our lamps be burning bright. When the Bridegroom comes?
night, that joyful night, With our lamps all burning bright, When the Bridegroom comes.
CHORUS.
May repeat pp.
O be ready! O be ready! O be ready when the Bridegroom comes!
Copyright, 1896, by Wm. J. Kirkpatrick.

# When for Me the Sunlight Gleams.

Jesse P. Tompkins. Wm. J. Kirkpatrick.

1. When for me the sunlight gleams, And life's fairest flowers bloom, Joy in-
2. When the fondest hopes shall die, And like ros- es scattered lie, When my
3. When for me the end shall come, And from earthly scenes I glide, When my

[and fair,
to my bosom streams, Driving out the mists and gloom; When the skies are bright
heart bowed down with grief, Sadly sighs for some relief; To his tender, loving heart
bark drifts slowly out, O'er the river's sullen tide; When my raptured vision falls

And sweet music fills the air, Then I'll praise his name so dear, Jesus, Jesus,
Would I then my grief impart; Then I rest, sweet rest shall find, Jesus, Jesus,
On the fair, celestial walls, Joy and peace shall then be mine, Jesus, Jesus,

Light of life to me, Je - sus, Je - sus, Love so full and free.
Light of life to me, Je - sus, Je - sus, Love so full and free.
I shall ev- er see, Je - sus, Je - sus, Thro' e-ter - ni - ty.

# The Heavenly Pilot.

H. L. G.
H. L. Gilmour.
1. With Jesus in the vessel, we can laugh at storm, Take the Pilot in,
2. This Jesus walks the billows with a conq'ring tread, Take the Pilot in,
3. He'll guide amid the breakers of a friendless world, Take the Pilot in,
4. And when we reach the haven, on the glassy sea, Take the Pi-lot in,
take the Pilot in; Tho' sleeping on a pillow, yet he saves from harm,
take the Pilot in; Inspiring songs of trust, tho' clouds are over- head,
take the Pilot in; And help us anchor safely, with our sails all furled,
take the Pilot in; We'll sing our happy rescue thro' e - ter - ni - ty,
CHORUS.
Take the heav'nly Pilot in. Take the Pi - lot, take the Pi - lot, For the
Take the heav'nly Pilot in.
Take the heav'nly Pilot in.
With the heav'nly Pilot in.
Take the heav'nly Pilot in, Take, oh, take him in,
reefs are close at hand, He'll bring us safe to land.
Tho' the threat'ning storms may cause alarm,

# My Father's in the Storm.

JOHNSON OATMAN, Jr. JNO. R. SWENEY.

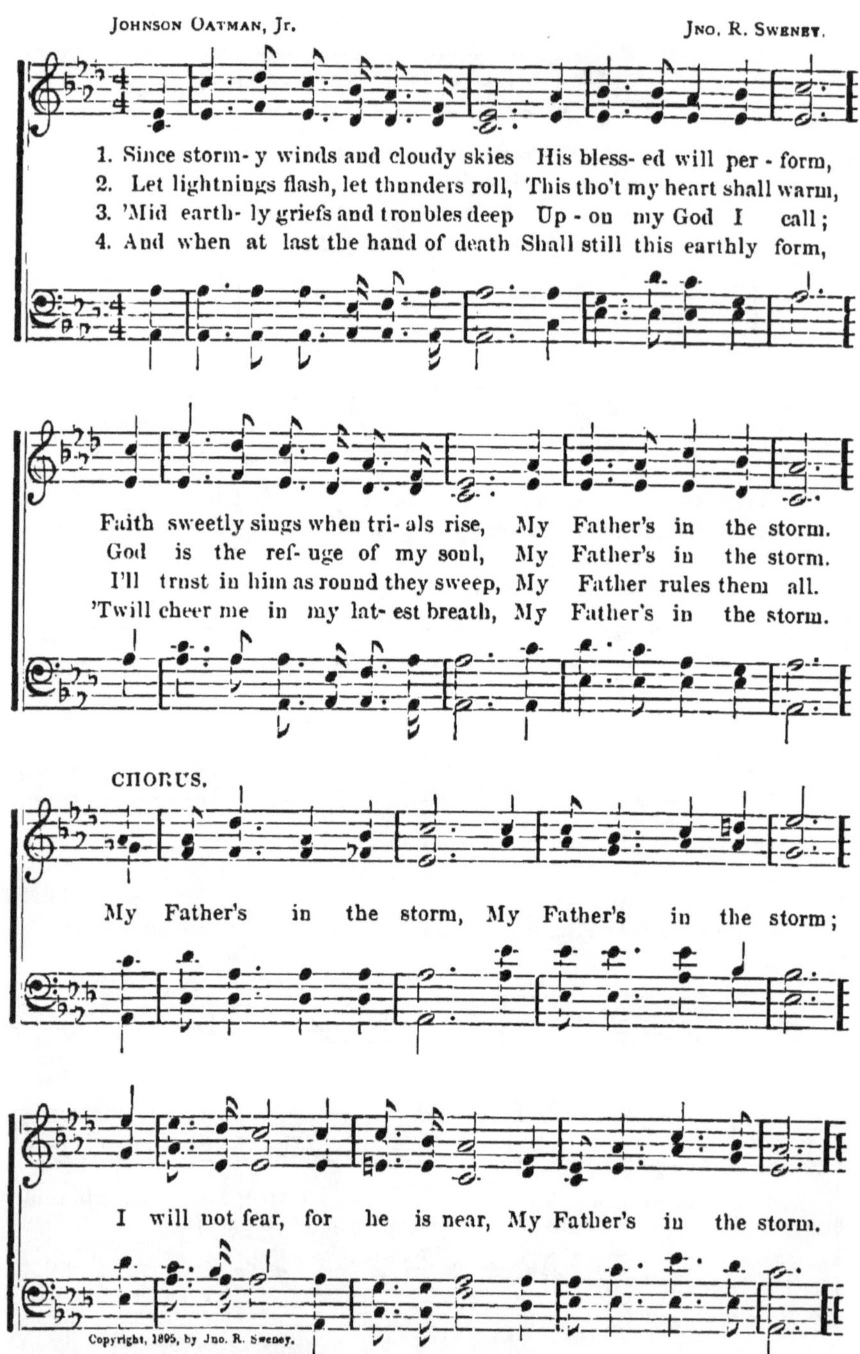
1. Since storm- y winds and cloudy skies His bless- ed will per - form,
2. Let lightnings flash, let thunders roll, This tho't my heart shall warm,
3. 'Mid earth- ly griefs and troubles deep Up - on my God I call;
4. And when at last the hand of death Shall still this earthly form,
Faith sweetly sings when tri- als rise, My Father's in the storm.
God is the ref- uge of my soul, My Father's in the storm.
I'll trust in him as round they sweep, My Father rules them all.
'Twill cheer me in my lat- est breath, My Father's in the storm.
CHORUS.
My Father's in the storm, My Father's in the storm;
I will not fear, for he is near, My Father's in the storm.

# Jesus Saves and Keeps Me.

F. S. Shepard.
Wm. J. Kirkpatrick.
1. My soul is re-joic-ing, the Sav-iour I know, Je-sus saves and keeps me ev-'ry day; My sins that were scarlet are white as the snow.
2. Oh, great is the peace that to me now is giv'n, Je-sus saves and keeps me ev-'ry day; It fills all my soul with the raptures of heav'n,
3. My life to his ser-vice I cheer-ful-ly give, Je-sus saves and keeps me ev-'ry day; I trust him each moment for pow-er to live,
4. I long for the day when his face I shall see, Je-sus saves and keeps me ev-'ry day; For then, he has promised, like him I shall be,
Jesus saves and keeps me ev-'ry day.
CHORUS.
Je-sus saves and keeps me ev'ry day, Jesus leads me safely all the way; And my soul would ever sing, Praises to my Lord and King, Jesus saves and keeps me ev'ry day. . . . .
Jesus saves
ev'ry day,
Jesus leads,
all the way;
Copyright, 1896, by Wm. J. Kirkpatrick.

# Beyond the Stars.

Jesse P. Tompkins
Jno. R. Sweney.
1. Beyond the stars that brightly gleam, Beyond life's short and shadow'd stream,
2. Beyond the stars no storms will beat, No thorns will pierce our weary feet,
3. Beyond the stars no toils or tears, No sombre skies or gloomy fears,
There is a land of fadeless bloom, And flow'rs of rich and rare per- fume;
No sad good-byes we e'er shall say, And see fond fa - ces glide a - way;
For he who trod life's weary way Shall wipe all sorrow's tears a - way;
Per- fect peace we there shall know, Like the riv - er's endless flow.
Forms that here we seek in vain There we'll clasp their hands a- gain.
End- less joys shall then be mine, When I see . . . his face di - vine.
CHORUS.
Beyond the stars sweet peace we'll know, Clear as the crys - tal river's flow;
Beyond the stars . sweet peace we'll know, Clear as the crys - tal river's flow;
Where rolls the sea . . of perfect love, Beyond the stars that gleam a- bove.
Where rolls the sea, the sea of perfect love, Beyond, beyond the stars
Copyright, 1896, by Jno. R. Sweney.

# Fulness of Joy.

E. E. Hewitt. Psalm xvi: 11. F. E Belden.

1. There is fulness of joy in the presence of the King, Where with
2. There is fulness of joy, e- ven "pleasures ev- ermore;" When the
3. There'll be fulness of joy in those blessed fields of light, When we
4. Of this fulness of joy, oh, what blessed foretastes here, In the

anthems of praise all the harps of glo- ry ring, And the numberless
waves of time break up - on the gold- en shore, When the beams of
walk with him in the robes of spotless white, Where no earth- ly
des - ert way, streams are flowing pure and clear, In the twi - light

hosts of re- deeming mercy sing, There is joy, joy, joy.
love their un- clouded radiance pour, There'll be joy, joy, joy.
stain shall of- fend his ho - ly sight, There'll be joy, joy, joy.
sky, smiles of ros - y dawn ap- pear, There is joy, joy, joy forevermore.

CHORUS.

Joy, bright joy, when we gather there, Joy, bright joy, in the mansions fair;

When glorified we stand, at the Lord's right hand, There'll be joy, joy, joy.

# Wonderful Story of Love.

M. TAYLOR. ARTHUR J. SMITH.

1. To-day God is tell - ing a won - derful sto - ry, The
2. He brings the as - sur - ance of present sal - va - tion, E-
3. This, then, is the day when with love far ex - ceeding, With

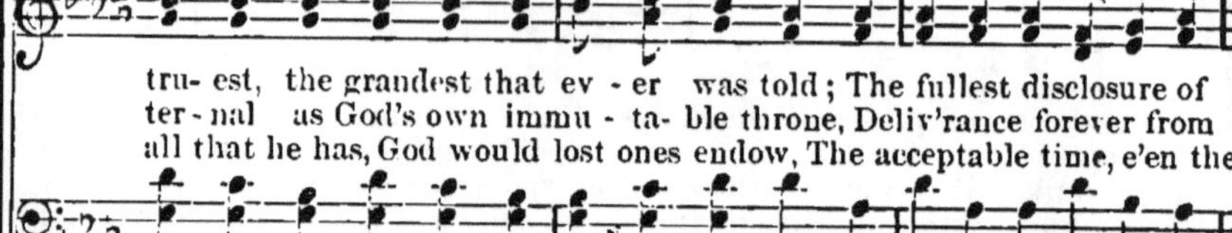
tru- est, the grandest that ev - er was told; The fullest disclosure of
ter - nal as God's own immu - ta- ble throne, Deliv'rance forever from
all that he has, God would lost ones endow, The acceptable time, e'en the

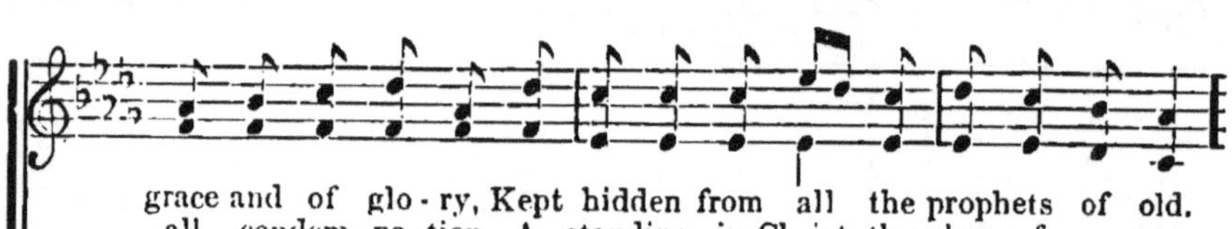
grace and of glo - ry, Kept hidden from all the prophets of old.
all condem- na- tion, A standing in Christ, the place of a son.
time of his pleading, The day of salvation, God's wonder- ful NOW.

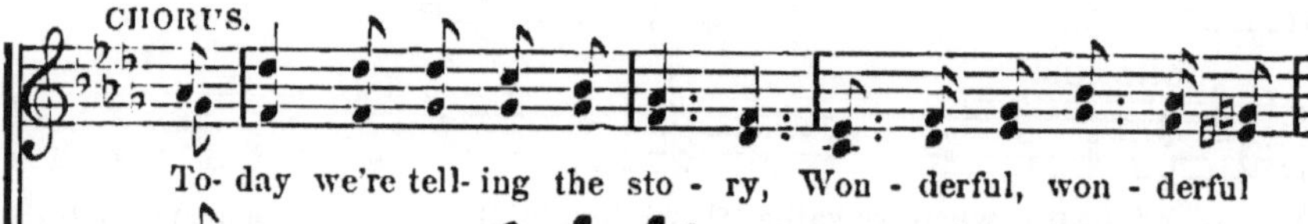
CHORUS.
To- day we're tell- ing the sto - ry, Won - derful, won - derful

sto - ry, To-day we're telling the story, The wonderful story of love.

# My Letters from Home.

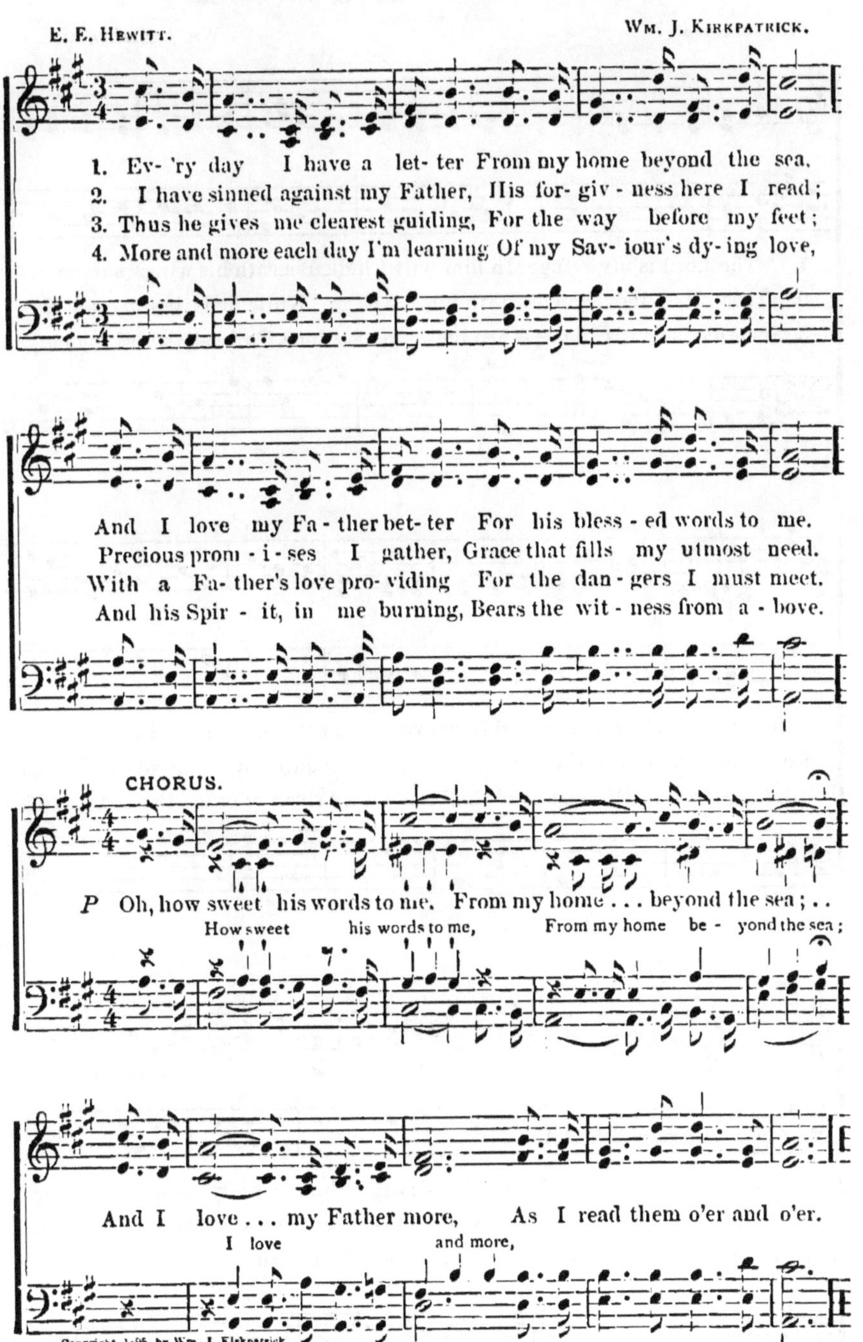
E. E. Hewitt.
Wm. J. Kirkpatrick.
1. Ev- 'ry day I have a let- ter From my home beyond the sea,
2. I have sinned against my Father, His for- giv - ness here I read;
3. Thus he gives me clearest guiding, For the way before my feet;
4. More and more each day I'm learning Of my Sav- iour's dy- ing love,
And I love my Fa - ther bet- ter For his bless - ed words to me.
Precious prom - i - ses I gather, Grace that fills my utmost need.
With a Fa- ther's love pro- viding For the dan - gers I must meet.
And his Spir - it, in me burning, Bears the wit - ness from a - bove.
CHORUS.
P Oh, how sweet his words to me. From my home . . . beyond the sea; . .
How sweet his words to me, From my home be - yond the sea;
And I love . . . my Father more, As I read them o'er and o'er.
I love and more,
Copyright, 1895, by Wm. J. Kirkpatrick.

# The Lord is My Refuge.

Ida. L. Reed. Wm. J. Kirkpatrick.

1. The Lord is my refuge, In him will I hide, Beneath his wings' shelter Se-
2. Thro' all of life's changes With him I will go, While he is beside me No
3. Some day he will call me, When life's cares are done, To dwell in his kingdom As

curely abide; There sheltered from evil. From error and wrong, I'll raise to him
fear I shall know; I'll rest in his promise, And tranquil and free, 'Neath life's weary
bright as the sun; His dear hand shall lead me By rivers of peace, Beyond this life's

ev- er A worship- ful song, I'll raise to him ev-er a worshipful song.
burdens, My spirit shall be, 'Neath life's weary burdens, My spirit shall be.
shadows, Where sorrows shall cease. Beyond this life's shadows, Where sorrows shall cease.

# Trust Thou in God.

Myron W. Morse. Jno. R. Sweney.

1. Do the cares of life press heav - i - ly up - on thee? Dost thou
2. Dost thou ev - er feel despond - ent or dis- couraged? Does the
3. There is joy and peace and rest in trusting Je - sus, He will
sometimes long for freedom from their hold? Do the burdens thou art
darkness cast up - on thy path a gloom? Look a - way to brighter
guide thee o'er life's ev - er- changing way; He will help thee if with
bearing almost crush thee? There is One to whom thy sorrow may be told.
things, and trust in Je- sus, Oh, remem- ber there is light beyond the tomb.
all thy heart thou trust him, And thy darkness he will turn to brightest day.
CHORUS.
Trust thou in God, . . thy friend most dear, Trust thou in God who still is near;
O trust and wait, . . for thou shalt prove His wondrous grace and boundless [love.

# Who will Follow Jesus?

E. E. Hewitt. Wm. J. Kirkpatrick.

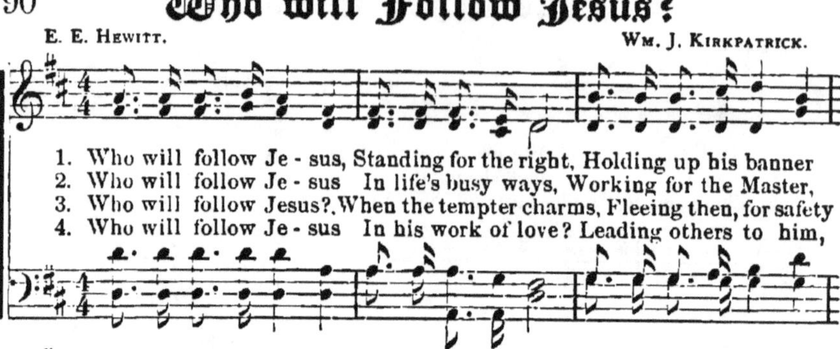

1. Who will follow Je - sus, Standing for the right, Holding up his banner
2. Who will follow Je - sus In life's busy ways, Working for the Master,
3. Who will follow Jesus?, When the tempter charms, Fleeing then, for safety
4. Who will follow Je - sus In his work of love? Leading others to him,

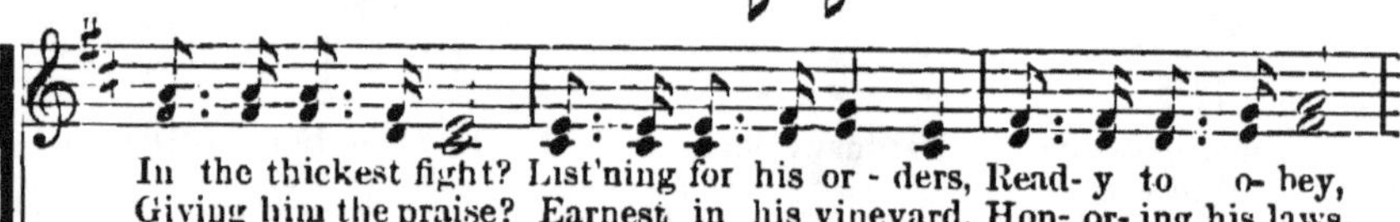

In the thickest fight? List'ning for his or - ders, Read- y to o- bey,
Giving him the praise? Earnest in his vineyard, Hon- or- ing his laws,
To the Saviour's arms; Trusting in his mer - cy, Trusting in his power,
Lifting prayers above; Courage, faithful servant; In his word we see,

CHORUS.

Who will follow Je - sus, Serving him to-day? Who will follow Je- sus?
Faithful to his counsel, Watchful for his cause?
Seeking fresh renewals Of his grace each hour.
On our side forev - er Will this Saviour be.

Who will make reply, "I am on the Lord's side, Master, here am I?" Who will follow

Je- sus? Who will make reply, "I am on the Lord's side, Master, here am I?"

# Is it Nothing to You?

Suggested on hearing the sermon by Rev. B. Fay Mills, from the text, "Is it nothing to you?" La. 1: 12, preached at the Ocean Grove Auditorium, Aug. 24, 1894.

Myron W. Morse, and Fanny J. Crosby. Jno. R. Sweney.

1. Our blessed Redeemer is passing this way, Is it nothing to you, is it nothing to you? Oh, hear him this moment so ten-der-ly say, Is it nothing, is it nothing to you? There is life for a look at the cru - ci- fied One, There is life for a look at the Father's own Son: Oh, hasten just now, to the dear Saviour come, Is it nothing, is it nothing to you?
2. The Master is calling, oh, list to his voice, Is it nothing to you, is it nothing to you? Awake from your slumber, believe and rejoice, Is it nothing, is it nothing to you? The sands of your life are fast pass- ing a- way, Oh, haste, quickly haste, ere the close of the day, Re- pent and receive him,oh,do not delay, Make it something make it something to you.
3. Yon region so lovely, where all will be song, Is it nothing to you, is it nothing to you? The Saviour's glad welcome, the glorified throng, Are they nothing, are they nothing to you? The an- gels are there, brother, where will you be?— 'Tis time that you halted on life's restless sea, And settled this question: "Did Christ die for me?" Is it nothing, is it nothing to you?
Copyright, 1894, by Jno R. Sweney.

# Zion's Song.

And there shall be no night there; and they need no candle, neither light of the sun; for the Lord God giveth them light; and they shall reign for ever and ever.

CHARLES S. STEVENS. Mrs. JAMES M. E. HILDRETH.

1. I love to hear the new, new song, Of mansions in the sky;
2. I love to hear that song so sweet, Of Zi - on's end-less day;
3. I love to hear it go a-broad, O'er ev - 'ry land and sea;
4. I'll love to hear it when I die, And when the grave is near;
That tells us of the white-robed throng In that blest home on high.
It draws us to the mer - cy- seat, And helps us on the way.
The prais - es of the Son of God, Who died for you and me.
To bear me to the realms on high, And con- quer ev - 'ry fear.
CHORUS.
We shall all join that song 'round the great white throne,
In praise of our Saviour King;
Oh, blessed assurance! that blood can atone, And precious salvation bring.

# Happy in Jesus on the Way.

"Blessed is the people that know the joyful sound: they shall walk, O Lord, in the light of thy countenance, and in thy name shall they rejoice all the day, and in thy righteousness shall they be exalted."—Psalm lxxxix: 15-16.

SAMUEL PEACH. JNO. R. SWENEY.

1. Come, ye blest of the Lord who know the joyful sound, Of sins forgiv-en, and can say, With a good hope of heaven thro' his mercy I am found,
2. On the straight, narrow track the ransomed host have trod, God's shining presence was their stay; The same light and glory shall lead us home to God,
3. In the old, blessed Book what promi-ses abound! Wait-ing to bless us ev-'ry day; Then rejoice in the Lord ev-er-more, and be found
4. We are bought with a price, we free-ly are forgiv'n, The heav'nly calling then o-bey; Come out now and live in the brighter joys of heaven,

*D.S.*—presence ever bright,

Happy in Jesus on the way. *Fine.*

CHORUS.

Happy in Je-sus, happy in Je-sus, Happy in Jesus on the way. Walking beside him all the day; all the day; I am living in the light of his *D.S.*

# Just Beyond these Earthly Scenes.

F. A. B. F. A. Blackmer.

1. { Just beyond these earthly scenes, Past the vale that intervenes, And the glory from us screens, Meet me there;
Where by faith my soul doth wing, Upward like a heav'n-bound thing, To the palace of the King. Meet me there.
2. { When shall pass this dreary night, And shall dawn that morning bright, And our faith shall end in sight, Meet me there;
When the mists shall clear away, And reveal that "perfect day," Brother, sister, then, I pray. Meet me there.
3. { Where he'll bid them welcome all, Rich and poor, and great and small, When the Lord his own shall call, Meet me there;
In that home of beauty rare, Which he left us to prepare, Where are many mansions fair, Meet me there.
1
2
CHORUS.
Meet me there. Meet me there, meet me there,
Meet me there, meet me there,
In that blessed home of promise, Meet me there,
Meet me there,
Where angelic harps shall ring, And the saints immortal sing, In the palace of the King,
Meet me there.
Copyright, 1895, by John J. Hood.

4 When those beauties shall unfold,
Gates of pearl and streets of gold,
Things to mortal ears untold,
Meet me there;
Where Life's River sparkles clear,
And the Tree of Life so near,
Yields its fruitage all the year,
Meet me there.

5 When the hosts redeemed return,
And of Jesus' triumphs learn,
And their hearts with rapture burn,
Meet me there;
Where each op'ning joy shall bring
Cause for ransomed ones to sing
Praises new unto their King,
Meet me there.

# I'll Not Be a Stranger Up There.

L. E. J.
L. E. Jones.
1. There's a beau- ti- ful homeland by Je - sus prepared, A cit - y all golden and fair; And when to its portals my spirit ascends, I shall not be a stranger up there.
2. To that bright sunny land man-y loved ones have gone, The rich - es of glo- ry to share; They are waiting for me at the portals of light, I shall
3. On that bright golden shore many friends gone before, In garments all spotless and fair, With Je- sus a - wait, just inside the gate, So I'll
CHORUS.
No shadows of night ever fall on that shore, No burden of sor- row and care; Yet sweeter than this the as- sur- ance to me, I shall not be a stranger up there.
Copyright, 1895, by John J. Hood.

# The Roll Call.

HATTIE I. WILDE.
JNO. R. SWENEY.
1. When the march of life is o- ver, And its battles all are fought, When we
2. What tho' sometimes we are weary, Let us courage take a- new, Pressing
3. Let us work and watch for Jesus, Seeking souls for whom he died, Till he
meet our Great Commander "in the air;" Praise to his redeeming mer- cy,
toward the shining mark with faith and pray'r; In my Saviour I am trusting,
comes with all his angels bright and fair; Then he'll take us home rejoicing,
What a soul-inspiring thought, When the roll is called in glory, I'll be there!
And I know his word is true, When he calls his people round him, I'll be there.
In his presence to abide; When the roll is called in glory, I'll be there.
CHORUS.
When the first trumpet sounds, And the roll is called in glo - ry, I'll be
there, I'll be there; When the first trumpet sounds,
hal - le - lu - jah, I'll be there, I'll be there;
Copyright, 1896, by Jno R. Sweney.

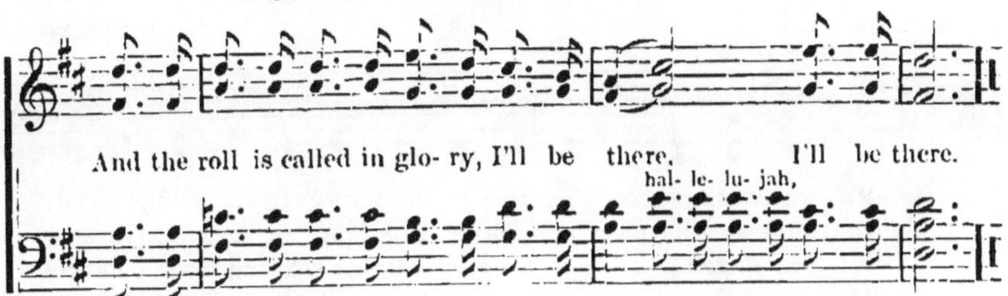
And the roll is called in glo- ry, I'll be there, I'll be there.
hal- le- lu- jah,

# Have a Little Talk with Jesus.

JOHNSON OATMAN, Jr. JNO. R. SWENEY.

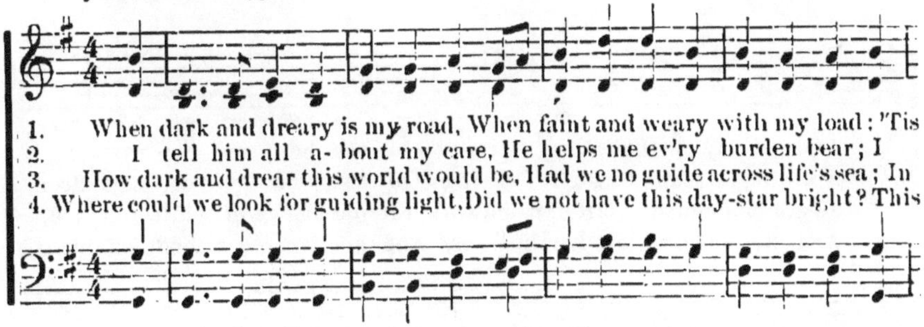

1. When dark and dreary is my road, When faint and weary with my load; 'Tis
2. I tell him all a- bout my care, He helps me ev'ry burden bear; I
3. How dark and drear this world would be, Had we no guide across life's sea; In
4. Where could we look for guiding light, Did we not have this day-star bright? This

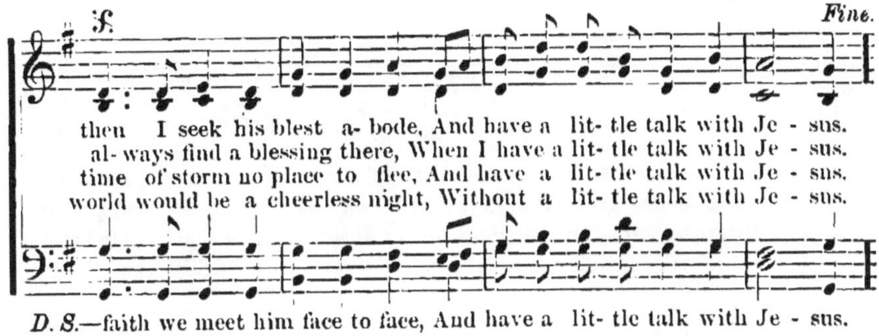

then I seek his blest a- bode, And have a lit- tle talk with Je- sus.
al- ways find a blessing there, When I have a lit- tle talk with Je - sus.
time of storm no place to flee, And have a lit- tle talk with Je - sus.
world would be a cheerless night, Without a lit- tle talk with Je - sus.

*Fine.*

*D. S.*—faith we meet him face to face, And have a lit- tle talk with Je - sus.

CHORUS.

O praise him for his wondrous grace, In ev- 'ry tri- al, in ev'ry place; By

*D.S.*

5 In times of peace, in times of strife,
Let joy prevail, or fears be rife;
I'll always seek this friend thro' life,
And have a little talk with Jesus.

6 And after life with me is o'er,
I'll enter in thro' mercy's door,
And with the millions gone before,
I'll ever live and talk with Jesus.

# The Patchwork Quilt.

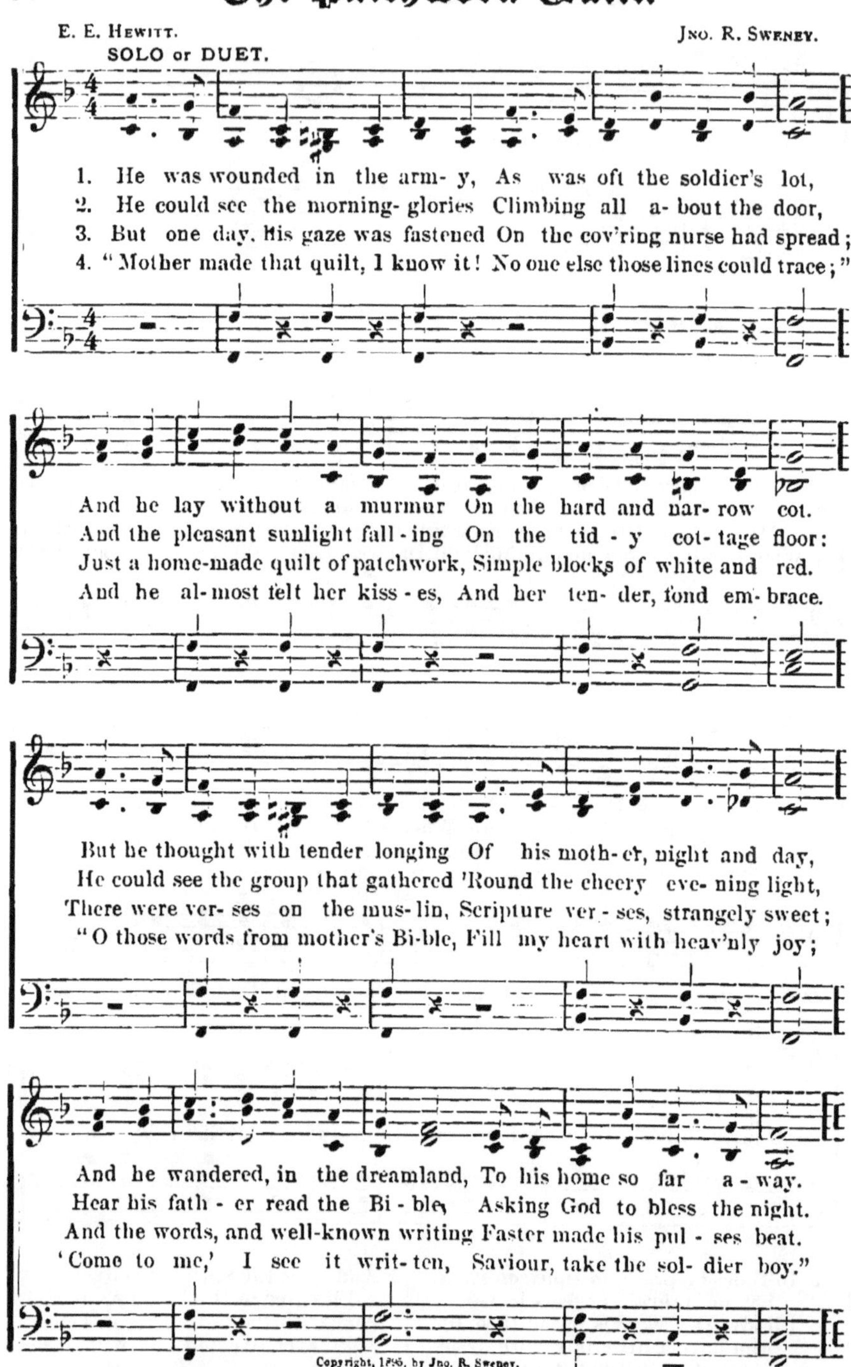
E. E. Hewitt.
Jno. R. Sweney.
SOLO or DUET.
1. He was wounded in the arm- y, As was oft the soldier's lot,
2. He could see the morning- glories Climbing all a- bout the door,
3. But one day, His gaze was fastened On the cov'ring nurse had spread;
4. "Mother made that quilt, I know it! No one else those lines could trace;"
And he lay without a murmur On the hard and nar- row cot.
And the pleasant sunlight fall - ing On the tid - y cot- tage floor:
Just a home-made quilt of patchwork, Simple blocks of white and red.
And he al- most felt her kiss - es, And her ten- der, fond em- brace.
But he thought with tender longing Of his moth- er, night and day,
He could see the group that gathered 'Round the cheery eve- ning light,
There were ver- ses on the mus- lin, Scripture ver - ses, strangely sweet;
"O those words from mother's Bi-ble, Fill my heart with heav'nly joy;
And he wandered, in the dreamland, To his home so far a - way.
Hear his fath - er read the Bi - ble, Asking God to bless the night.
And the words, and well-known writing Faster made his pul - ses beat.
'Come to me,' I see it writ- ten, Saviour, take the sol- dier boy."

# He Left the Ninety and Nine.

Johnson Oatman. Op. 99. H. L Gilmour.

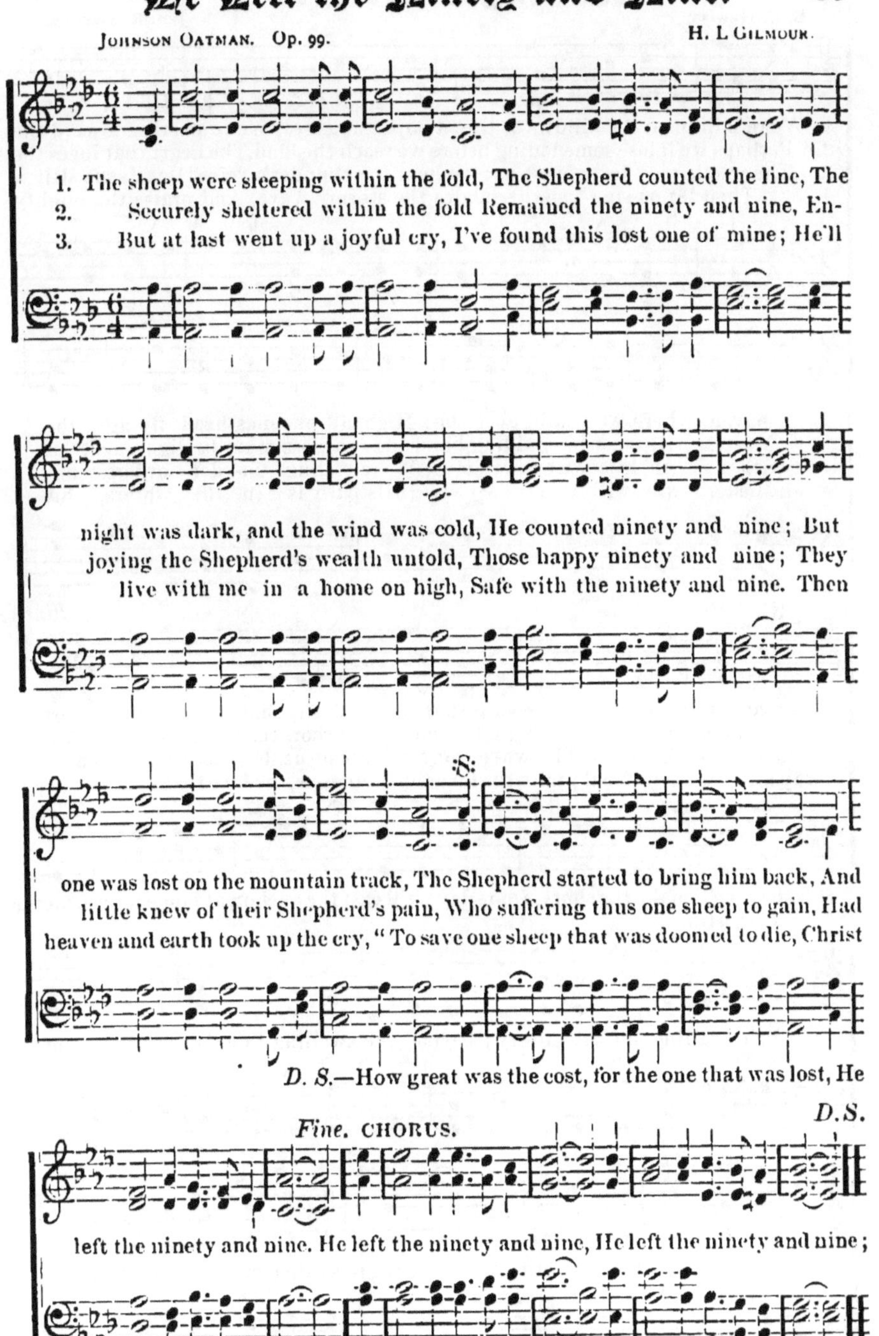
1. The sheep were sleeping within the fold, The Shepherd counted the line, The
2. Securely sheltered within the fold Remained the ninety and nine, En-
3. But at last went up a joyful cry, I've found this lost one of mine; He'll
night was dark, and the wind was cold, He counted ninety and nine; But
joying the Shepherd's wealth untold, Those happy ninety and nine; They
live with me in a home on high, Safe with the ninety and nine. Then
one was lost on the mountain track, The Shepherd started to bring him back, And
little knew of their Shepherd's pain, Who suffering thus one sheep to gain, Had
heaven and earth took up the cry, "To save one sheep that was doomed to die, Christ
D. S.—How great was the cost, for the one that was lost, He
Fine. CHORUS.
D.S.
left the ninety and nine. He left the ninety and nine, He left the ninety and nine;

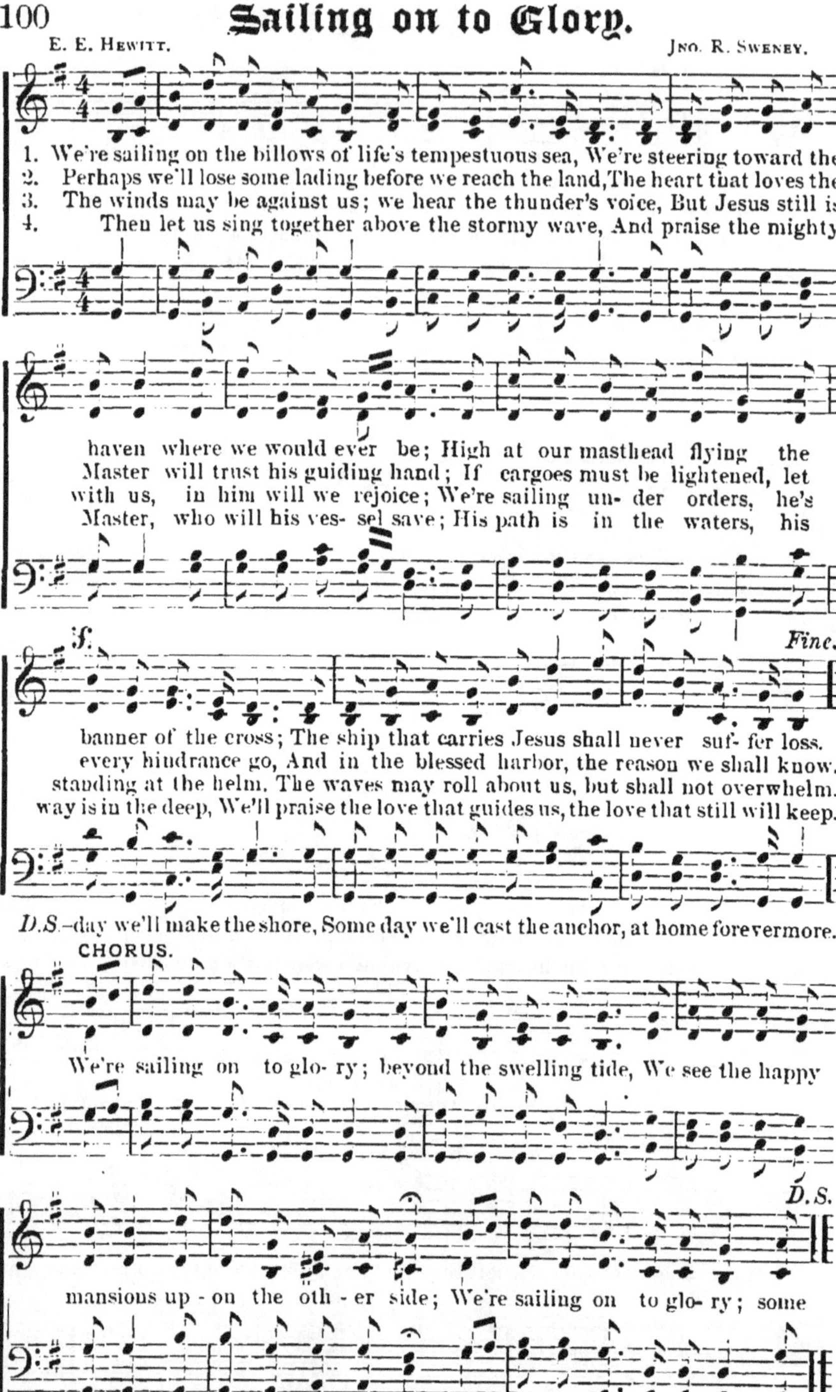
100
Sailing on to Glory.
E. E. Hewitt.
Jno. R. Sweney.
1. We're sailing on the billows of life's tempestuous sea, We're steering toward the haven where we would ever be; High at our masthead flying the banner of the cross; The ship that carries Jesus shall never suf- fer loss.
2. Perhaps we'll lose some lading before we reach the land, The heart that loves the Master will trust his guiding hand; If cargoes must be lightened, let every hindrance go, And in the blessed harbor, the reason we shall know.
3. The winds may be against us; we hear the thunder's voice, But Jesus still is with us, in him will we rejoice; We're sailing un- der orders, he's standing at the helm. The waves may roll about us, but shall not overwhelm.
4. Then let us sing together above the stormy wave, And praise the mighty Master, who will his ves- sel save; His path is in the waters, his way is in the deep, We'll praise the love that guides us, the love that still will keep.
Fine.
D.S.—day we'll make the shore, Some day we'll cast the anchor, at home forevermore.
CHORUS.
We're sailing on to glo- ry; beyond the swelling tide, We see the happy mansions up - on the oth - er side; We're sailing on to glo- ry; some
D.S.
Copyright, 1895, by Jno. R. Sweney.

# Look for the Beautiful.

E. E. Hewitt. Wm. J. Kirkpatrick.

1. Look for the beau- ti- ful; day af- ter day Angels are scattering flowers by the way; Mercies so numberless, sent from above, Making the wilderness fragrant with love.
2. Look for the beau- ti- ful; seek ev'rywhere Hints of the heaven- ly, dropped here and there; Labor on cheer- ily where'er thou art, Sweet hopes and mem- o- ries filling thy heart.
3. Look for the beau- ti- ful; under the snow Seedlets are quickening, may blossoms grow; Oft- en in lowliness, hidden from view, Lives too are blossoming, lives pure and true.
4. Look for the beau- ti- ful; when falls the night, Finding the promi- ses sparkling and bright; Prayerfully, trustfully lift up thine eye, See the stars glit- tering, lighting the sky.
CHORUS.
Look! look! look for the beautiful,
Look for the beautiful, Look! look!
Look! look! life's pathway thro'; Look for the beau - ti- ful,
Look for the beau - ti - ful,
Look! look!
look for the beauti- ful, Look for the beau - ti - ful, cherish the true.
look! look!
ritard.

# His Glorious Praise.

"Make his praise glorious."

E. E. Hewitt. F. E. Belden.

1. Ser - a - phic hosts, be- fore the throne, Where living jewels blaze,
2. Bright saints a- bove, arrayed in white, Thro' ev - er - lasting days,
3. Sing, Church of God! up - on the march, An answ'ring chorus raise,
4. Come, ev - 'ry burdened, wea- ry heart, On Cal- va - ry now gaze;
Enraptured, sweep their harps of gold, And glorious make his praise.
Ring out the grand re- demption song, And glorious make his praise.
His roy - al standard high up - lift, And glorious make his praise.
"Be- hold the Lamb" for sinners slain, And glorious make his praise.
CHORUS.
Sing to the Lord in all life's ways, His glorious praise, glorious praise;
Praise him, praise him;
Come, ev- 'ry heart, a song up- raise, And glorious make his praise.

# Shout the Victory.

Rev. D. H. Kenney. Jno. R. Sweney.

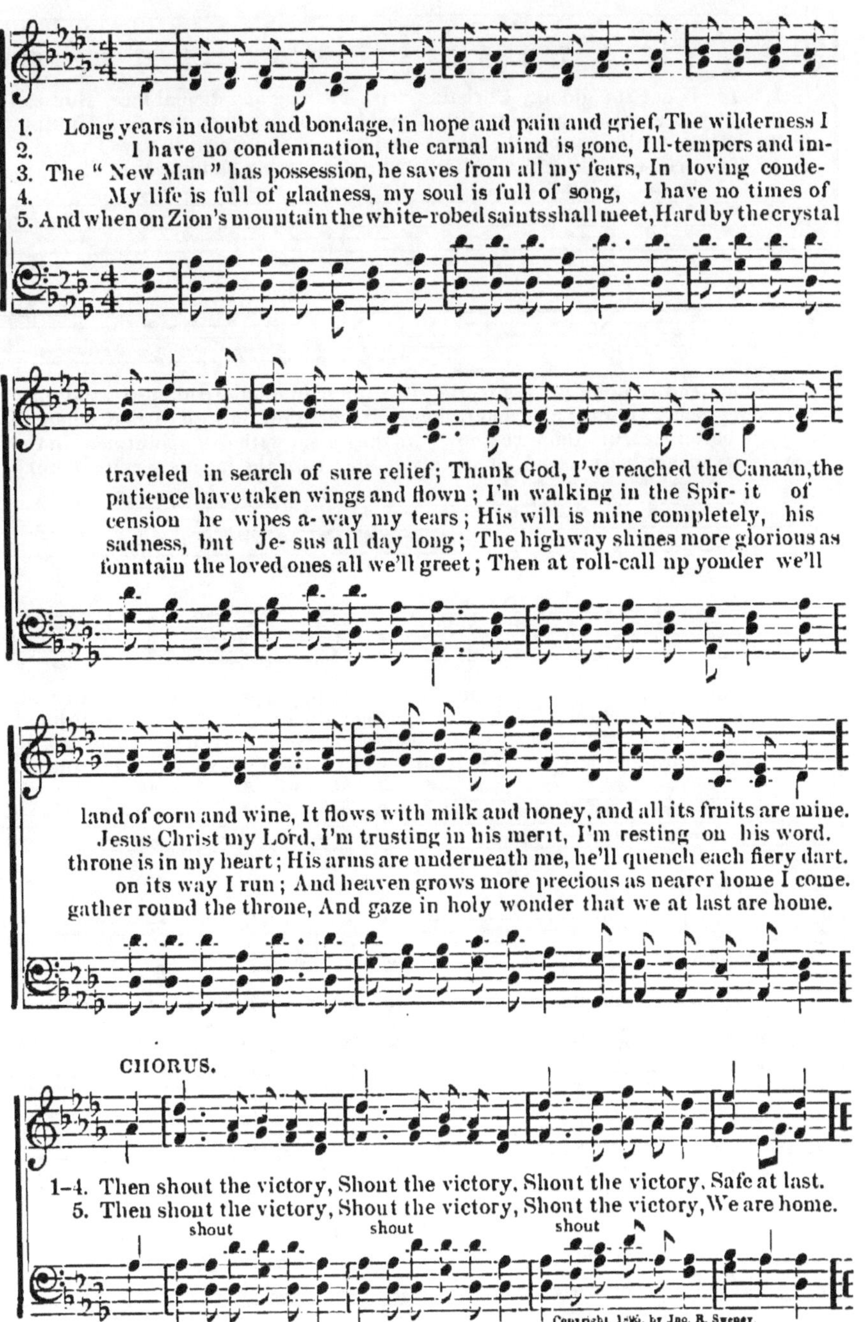
1. Long years in doubt and bondage, in hope and pain and grief, The wilderness I traveled in search of sure relief; Thank God, I've reached the Canaan, the land of corn and wine, It flows with milk and honey, and all its fruits are mine.
2. I have no condemnation, the carnal mind is gone, Ill-tempers and impatience have taken wings and flown; I'm walking in the Spir- it of Jesus Christ my Lord, I'm trusting in his merit, I'm resting on his word.
3. The "New Man" has possession, he saves from all my fears, In loving condescension he wipes a- way my tears; His will is mine completely, his throne is in my heart; His arms are underneath me, he'll quench each fiery dart.
4. My life is full of gladness, my soul is full of song, I have no times of sadness, but Je- sus all day long; The highway shines more glorious as on its way I run; And heaven grows more precious as nearer home I come.
5. And when on Zion's mountain the white-robed saints shall meet, Hard by the crystal fountain the loved ones all we'll greet; Then at roll-call up yonder we'll gather round the throne, And gaze in holy wonder that we at last are home.
CHORUS.
1-4. Then shout the victory, Shout the victory, Shout the victory, Safe at last.
5. Then shout the victory, Shout the victory, Shout the victory, We are home.
shout
shout
shout

# A Joyful Religion.

H. B. Beegle. Jno. R. Sweney.

1. It is not the gloomy Christian, with his long and dismal face, That can
2. Did you ever see the mortal that could strength or comfort find, Taking
3. It's the really happy Christians who compel the world to say They en-
4. Then cease all dark forebodings, which so deeply shadow life, They are
recommend religion to the world; But the man of cheerful spirit and of
dark and gloomy views of men and things? Sitting in the darkest corners, where the
joy a better treasure than we know; As they meet with disappointment in the
good for neither body, mind, or soul; For they turn the joyous service of our
kind and gentle ways, Who can show a happy face with smiles unfurled.
sunlight seldom shines, Then complain that life so lit - tle comfort brings?
pleasures of this life, They will turn and on to heaven with you go.
blessed Lord and King In - to du- ties that have lit- tle to console.
CHORUS.
Would you rec-ommend re - lig - ion to an un - be- lieving world? Then
bathe in gospel sunshine ev'ry day; Keep a loving, cheerful spirit, and a
Copyright, 1896, by Jno. R. Sweney.

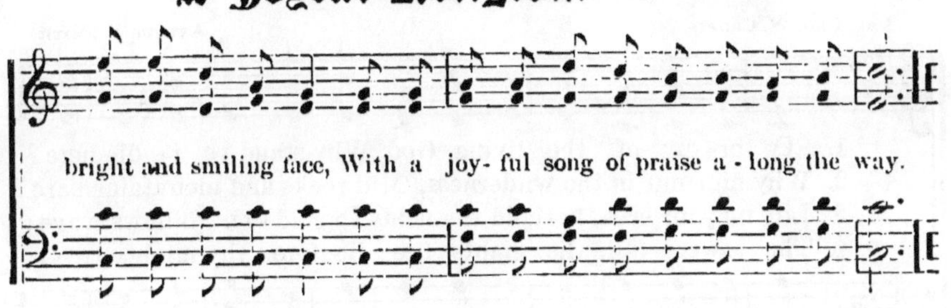
bright and smiling face, With a joy- ful song of praise a - long the way.

# Jesus, I will Trust Thee.

Anon. A. J. Showalter. By per.

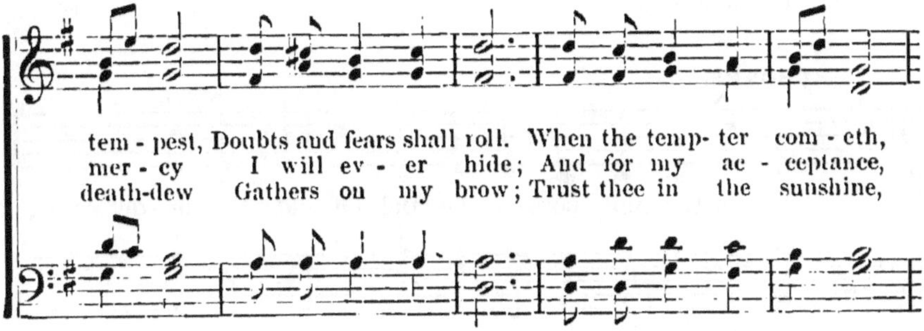

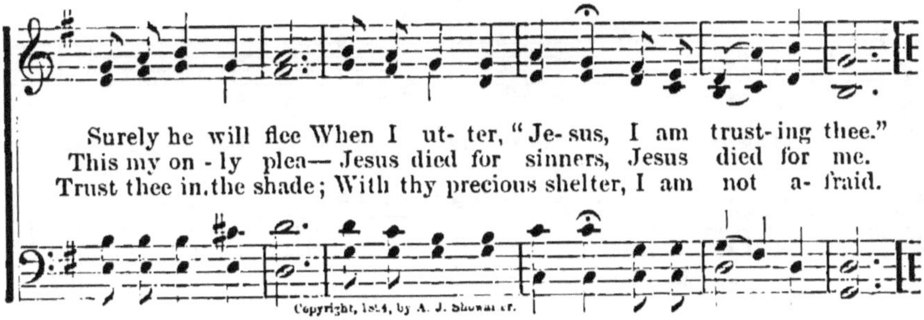

1. Je- sus, I will trust thee, When across my soul, Like a fearful tem - pest, Doubts and fears shall roll. When the temp- ter com - eth, Surely he will flee When I ut- ter, "Je- sus, I am trust- ing thee."

2. Je- sus, I will trust thee, There is none be - side; In thine arms of mer - cy I will ev - er hide; And for my ac - ceptance, This my on - ly plea— Jesus died for sinners, Jesus died for me.

3. Je- sus, I will trust thee, Trust thee e- ven now; Trust thee when the death-dew Gathers on my brow; Trust thee in the sunshine, Trust thee in the shade; With thy precious shelter, I am not a- fraid.

# Possess the Land.

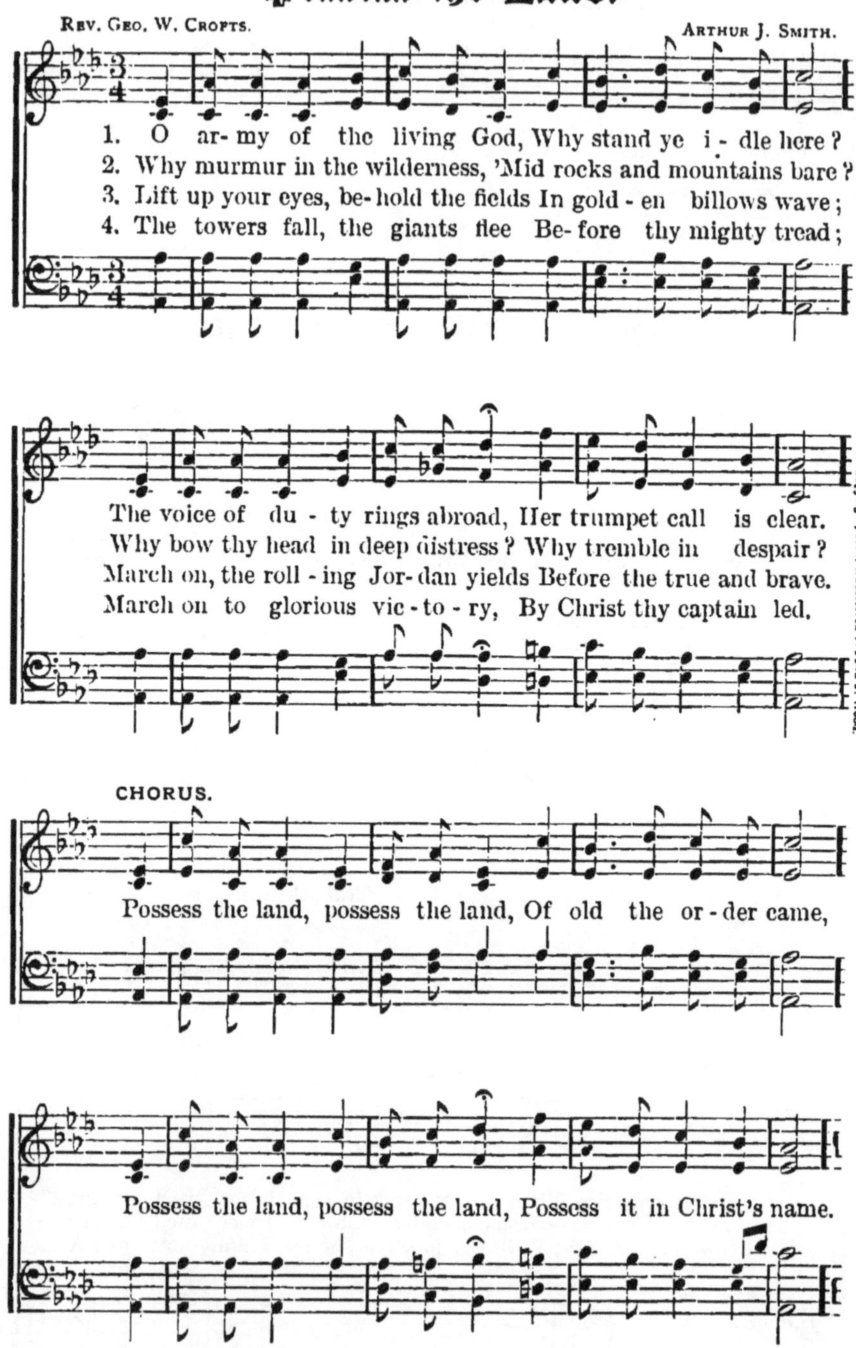
Rev. Geo. W. Crofts.
Arthur J. Smith.
1. O ar- my of the living God, Why stand ye i - dle here? The voice of du - ty rings abroad, Her trumpet call is clear.
2. Why murmur in the wilderness, 'Mid rocks and mountains bare? Why bow thy head in deep distress? Why tremble in despair?
3. Lift up your eyes, be- hold the fields In gold - en billows wave; March on, the roll - ing Jor- dan yields Before the true and brave.
4. The towers fall, the giants flee Be- fore thy mighty tread; March on to glorious vic - to - ry, By Christ thy captain led.
CHORUS.
Possess the land, possess the land, Of old the or - der came,
Possess the land, possess the land, Possess it in Christ's name.
Copyright, 1890, transferred to John J. Hood.

# Speed Away! Speed Away!

Rev. C. Cooke. (Arr. by W. J. K., 1859.) I. B. Woodbury.

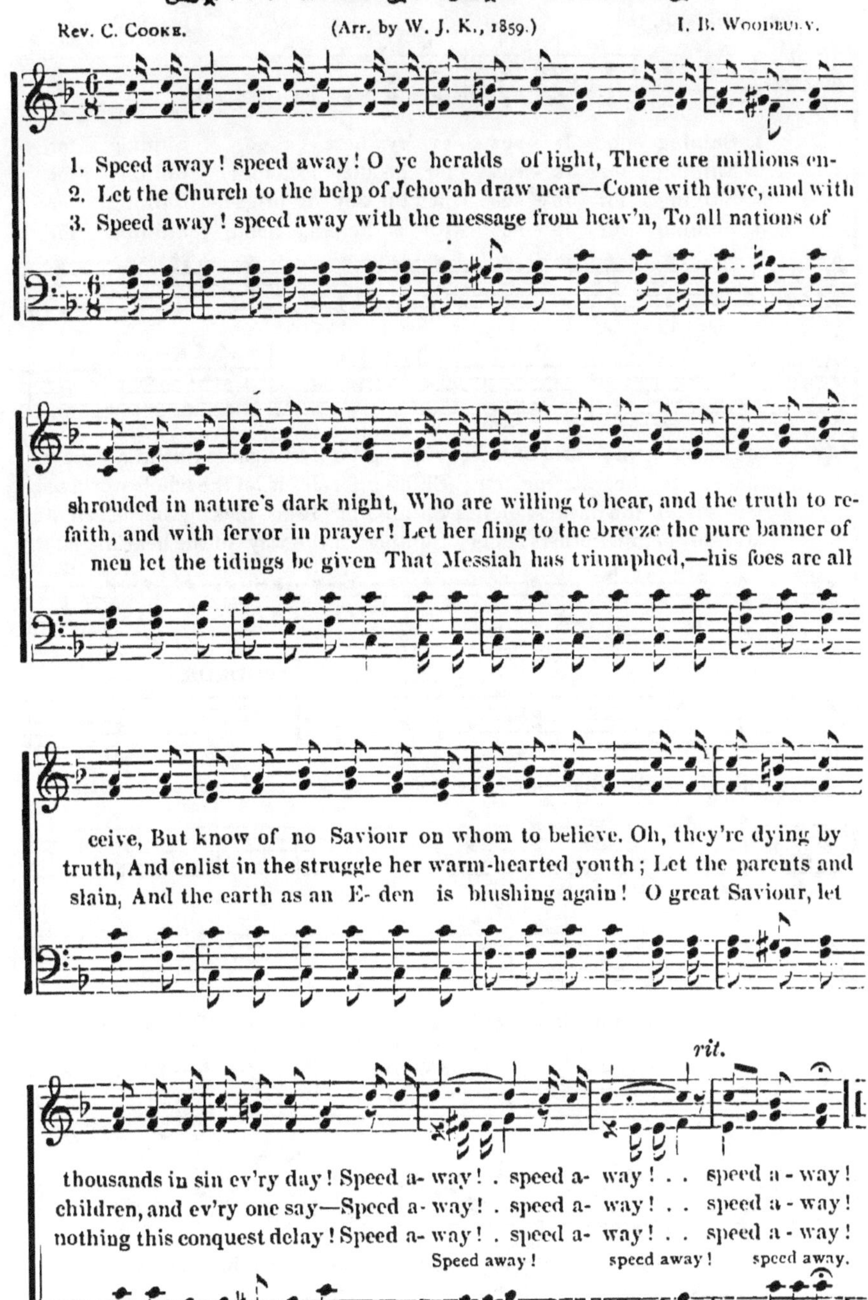

1. Speed away! speed away! O ye heralds of light, There are millions en-
2. Let the Church to the help of Jehovah draw near—Come with love, and with
3. Speed away! speed away with the message from heav'n, To all nations of
shrouded in nature's dark night, Who are willing to hear, and the truth to re-
faith, and with fervor in prayer! Let her fling to the breeze the pure banner of
men let the tidings be given That Messiah has triumphed,—his foes are all
ceive, But know of no Saviour on whom to believe. Oh, they're dying by
truth, And enlist in the struggle her warm-hearted youth; Let the parents and
slain, And the earth as an E- den is blushing again! O great Saviour, let
rit.
thousands in sin ev'ry day! Speed a- way! . speed a- way! . . speed a - way!
children, and ev'ry one say—Speed a- way! . speed a- way! . . speed a - way!
nothing this conquest delay! Speed a- way! . speed a- way! . . speed a - way!
Speed away! speed away! speed away.

From "Devotional Melodies," by per.

# Shining for Jesus.

Johnson Oatman, Jr. Jno R. Sweney.

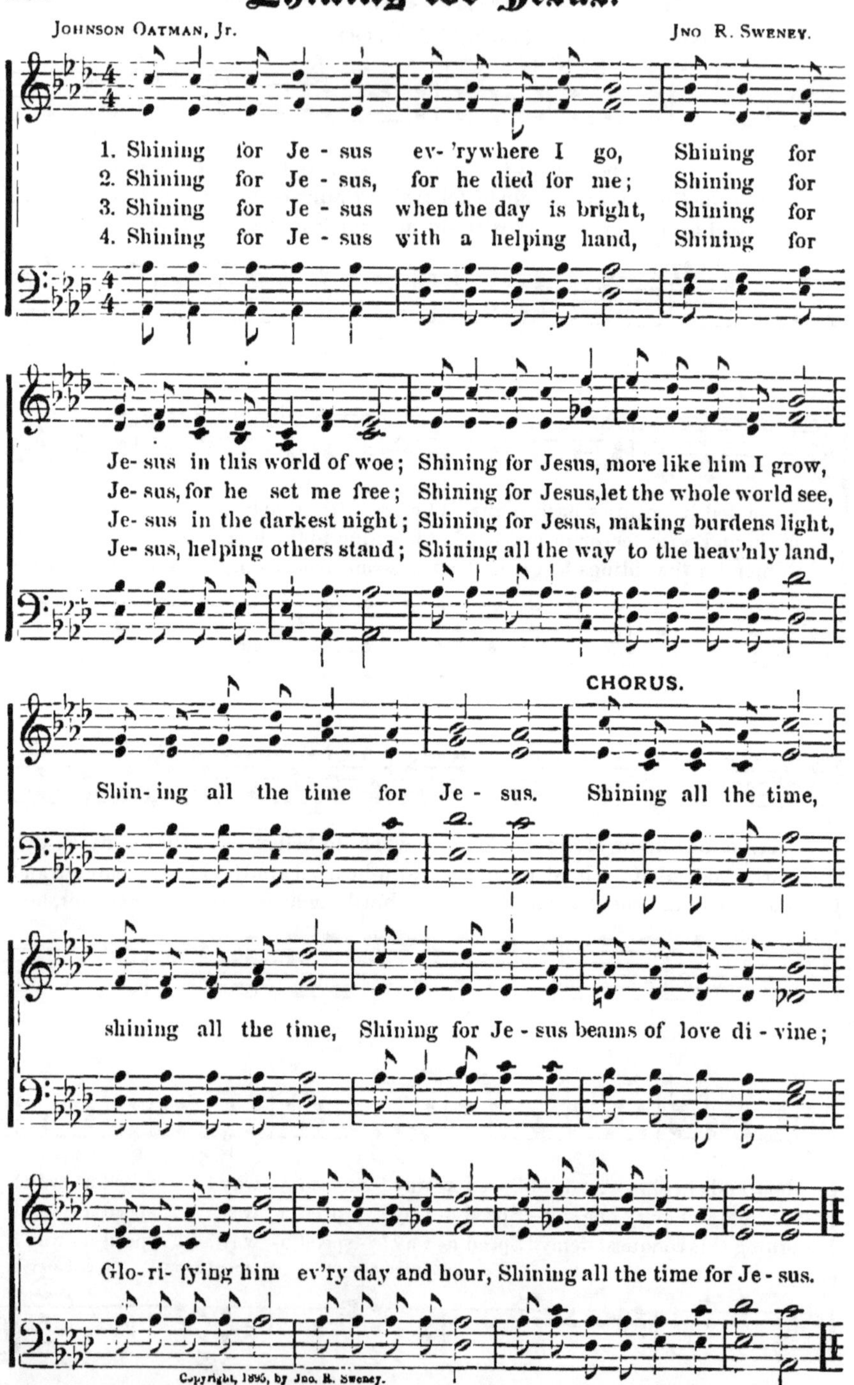

1. Shining for Je - sus ev- 'rywhere I go, Shining for Je- sus in this world of woe; Shining for Jesus, more like him I grow,
2. Shining for Je - sus, for he died for me; Shining for Je- sus, for he set me free; Shining for Jesus,let the whole world see,
3. Shining for Je - sus when the day is bright, Shining for Je- sus in the darkest night; Shining for Jesus, making burdens light,
4. Shining for Je - sus with a helping hand, Shining for Je- sus, helping others stand; Shining all the way to the heav'nly land,
Shin- ing all the time for Je - sus.
CHORUS.
Shining all the time, shining all the time, Shining for Je - sus beams of love di - vine; Glo- ri- fying him ev'ry day and hour, Shining all the time for Je - sus.

# Christ All and In All.

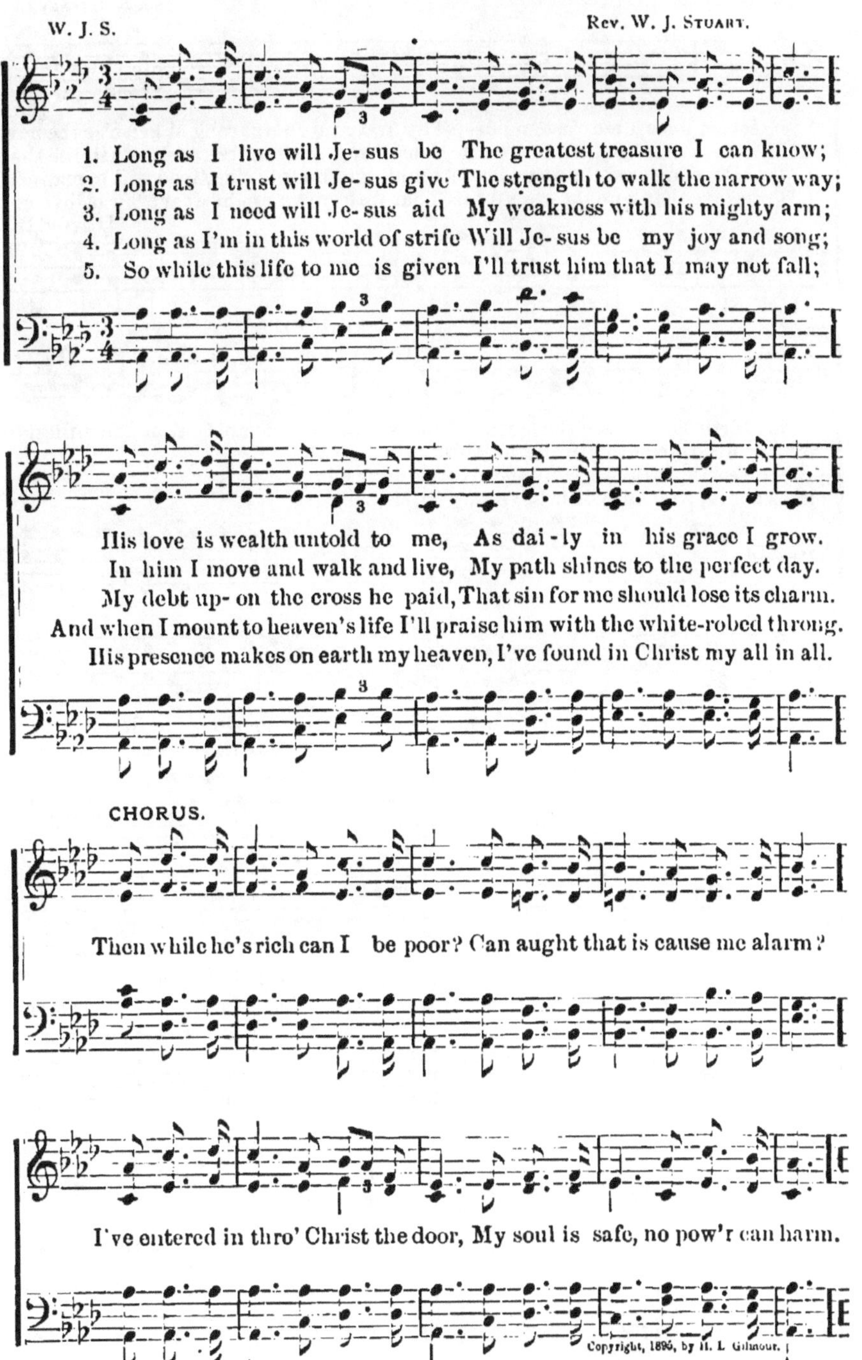
W. J. S.
Rev. W. J. Stuart.
1. Long as I live will Je- sus be The greatest treasure I can know;
2. Long as I trust will Je- sus give The strength to walk the narrow way;
3. Long as I need will Je- sus aid My weakness with his mighty arm;
4. Long as I'm in this world of strife Will Je- sus be my joy and song;
5. So while this life to me is given I'll trust him that I may not fall;
His love is wealth untold to me, As dai-ly in his grace I grow.
In him I move and walk and live, My path shines to the perfect day.
My debt up- on the cross he paid, That sin for me should lose its charm.
And when I mount to heaven's life I'll praise him with the white-robed throng.
His presence makes on earth my heaven, I've found in Christ my all in all.
CHORUS.
Then while he's rich can I be poor? Can aught that is cause me alarm?
I've entered in thro' Christ the door, My soul is safe, no pow'r can harm.
Copyright, 1895, by H. L. Gilmour.

FANNY J. CROSBY. JNO. R. SWENEY.

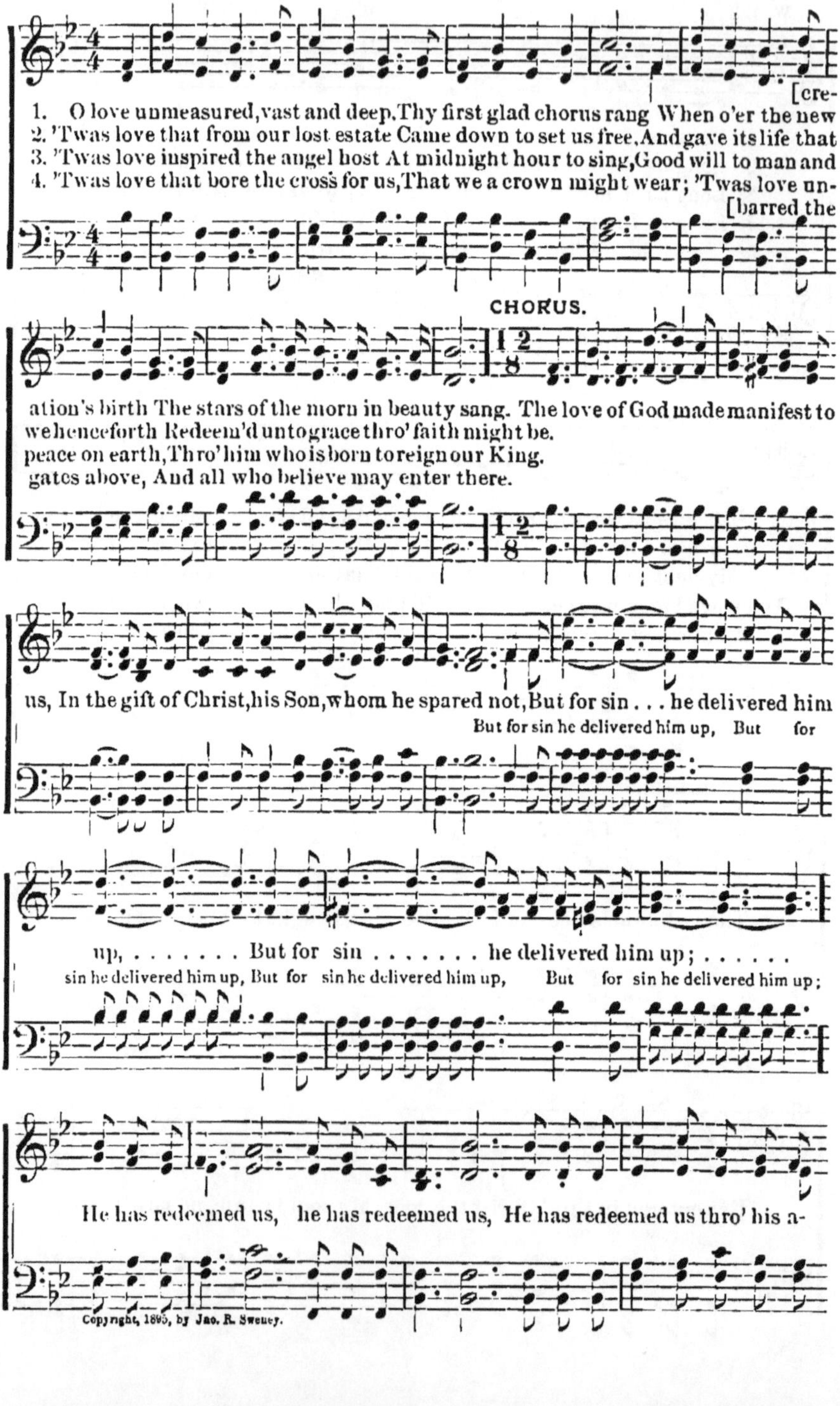

[cre-
1. O love unmeasured, vast and deep, Thy first glad chorus rang When o'er the new
2. 'Twas love that from our lost estate Came down to set us free, And gave its life that
3. 'Twas love inspired the angel host At midnight hour to sing, Good will to man and
4. 'Twas love that bore the cross for us, That we a crown might wear; 'Twas love un-
[barred the

CHORUS.

ation's birth The stars of the morn in beauty sang. The love of God made manifest to
we henceforth Redeem'd unto grace thro' faith might be.
peace on earth, Thro' him who is born to reign our King.
gates above, And all who believe may enter there.

us, In the gift of Christ, his Son, whom he spared not, But for sin . . . he delivered him
But for sin he delivered him up, But for

up, . . . . . . . But for sin . . . . . . . he delivered him up; . . . . . .
sin he delivered him up, But for sin he delivered him up, But for sin he delivered him up;

He has redeemed us, he has redeemed us, He has redeemed us thro' his a-

tonement once for all, . . . . He has redeemed us, he has re-
once for all, He has redeemed us,
deemed us, He has redeemed us thro' his atonement once for all. . . .
he has redeemed us,
once for all.
True Rest.
Jessie P. Tompkins.
John R. Thomas.
1. O weary souls who long for rest, O troubled, restless hearts, There is a
2. The shadows dark that cloud thy sky, The burdens hard to bear, The joys that
3. He trod the wine-press all alone, Sorrow and grief he knew; The hands that
4. Rest only comes when his dear voice Bids calm the troubled sea; 'Tis when we
5. Then do not slight the proffered hand, And drive the nails anew; Look thou, and
D. S.—love that
D.S.
Fine. REFRAIN. ritard. a'tempo.
p
pp
kind and loving breast, Where pity ne'er departs. Rest, rest, sweet, sweet rest; The
bloom to fade and die, He marks with tender care.
felt the cruel nails He reaches down to you.
hear his "Peace, be still!" Earth's darkest shadows flee.
see your Saviour stand And offer rest to you.
Copyright, 1885, by Wm. J. Kirkpatrick.
calms life's troubled sea Will give you rest, sweet rest.

# The Comforter has Come.

"I will pray the Father, and he shall give you another Comforter, that he may abide with you for ever."—John xiv: 16.

Rev. F. Bottome, D. D. | Wm. J. Kirkpatrick.

1 Oh, spread the tid-ings 'round, wher-ev - er man is found, Wher-
2. The long, long night is past, the morn-ing breaks at last; And
3. Lo, the great King of kings, with heal-ing in his wings, To
4. Oh, boundless love di-vine! how shall this tongue of mine To
5. Sing, till the ech-oes fly a-bove the vaulted sky, And
ev - er human hearts and hu-man woes abound; Let ev-'ry Christian
hushed the dreadful wail and fu - ry of the blast, As o'er the golden
ev - 'ry captive soul a full deliv'rance brings; And thro' the vacant
wond'ring mortals tell the matchless grace divine—That I, a child of
all the saints a-bove to all be-low re-ply, In strains of endless
D. S.—Holy Ghost from heav'n, The Father's promise giv'n; Oh, spread the tidings
Fine.
tongue proclaim the joy-ful sound: The Com - fort - er has come!
hills the day ad - vances fast! The Com - fort - er has come!
cells the song of triumph rings: The Com - fort - er has come!
hell, should in his im-age shine! The Com - fort - er has come!
love, the song that ne'er will die: The Com - fort - er has come!
round, Wher-ev - er man is found—The Com - fort - er has come!
CHORUS.
D.S.
The Com-fort-er has come, The Com-fort-er has come! The

# Saviour, Take My Hand.

JOHNSON OATMAN, Jr. H. L. GILMOUR.

1. Sav - iour, take my hand and lead me, For this world is cold,
2. Sav - iour, take my hand and lead me, Where there's perfect rest;
3. Sav - iour, take my hand and lead me, Thro' this world of sin;
And I need thee, yes, I need thee, Lead me to thy fold.
Let me find it, O I plead thee, On thy lov- ing breast.
Thou from ev -'ry sin canst free me, Make me pure with - in.
Fierce the winds are sweeping 'round me, Death and danger seem to bound me;
Where I fain would stay forev - er, Hidden there, no sin can sev - er;
O, I pray thee, do not leave me, In thy lov- ing arms receive me;
I'm so glad that thou hast found me, Lead me safe- ly on.
Bless- ed ref - uge, I'll leave nev - er, Sav - iour, lead me on.
By thy help I'll nev- er grieve thee, Sav - iour, lead me home.
rit.

# Come, Work in My Vineyard.

H. D. L. HERBERT D. LOTHROP.

1. Come, work in my vineyard, 'tis the Mas- ter calls for you,
2. Come, work in my vineyard, there is la- bor now for all.
3. Come, work in my vineyard and re- ceive the great re- ward,

The har- vest fields are whit'ning, but the la- bor- ers are few;
Be faith- ful in his ser- vice and the power of sin shall fall;
"Well done, my faithful ser- vant," is the hap- py, welcome word;

The night is fast approaching, and there's plen- ty now to do,
Be wise and keep the ar- mor bright un - til we hear the call,
We'll en - ter joys un- end- ing in the pres- ence of the Lord

*D.S.*—The Lord of the har - vest is com- ing by and by,

*Fine.* CHORUS.

Let us work till the Master comes. The Lord of the harvest is
Let us work till the Master comes.
If we work till the Master comes.

Let us work till the Master comes.

*D.S.*

coming by and by, To bear the reapers homeward to dwell with him on high;

# Up and Be Doing.

L. E. J. L. E. Jones.

1. Why stand ye i - dle, my brother, to - day, While there are millions in darkness a- way? Hark to the cry, ringing out o'er the wave, Send us the tidings of him who can save.
2. Will you not list to the Master's com - mand, Car- ry the gos- pel light over the wave; How can you linger when he bids you go? Dare you refuse him, and answer him, no?
3. Give of your la - bor, and give of your store, As he doth prosper you giving the more; 'Till ev'ry creature shall hear of the Lord, 'Till all the nations shall honor his Word.
CHORUS.
Up and be do - ing, up and be do - ing, It is the Master's com - mand; Up and be do - ing, up and be do- ing, Spreading the truth o'er the land.
Up and be do- ing, up and be doing, It is the Master's, the Master's command; Up and be doing, up and be doing, Spreading the gospel truth over the land.

# Let Me Tell You.

"But now abideth faith, hope, love, these three; but the greatest of these is love."
1 Cor. xiii: 13.

A. Rosalthe Carey. Wm. J. Kirkpatrick.

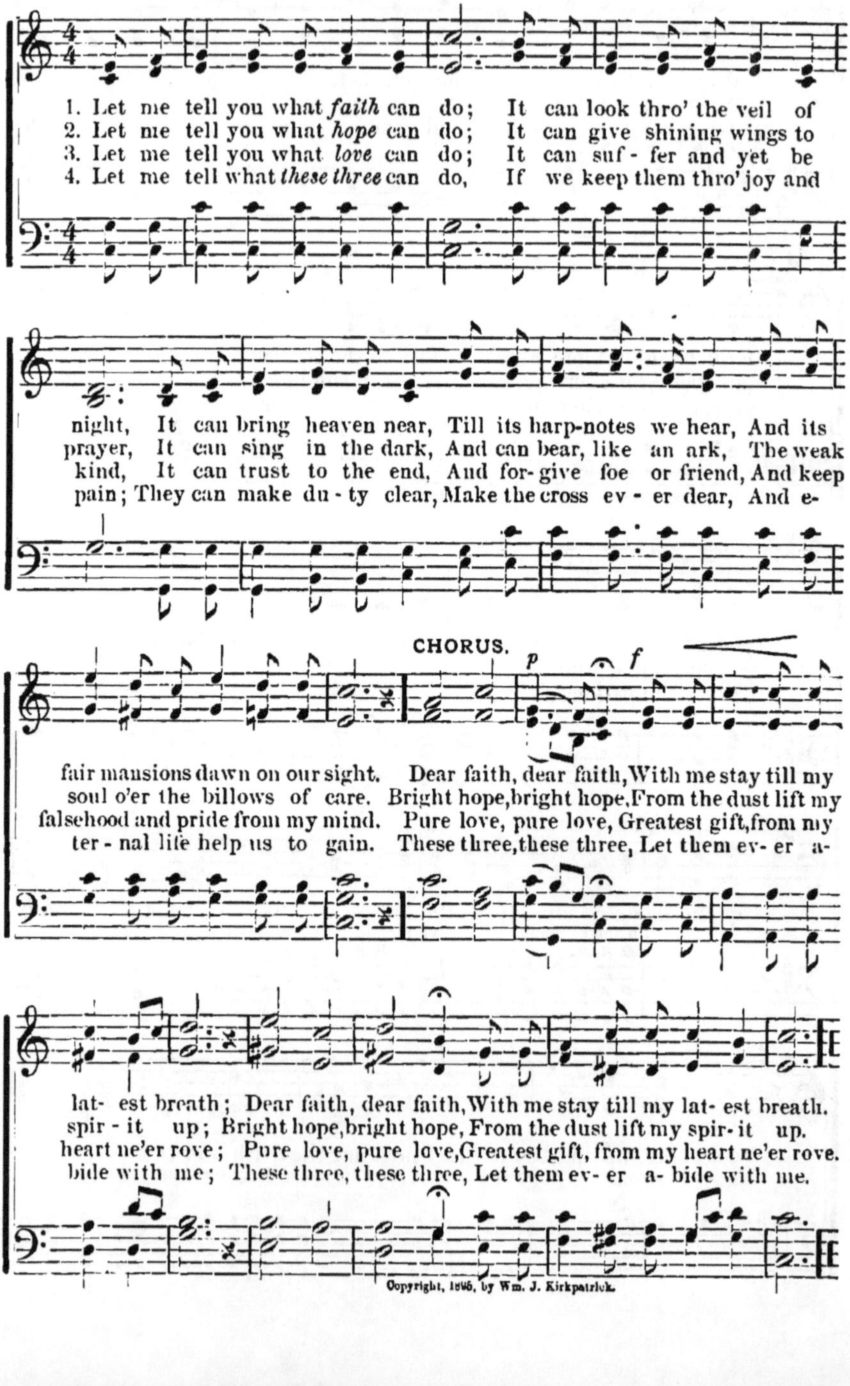

1. Let me tell you what *faith* can do; It can look thro' the veil of night, It can bring heaven near, Till its harp-notes we hear, And its fair mansions dawn on our sight.
2. Let me tell you what *hope* can do; It can give shining wings to prayer, It can sing in the dark, And can bear, like an ark, The weak soul o'er the billows of care.
3. Let me tell you what *love* can do; It can suf-fer and yet be kind, It can trust to the end, And for-give foe or friend, And keep falsehood and pride from my mind.
4. Let me tell what *these three* can do, If we keep them thro' joy and pain; They can make du-ty clear, Make the cross ev-er dear, And e-ter-nal life help us to gain.

CHORUS.

Dear faith, dear faith, With me stay till my lat-est breath; Dear faith, dear faith, With me stay till my lat-est breath.
Bright hope, bright hope, From the dust lift my spir-it up; Bright hope, bright hope, From the dust lift my spir-it up.
Pure love, pure love, Greatest gift, from my heart ne'er rove; Pure love, pure love, Greatest gift, from my heart ne'er rove.
These three, these three, Let them ev-er a-bide with me; These three, these three, Let them ev-er a-bide with me.

# Why Art Thou Wandering?

Ida L. Reed.
H. L. Gilmour.
1. Why art thou wand'ring alone in the darkness? Je - sus is calling thee,
2. Why art thou wand'ring so sin-sick and weary, Out in the wilderness,
3. Cease from thy wand'rings, turn now unto Jesus, Come while he calleth, and
"Come un - to me;" Why art thou straying, still houseless and homeless,
far from the fold? Out of the darkness the Saviour will lead thee,
cri - eth to thee; Wait - ing he standeth, still off'ring sal - va - tion,
D.S.—Won - der-ful mer - cy and love he is off'ring,
Fine.
CHORUS.
When there a- waiteth such shel- ter for thee? Why art thou wand'ring? when
Thro' his great love and compassion un-told.
Come un - to Je - sus, his blood is thy plea.
Come, and its fullness thine ev- er shall be.
D.S.
Je - sus is pleading, Come! come! come un - to me.
Come un - to me, oh,

# Over the River.

L. H. EDMUNDS. Spanish Melody, arr.

1. O - ver the riv - er Hangs a cloud so dark and drear, Till Je- sus
2. O - ver the riv - er Loved ones pass from day to day; To realms im-
3. O - ver the riv - er Blissful chords of mu- sic float, O - ver the
comforts, Till his voice we hear; Then his smile, il- lum - ing,
mor - tal, Bear our hearts a - way; O the sweet re- un - ions,
riv - er Sounds the harp's glad note; There, at home with Je - sus,
Floods the waves with gold - en light, Then a path of glo - ry
Just be- yond the si - lent tide! O the songs of welcome,
End- less a - ges of de- light; There the shin - ing mansions,
Slower.
O- pens to the sight.
On the oth - er side.
Robes of radiant white.
CHORUS.
O - ver the riv - er, Saviour, close be-
side us stand; O - ver the riv - er, To the heavenly land.
ritard.

# Be Not Afraid.

Rev. Alfred J. Hough.
Chas. H. Gabriel.
1. Come weal, come woe wher'er we go, God is not far a- way; He holds the stormy winds that blow, And moulds the golden day. The darkest night to him is light, And thro' the shine or shade, He speaks in tones of tender might, "My child, be not afraid."
2. Tho' clouds may veil the stars that sail O'er boundless seas of space, And lights along all shores may fail, God will not hide his face: But sweetly whispers while his hands Up-on his own are laid,—"Lo! at thy side thy Father stands, My child, be not afraid."
3. Thro' changing years, in joy and tears, The changeless One abides, And safe the soul from doubts and fears That in his bosom hides. On noisy street, in still retreat, Thro' vales of deepest shade, That voice is heard with accents sweet, "My child, be not afraid."
CHORUS.
Be not a - fraid, . . . be not a - fraid, . . The darkest night to him is light, And thro' the shine or shade,
Be not a - fraid, . . . be not a - fraid, . . He speaks in tones of tender might, "My child, be not afraid."
Child, be not, be not afraid, Child, be not, be not afraid,
Used by per. of Geo. F. Rosche, owner of copyright.

# The Days of My Childhood.

Rev E. H Stokes, D.D., L.L D. Josephine H. Sweney.

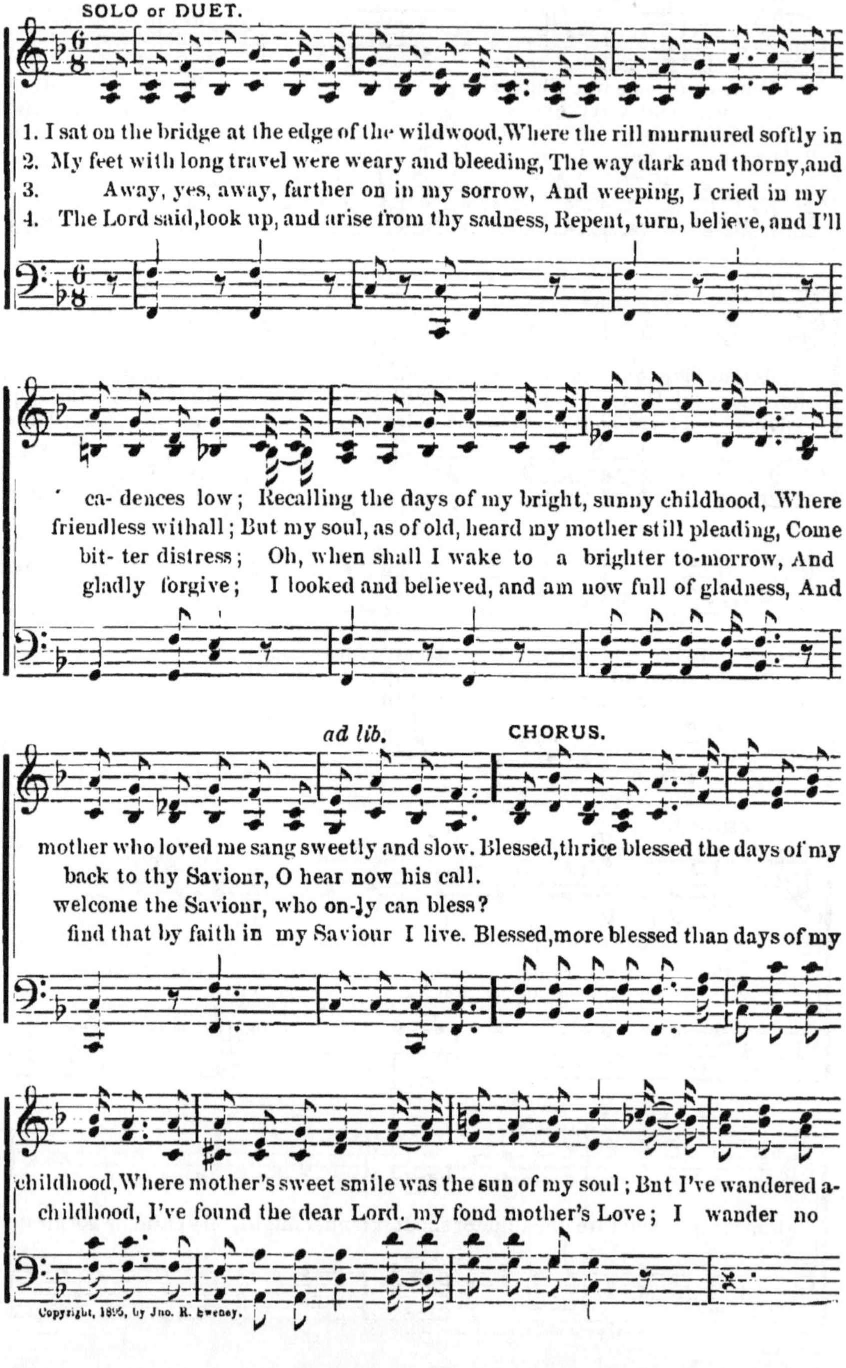

SOLO or DUET.

1. I sat on the bridge at the edge of the wildwood, Where the rill murmured softly in ca- dences low; Recalling the days of my bright, sunny childhood, Where mother who loved me sang sweetly and slow.
2. My feet with long travel were weary and bleeding, The way dark and thorny, and friendless withall; But my soul, as of old, heard my mother still pleading, Come back to thy Saviour, O hear now his call.
3. Away, yes, away, farther on in my sorrow, And weeping, I cried in my bit- ter distress; Oh, when shall I wake to a brighter to-morrow, And welcome the Saviour, who on-ly can bless?
4. The Lord said, look up, and arise from thy sadness, Repent, turn, believe, and I'll gladly forgive; I looked and believed, and am now full of gladness, And find that by faith in my Saviour I live.

*ad lib.*

CHORUS.

Blessed, thrice blessed the days of my childhood, Where mother's sweet smile was the sun of my soul; But I've wandered a-

Blessed, more blessed than days of my childhood, I've found the dear Lord, my fond mother's Love; I wander no

ad lib.
way in sin's dreary wildwood, Led on by a force which I could not control.
more in the world's dreary wildwood, But thro' bowers of bliss to her Eden above

# Oh, Come Home To-day.

L. E. J. L. E. Jones.

1. Come to Jesus, come, ye lost ones, Je-sus calls so tender- ly; Why de-
2. Come to Jesus and find mercy, Come with all your guilt and woe; On the
3. Come to Jesus, do not lin - ger, Come and his disciple be; He who

Fine. CHORUS.

lay while he is waiting. Waiting, calling now for thee? Oh, come home to-day, ye
cross he sealed your pardon, And his blood makes white as snow.
marks the sparrow's falling Will accept and care for thee.

*D. S.*—To the homeland enter in.

D. S.
wand'rers, Leave the barren ways of sin; Come while Jesus yet is calling,

# Over the Dead-Line.

When urging an exceedingly wicked man to flee from the wrath to come, I was met by this statement: "I was brought up to honor God, and I have ended by hating him; I have blasphemed his name, and resisted his Spirit until I can no longer repent or believe, if there is a dead-line to God's grace I have drifted over it, and am lost."—W. G. M.

VIRGINIA W. MOYER. H. L. GILMOUR.

1. O sinner, the Saviour is calling for thee, Long, long has he called thee in vain;
2. O sinner, thine ears have been deaf to his voice, Thine eyes to his glory been dim;
3. O sinner, the Spirit is striving with thee; What if he should strive never more,
4. O sinner, God's patience may weary some day, And leave thy sad soul in the blast;

He called thee when joy lent its crown to thy days, He called thee in sorrow and pain.
The calls of thy Saviour have so wearied thee, Oh, what if they should weary him?
But leave thee alone, in thy darkness to dwell, In sight of the heavenly shore?
By willful resistance you've drifted away, O- ver the dead-line at last.

CHORUS.

O turn, while the Saviour in mercy is waiting, And steer for the harbor light;

*ritard.*

For how do you know but your soul may be drifting Over the dead-line to-night?

# It must be Settled to-night.

A miner in England went to Church one night and became deeply concerned for the salvation of his soul. When the services were ended he refused to leave the house, although the minister told him it was late, and he must go home and seek the Saviour there, and come again the next night. "No," said the miner, "It must be settled to-night, to-morrow night may be too late." So the minister stayed with him until he found peace. The next day while at work in the mines a mass of rock fell upon him, and he was killed. His last words were, "Thank God, it was settled last night, to-night it would have been too late."

Rev. C. B. KENDALL. JOHN J. HOOD.

1. "It must be settled to - night, To-morrow may be too late;"
2. A bur - den weighs my soul I can no long - er bear;
3. I can - not rest till peace En - folds me from a - bove,—
4. Oh, now I know 'tis done! My peace is made with God;
The an - gel of death may come, And seal for - ev - er my fate.
Un - less removed this night, 'Twill sink me in - to de - spair.
Till my Redeem - er speaks to me As - sur - ance of his love.
My par - don's found in Je - sus' name, Thro' faith in Je - sus' blood.
CHORUS.
It must be set - tled to - night, I can no long - er wait,
4th v. Oh, now I know 'tis done! Sweet joy pervades my soul;
to-night,
Peace with my God I now must have, To-morrow may be too late.
Peace with my God I now have found; His blood hath made me whole.

# There are Lights on the Shore.

H. D. L.
Herbert D. Lothrop.
1. I am nearing that heaven - ly land of delight That for a- ges e-
2. I am nearing that land where the armies of God Shall return when their
3. I am nearing that land where my Saviour has gone To prepare a bright
ter- nal shall stand, Where the saints are rejoic- ing by riv- ers of life,
warfare is done; Where the cross they have borne shall be changed for a crown,
mansion for me, And the raptures of heaven can nev- er be known
And are singing, an un - broken band; Where the flow'rs never fade, and the
And the righteous shall shine like the sun. I am nearing that land where all
Till the blessed Redeem - er I see. In the noontide of glo - ry, I
springs never fail, Where the skies are unclouded and bright; Where the dear ones [are
storms are at rest, I shall sing when the journey shall cease, Glory, glo- ry to
soon shall be there, In the shade of the sheltering fold; And the joys that the
waiting to welcome me home, In the beauti - ful country of light.
Je - sus, for - ev - ermore blest, By the clear, flowing riv - er of peace.
faithful for - ev - er shall share Un- to mortals can nev - er be told.

CHORUS.
There are lights on the shore that are beaming for me, As over the river I go;
There are friends over there whose faces I'll see,
Whose robes have been washed white as snow.
'Tis My Home.
FANNY J. CROSBY.
FRANCIS BURGETTE SHORT.
1. There is a place where I would be, 'Tis my home, 'tis my home;
Where pure, unmin - gled joy I see, 'Tis my home, 'tis my home.
2. There is a place where mem'ry clings, 'Tis my home, 'tis my home;
Where gen- tle peace delight - ed sings, 'Tis my home, 'tis my home.
3. There is a place that most I love, 'Tis my home, 'tis my home;
It links my soul with heaven a- bove, 'Tis my home, 'tis my home.
There kindred hearts with tender care My ev'- ry thought and feeling share;
Oh, there I find a calm re- pose That stays the ties of human woes,
There kindly words, like music sweet, And cheerful smiles my coming greet;
If earth can boast an E - den fair, 'Tis my home, 'tis my home.
And o - ver all a beau- ty throws, 'Tis my home, 'tis my home.
O hallowed spot! O blest re - treat! 'Tis my home, 'tis my home.

# Like an Army Strong.

FANNY J. CROSBY.
FRANCIS BURGETTE SHORT.
1. We are marching on like an ar- my strong, We are marching in the King's highway; And our hearts break forth in a joy- ful song, We are marching in the King's highway.
2. We are marching on thro' a world of care, We are marching in the King's highway; But the shield of faith on our hearts we bear, While we're marching in the King's highway.
3. We are marching on thro' the ranks of sin, We are marching in the King's highway; O the victor crowns that we all may win, While we're marching in the King's highway.
4. We are marching on to the realms of light, We are marching in the King's highway; And the morning star is our beacon light, For it shin - eth in the King's highway.
CHORUS.
We are marching, marching on, marching, marching on, Hap- py in the Lord to - day; Like an army brave and strong we can sing our song, We are marching in the King's highway.

# Soldiers of Jesus, Press On.

L. H. Edmunds.
Wm. J. Kirkpatrick.
1. Soldiers of Je- sus, be "strong in the Lord," Follow the or- ders you
2. Have you looked back with the course just begun? Wearied of conflict? the
3. Do not lose time in the heavenward way, Upward and onward, ad-
4. Car - ing for oth- ers, with hearts all aglow, Tell this sal- vation wher-
find in his word; Trust- ing in him for his boun- ti - ful grace,
crown is not won; Marching to Zi - on, be steadfast and brave,
vanc- ing each day; Strive to keep pace with the faithful and pure,
ev - er you go, Ask - ing your friends in the ranks to take place,
Turn from all e - vil, press on in the race.
Look- ing to Je - sus, he's might-y to save.
Watching and praying, the blessing secure.
Marching with those who shall triumph thro' grace.
CHORUS.
On, press on!
On, press on, on, press on!
Soldiers of Je- sus, press on, press on, Till in his pal - ace the
vic- tor-shouts ring, Hold up the ban - ner of Je - sus our King.

# Let us Adore Him Forever.

Geo. Shadwick.
Isaiah lxiii: 1.
Mrs. Grace Weiser Davis.
1. Who is this that cometh with garments died in blood, Trav'ling in the greatness of his strength and mighty love? This? O this is Je - sus, the blessed Son of God! Let us adore him for- ev - er.
2. Once a lit- tle stranger babe in Bethlehem he lay, Shepherds bow'd and wise men knelt to worship him that day; But his own for whom he came their faces turned away, Let us adore him for- ev - er.
3. None can tell the life of toil and pain on earth he led, No one knows how ma- ny hearts by him were comforted; There upon the cruel cross for you and me he bled, Let us adore him for- ev - er.
4. O'er the grave tri- um - phant, a mighty vic- tor, he Burst the bars of death and captive led captiv - i- ty, Lift your heads, ye gates! he comes to make his people free, Let us adore him for- ev - er.
5. Pardon, cleansing, peace and joy for all the world abound, Rest of soul, oh, wondrous rest! by faith in him is found; Full salvation from all sin, O spread the joyful sound, Let us adore him for- ev - er.
CHORUS.
For he looked, and there was none to save, He saw, and there was none to deliv - er: Then his

own right arm sal - vation gave, Let us adore him for - ev - er.

# More of Thee.

E. E. Hewitt. H. L. Gilmour.

1. Come, Lord, and fill my waiting soul, More, more of thee; Let love in mighty billows roll, More, more of thee.
2. Take self away, that I may hold More, more of thee; And to my emptied heart unfold, More, more of thee.
3. O teach me by the "still, small voice" More, more of thee; Thy spirit will my soul rejoice, More, more of thee.
4. Whatev - er else may be denied, More, more of thee; Thyself bestow'd, 'tis heav'n supplied, More, more of thee.
5. In sorrow's night, in sparkling day, More, more of thee; Till earthly shadows flee a-way, More, more of thee.

CHORUS.

More of thy grace afford, More of thy-self, dear Lord; No gift like this can ev- er be, More, more of thee.

# Surely, No!

E. E. Hewitt. H. C. Rowell.

1. Earthly blossoms quickly per - ish, Earthly ros - es soon will fade;
2. Blessed comfort he hath spo - ken, To the wea - ry and the sad;
3. Ev - er in his grace a - bid - ing, Life grows richer day by day;

And the hopes we fond - ly cher - ish, Un - der drifting snows be laid.
And his prom - ise, nev - er bro - ken, Makes the trustful spir - it glad.
Naught can come, our souls divid - ing From the Life, the Truth, the Way.

But will Je - sus ev - er leave us When our passing lights grow dim?
Let us ev - 'ry fear sur - ren - der, Sweet - ly leaning on his breast;
Like the glitt'ring stars a - bove us, Shall his ransomed peo - ple be;

Shall we fail, when troubles grieve us, Fail to find a friend in him?
From his love, so strong and ten - der, Can we turn a - way un - blessed?
Will our Saviour cease to love us, Thro' the long e - ter - ni - ty?

CHORUS.

Surely, no! . . . . oh, surely no! He will not . . . . forsake us so;
Surely, no! oh, surely, no! He will not forsake us so;

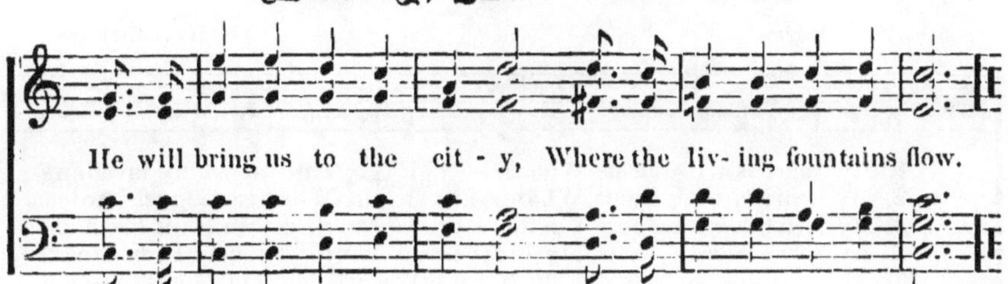
He will bring us to the cit - y, Where the liv- ing fountains flow.

# I'm Rich To-day.

JOHNSON OATMAN, Jr. JNO. R. SWENEY.

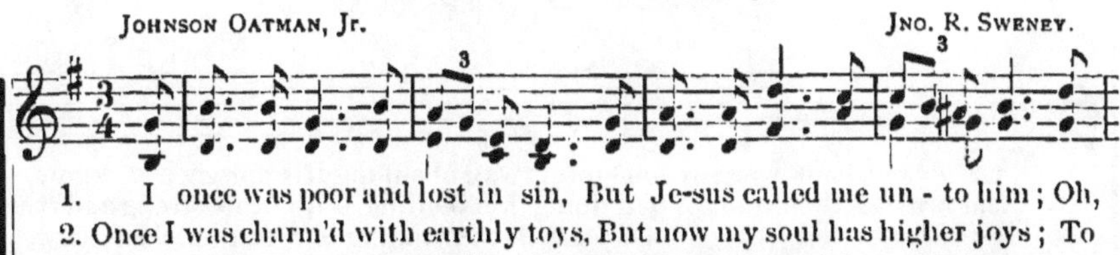
1. I once was poor and lost in sin, But Je-sus called me un - to him; Oh,
2. Once I was charm'd with earthly toys, But now my soul has higher joys; To
3. What tho' I have no earthly gold? My Saviour's wealth cannot be told; In
4. What tho' a cot- tage here below? Soon to a mansion I will go; Still

praise his name, I now can say, I'm rich to- day, I'm rich to- day.
feed on husks I can - not stay, I'm rich to- day, I'm rich to- day.
things that can - not pass a - way, I'm rich to- day, I'm rich to- day.
shouting this same joy- ful lay, I'm rich to- day, I'm rich to- day.

*D.S.*—paid the debt I could not pay, I'm rich to- day, I'm rich to- day.

CHORUS.

I'm rich to-day, I'm rich to-day, Since Je- sus took my sins a- way; He

# My Heart is with Jesus.

Mrs. V. M. Moyer. H. L. Gilmour.

1. My heart is with Jesus Wherev - er I go, Thro' sunshiny meadows,
2. My heart is with Jesus Whatev - er I do, When casting off burdens,
3. My heart is with Jesus Whatev - er I bear, Sweet smiles of his favor,
4. My heart is with Jesus, My heart is not here; When may I come to thee,
5. O who can take from me The life of my heart, The joy of my bos - om,

Or des- erts of woe; When storms wail about me His presence I know,
And bearing them too; When doing his bidding, With heart strong and true,
Or sorrows that wear; When joybells are ringing Or sad notes of care,
O Saviour most dear? O nev - er to wander, O nev - er to fear,
Tho' all else depart? A- drift on his promise, A- float on his love,

REFRAIN.

My heart is with Je- sus Wherev - er I go. Wherev - er I go,
My heart is with Je- sus Whatev - er I do. Whatev - er I do,
My heart is with Je- sus Whatev - er I bear. Whatev - er I bear,
My heart is with Je- sus, My heart is not here. My heart is not here,
My heart is with Je- sus, My home is a - bove. My home is a - bove,

Wherev - er I go, My heart is with Jesus Wherev - er I go.
Whatev - er I do, My heart is with Jesus Whatev - er I do.
Whatev - er I bear, My heart is with Jesus Whatev - er I bear.
My heart is not here, My heart is with Jesus, My heart is not here.
My home is a - bove, My heart is with Jesus, My home is a - bove.

# I Have the Glory in My Soul.

Rev. Geo. A. McLaughlin.
Wm. J. Kirkpatrick.
1. O bless-ed tide that cleanses sin, Thy mighty billows o'er me roll;
2. My aching heart has known thy skill, From ev'ry wound I'm now made whole;
3. Freedom from sins and doubts and fears—I long have sought to reach this goal;
4. The world and all its trifling joys No more my spir - it shall console;
I feel the power and joy with-in, I have the glo - ry in my soul.
With perfect love, I dread no ill, I have the glo - ry in my soul.
Thy blessed love has dried my tears, I have the glo - ry in my soul.
Thy comfort comes to me; tho' weak, I have the glo - ry in my soul.
CHORUS.
I have the glo-ry in my soul, I
I have the glo - ry, have the glo - ry in my soul,
have the glo-ry in my soul, I feel the
I have the glo - ry, have the glo - ry in my soul,
poco ritard.
power and joy with-in, I have the glo-ry in my soul.
have the glo - ry in my soul.

# Soldiers are Needed.

BIRDIE BELL. JNO. R. SWENEY.

1. Soldiers are needed, is your name enrolled? Say, is it written with names of the bold? And are you marching in Christ's ar - my true, With his dear standard a - float o - ver you?
2. Soldiers are needed, the brave and the true, Je- sus the Captain is call - ing for you; Tak - ing the sword that he gives, for- ward go, Fear- less in spir- it, tho' might- y the foe!
3. Soldiers are needed, oh, haste to the field! Sal-vation's helmet and faith's gold- en shield Christ gives each war- rior, take them from his hand, March then to triumph with his trust- y band.
4. Soldiers are needed, oh, loud, clear the cry! Fear not, be valiant, our Cap - tain is nigh! Steadfast, unmind - ful of en - e-mies' frown, Fight, that at last you may win vict'ry's crown.
D. S.—'Neath Je - sus' ban- ner do you march to- day? Foll'wing the Captain each step of the way?
Fine.
CHORUS.
Soldiers are needed, oh, yes, not a few! Hearts that are earnest, and hearts that are true;
D.S.

# Comrades of the Battlefield.

W. A. S. Rev. W. A. Spencer, D. D.

1. Com- panions in this ho - ly war, With man-y bat- tles won;
2. In fightings oft, and marches sore, The conflict seemeth long;
3. 'Tis wea- ry watching wave on wave Be- side an al - ien sea;
4. We soon shall camp by heaven's sea, When all our warfare's past;

Heav'n's victors call us from a - far, And Je - sus leads us on.
Our comrades hail us from yon shore, And cheer us with their song.
We see a - far, beyond the grave Our blest e - ter - ni - ty.
We'll praise his love so full and free, When we get home at last.

CHORUS.

Comrades of the battlefield, Soldiers of Je - sus, Tho' long the battle seems, Still our hearts are brave; Soon we shall see him, The won- der- ful Je - sus, Je- sus, the Conqueror, Mighty to save.

# When We Enter the Pearly Gates.

L. H. Edmunds. Wm. J. Kirkpatrick.

1. Nevermore a sorrow, nevermore a fear, When we enter the pearly gates;
2. Nevermore to grieve him, nevermore to stray, When we enter the pearly gates;
3. Oh, the happy meetings with the friends we love, When we enter the pearly gates!
4. Let this hope revive us, pressing on anew, Till we enter the pearly gates;

For the loving Father dries the ling'ring tear, When we enter the pearly gates.
Not a shadow darkens ev-erlasting day, When we enter the pearly gates.
Oh, the glorious mansions of the home above, When we enter the pearly gates!
He will not forsake us, he will bear us thro', Till we enter the pearly gates.

CHORUS.

O some day the gates will to us unfold, With the ransomed host we shall be enrolled,

And with angels walk in the streets of gold, When we enter the pearly gates.

# Jesus is All that You Need. 

Mrs. Frank A. Breck.
Frank M. Davis.
1. Come to the Saviour, believe in his name, Jesus is all that you need;
2. Jesus has triumph'd o'er sin and the grave, Jesus is all that you need;
3. Give your life o- ver to Je- sus' control, Jesus is all that you need;
Je- sus is now and for- ev- er the same, Je- sus is all that you need.
He is a- bundant- ly a- ble to save, Je- sus is all that you need.
Je- sus will meet ev'ry want of the soul, Je- sus is all that you need.
Claim his sure promise, oh, fully believe, Ask for his blessing and you shall receive,
Jesus will pardon if you will confess, Jesus will comfort in time of distress,
Jesus is calling, oh, turn not away, Make him forever your life and your stay,
Fine.
Je- sus will help you the past to retrieve, Je- sus is all that you need.
He will be with you for- ev- er to bless, Je- sus is all that you need.
Will you belong to him wholly to- day? Je- sus is all that you need.
D.S.—why turn away from the Saviour to-day, When Jesus is all that you need?
CHORUS.
D.S.
Je- sus is all that you need, . . . All that you ever can need; . . . Oh,
you need,
can need;

# Glory to the Saviour.

JAMES L. BLACK. FRANCIS BURGDETTE SHORT.

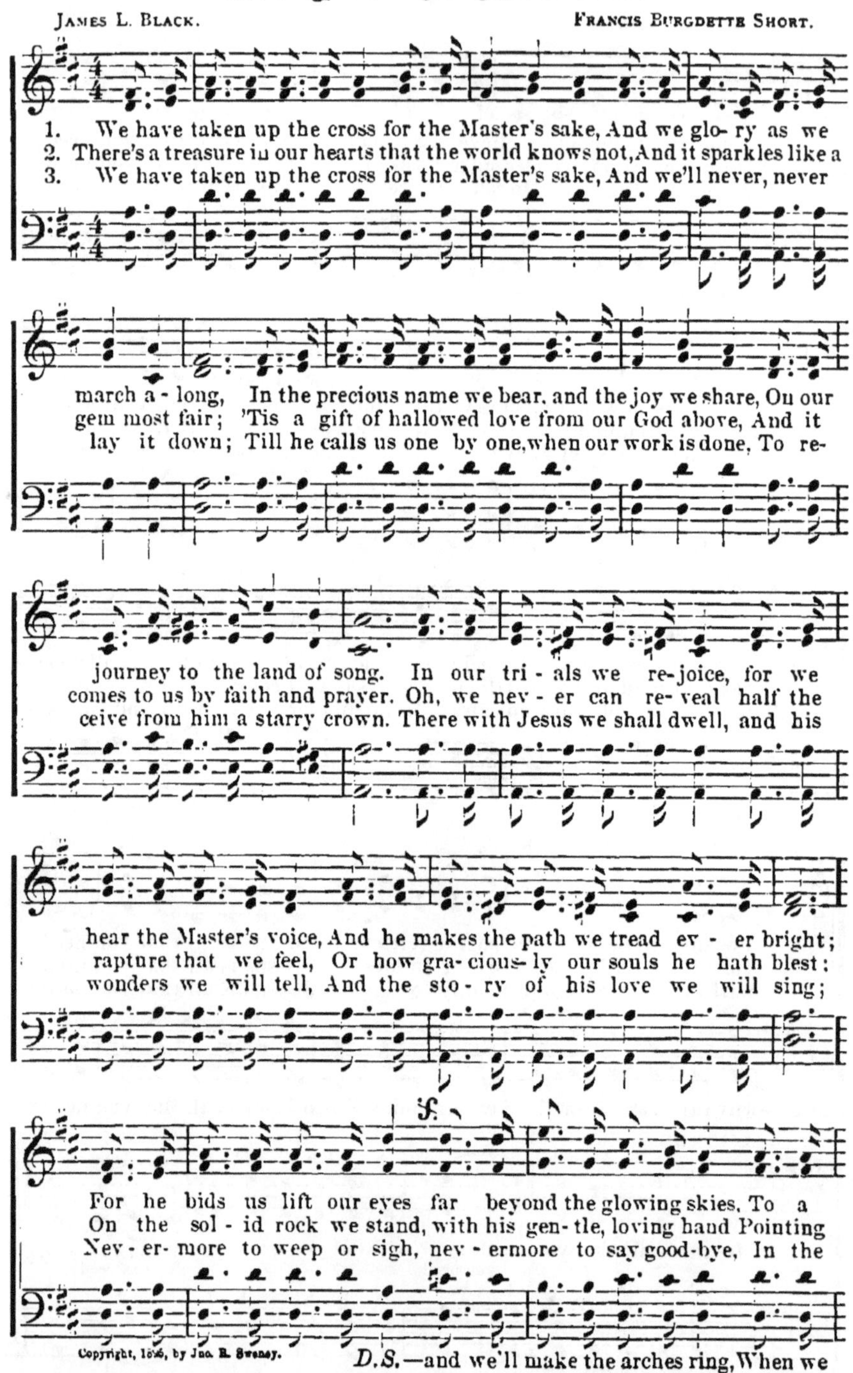
1. We have taken up the cross for the Master's sake, And we glo- ry as we march a - long, In the precious name we bear, and the joy we share, On our journey to the land of song. In our tri - als we re-joice, for we hear the Master's voice, And he makes the path we tread ev - er bright;
2. There's a treasure in our hearts that the world knows not, And it sparkles like a gem most fair; 'Tis a gift of hallowed love from our God above, And it comes to us by faith and prayer. Oh, we nev - er can re - veal half the rapture that we feel, Or how gra - cious- ly our souls he hath blest;
3. We have taken up the cross for the Master's sake, And we'll never, never lay it down; Till he calls us one by one, when our work is done, To re- ceive from him a starry crown. There with Jesus we shall dwell, and his wonders we will tell, And the sto - ry of his love we will sing;
For he bids us lift our eyes far beyond the glowing skies, To a
On the sol - id rock we stand, with his gen- tle, loving hand Pointing
Nev - er- more to weep or sigh, nev - ermore to say good-bye, In the
D.S.—and we'll make the arches ring, When we

Fine. CHORUS.
cit - y that is filled with light. Glo - ry to the Saviour, we shall soon be there,
upward to the vale of rest.
palace of the Lord our King.
anchor by the crystal sea.
D.S.
Shouting hal - le - lu - jah in the land so fair; Glo - ry we will sing,

# Oh, for Converting Grace!

ANDREW REED. Adapted and arr. by WM. J. KIRKPATRICK.

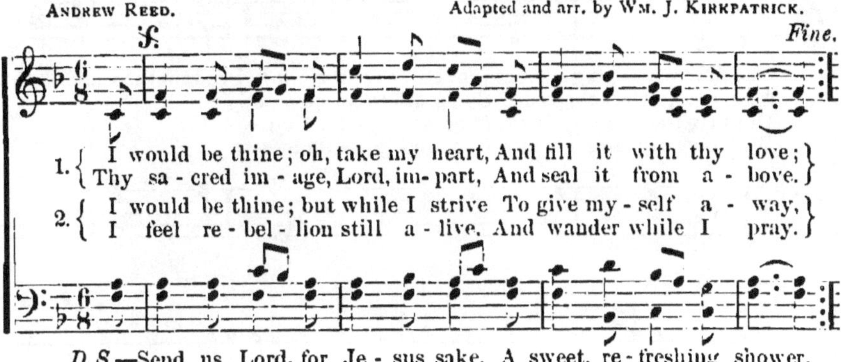
Fine.
1. { I would be thine; oh, take my heart, And fill it with thy love;
Thy sa - cred im - age, Lord, im - part, And seal it from a - bove. }
2. { I would be thine; but while I strive To give my - self a - way,
I feel re - bel - lion still a - live, And wander while I pray. }
D.S.—Send us, Lord, for Je - sus sake, A sweet, re - freshing shower.

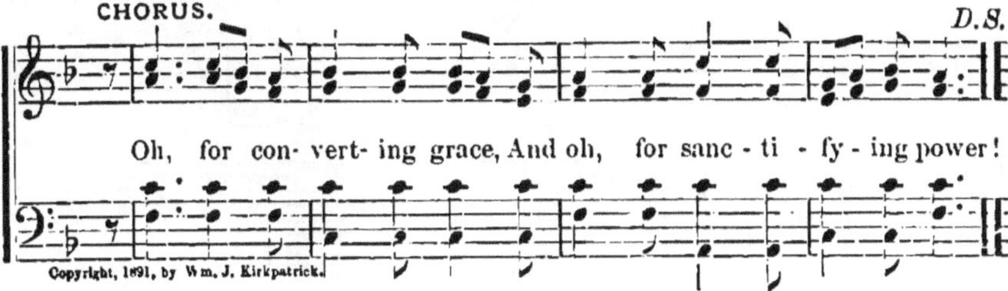
CHORUS.
D.S.
Oh, for con - vert - ing grace, And oh, for sanc - ti - fy - ing power!

3 I would be thine; but, Lord, I feel
Evil still lurks within;
Do thou thy majesty reveal,
And banish all my sin.

4 I would be thine; I would embrace
The Saviour, and adore;
Inspire with faith, infuse thy grace,
And now my soul restore.

# Send Out the Search-Light.

E. E. Hewitt.
Jno. R. Sweney.
1. Send out the search-light in sin's storm-y night, Where, lashed by the tempest, the breakers are white; Keep steady the beacon, revealing the shoal, The fierce, sweeping currents en-gulf-ing the soul.
2. Send out the search-light, brave hearts, we implore, A ves-sel is sinking in sight of the shore; Far o-ver the deep sounds the cry of distress, Who springs to the rescue? God grant them success.
3. Send out the search-light, the sig-nal of love, The Mas-ter will give us his help from a-bove; Our lantern was kindled at Bethlehem's star, And brightened at Calv'ry, its rays spread a-far.
4. Send out the search-light, tho' cloudy the sky, We'll scat-ter the darkness with light from on high; The life-giving gospel, the light of the cross, Will save dy-ing sinners from in-fi-nite loss.
CHORUS.
Send out the search-light, Send out the search-light, O-ver the dark, rolling wave; rolling wave; Send out the search-light, Send out the search-light, Je-sus is mighty, he's mighty to save.
Copyright, 1895, by Jno R. Sweney.

# Tell it Over Again.

"The time is fulfilled, and the kingdom of God is at hand; repent ye, and believe the gospel."
St. Mark i: 15.

A. Rosalthe Carey. Wm. J. Kirkpatrick.

1. It is new, it is new ev-'ry mo-ment, Half its marvels have nev-er been told; This glad mes-sage of hope and re-demption, This sweet gospel that nev-er grows old.
2. 'Tis a message of bount-y and mer-cy, Full of heart-throbs of love from the throne; They who quaff at its fountain of prom-ise, Make the glo-ries of heaven their own.
3. It has balm for the wounds of life's bat-tle, For the great Heal-er left it be-low; And it tells how the heart, sin makes crim-son Grows, by faith in his blood, white as snow.
4. Happy souls, happy souls that re-ceive it, They have on-ly to learn and be-lieve; Just to turn from earth-i-dols to Je-sus, Keep his word, and sal-va-tion receive.

CHORUS.

Tell it o-ver and o-ver, Tell it o-ver a-gain; Tell of mer-cy and love and sal-va-tion, Till all earth shall reply, a-men!

(o-ver and o-ver, o-ver and o-ver, O-ver and o-ver a-gain, and a-gain; mercy and love,)

# I Want to Get Closer to Jesus.

E. E. Hewitt. Wm. J. Kirkpatrick.

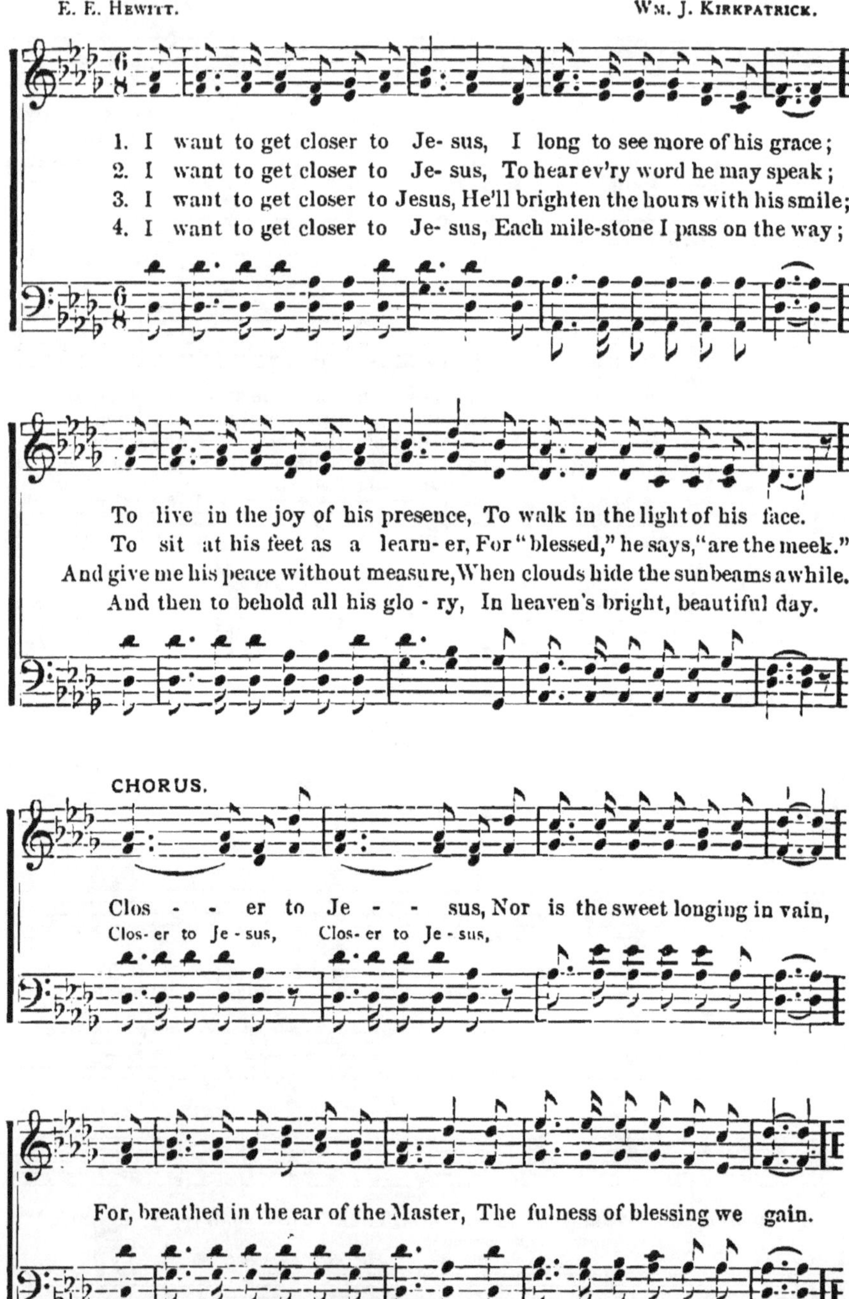
1. I want to get closer to Je- sus, I long to see more of his grace;
2. I want to get closer to Je- sus, To hear ev'ry word he may speak;
3. I want to get closer to Jesus, He'll brighten the hours with his smile;
4. I want to get closer to Je- sus, Each mile-stone I pass on the way;
To live in the joy of his presence, To walk in the light of his face.
To sit at his feet as a learn- er, For "blessed," he says, "are the meek."
And give me his peace without measure, When clouds hide the sunbeams awhile.
And then to behold all his glo - ry, In heaven's bright, beautiful day.
CHORUS.
Clos - - er to Je - - - sus, Nor is the sweet longing in vain,
Clos- er to Je - sus, Clos- er to Je - sus,
For, breathed in the ear of the Master, The fulness of blessing we gain.

# Joy Divine.

J. B. Mackay. Jno. R. Sweney.

1. Going on with Jesus, where he leads the way, Keeping close beside him,
2. What if foes assail, when Jesus is my friend? He is ev - er near me,
3. Passing thro' the valley, tho' it may be drear, I shall journey onward,
where I cannot stray; Peace that passeth knowledge ev-'ry day is mine,
might-y to de-fend; On his strength rely - ing, tho' the fight be long,
thinking not of fear, Knowing that my Saviour leads me by the hand
D.S.—hap-py ev-'ry day,
Fine.
CHORUS.
Je-sus gives me joy di- vine.
I shall sing the victor's song.
To the bright and sunny land.
Joy, joy, joy, oh, what joy is mine!
Je-sus gives me joy di- vine.
D.S.
Joy, joy, joy, won-der-ful, di-vine; Go-ing on re-joic-ing,

# We are Almost Home.

JOHNSON OATMAN, Jr. JNO. R. SWENEY.

1. Just o - ver the ocean is our home on high, Where we all will gath- er and rest by and by; We've a mansion far above the vaulted dome, We shall soon be o - ver, we are al - most home.
2. Our house is all ready in the promised land, It was built and modeled by the Lord's own hand; He will lead us o- ver when this life is o'er, Where beneath its portals we will rest ev- ermore.
3. The road has been weary, and the way been long, But our hearts are cheer- y with the Lord's own song; See, the lights are gleaming o'er the o - cean foam, And our joy is beaming, we are al - most home.
4. Our dear ones are watching as we near the shore, How we long to join them, to part never more; Thro' the golden cit- y with them we will roam, Don't you hear the singing? we are al - most home.
CHORUS.
We are al - most home, we are al - most home,
almost home, almost home, we are al - most home,
Just a few more tri- als, just a few more tears, Just a few more

troubles, just a few more fears, Then we'll cast the anchor, never more to roam;
We will soon be over, we are almost home, we are al - most home.
almost, almost home.
Hosanna to His Name.
Jas. L. Smith.
F. B. Short.
1. Give praise to God's a - nointed One, The ho - ly, great, and just;
2. He came to lift the heav- y chains, From captive souls oppressed;
3. He bore our sins up - on the cross, And died that we might live;
4. 'Tis he, whose precious love hath paid Our ran- som from the fall;
Fine.
O sing a - loud his wondrous love, In whom a - lone we trust.
He came to bind the brok- en heart, And give the wea - ry rest.
He rose, the Lord our righteousness, E - ter - nal life to give.
And ev - 'ry tongue shall yet con- fess, And hail him Lord of all.
D. S.—I'll sing his praise thro' endless days, Ho - san - na to his name.
CHORUS.
D.S.
Ho - san - na to his name, Let heaven and earth proclaim;

# Trusting in the Darkness.

E. E. Hewitt. F. E. Belden.

1. Let us trust him in the darkness, Just the same as in the light, Trust our
2. Let us trust him in the darkness, Just the same as in the light; Let us
3. Let us trust him in the darkness, Just the same as in the light, Since his
4. Let us trust him in the darkness, Just the same as in the light, For he

Father's lov- ing kindness, And his ev - er - lasting might; Trust the
walk by faith, re- joic- ing, When we can- not walk by sight; For we
ten- der arms en- fold us, Why should an- y fear affright? For the
leads us to the country Where there never falls a night; Leads us

faithful words of promise, Stars up- on the midnight sky, For some
know his glo - ry shin-eth, Just beyond the cloud - y veil; Oh, the
eyes that nev- er slumber Watch us thro' the shadows dim, Tho' all
on by ways we know not, 'Tis enough he sees and knows, There we'll

CHORUS.

gleams of brightness ever Greet the hearts that look on high. Trusting in the
precious love of Jesus, Light that never shall grow pale. darkness,
else in gloom is shrouded, Joy and gladness stream from him.
praise his name in rapture, Where eternal noon-day glows.

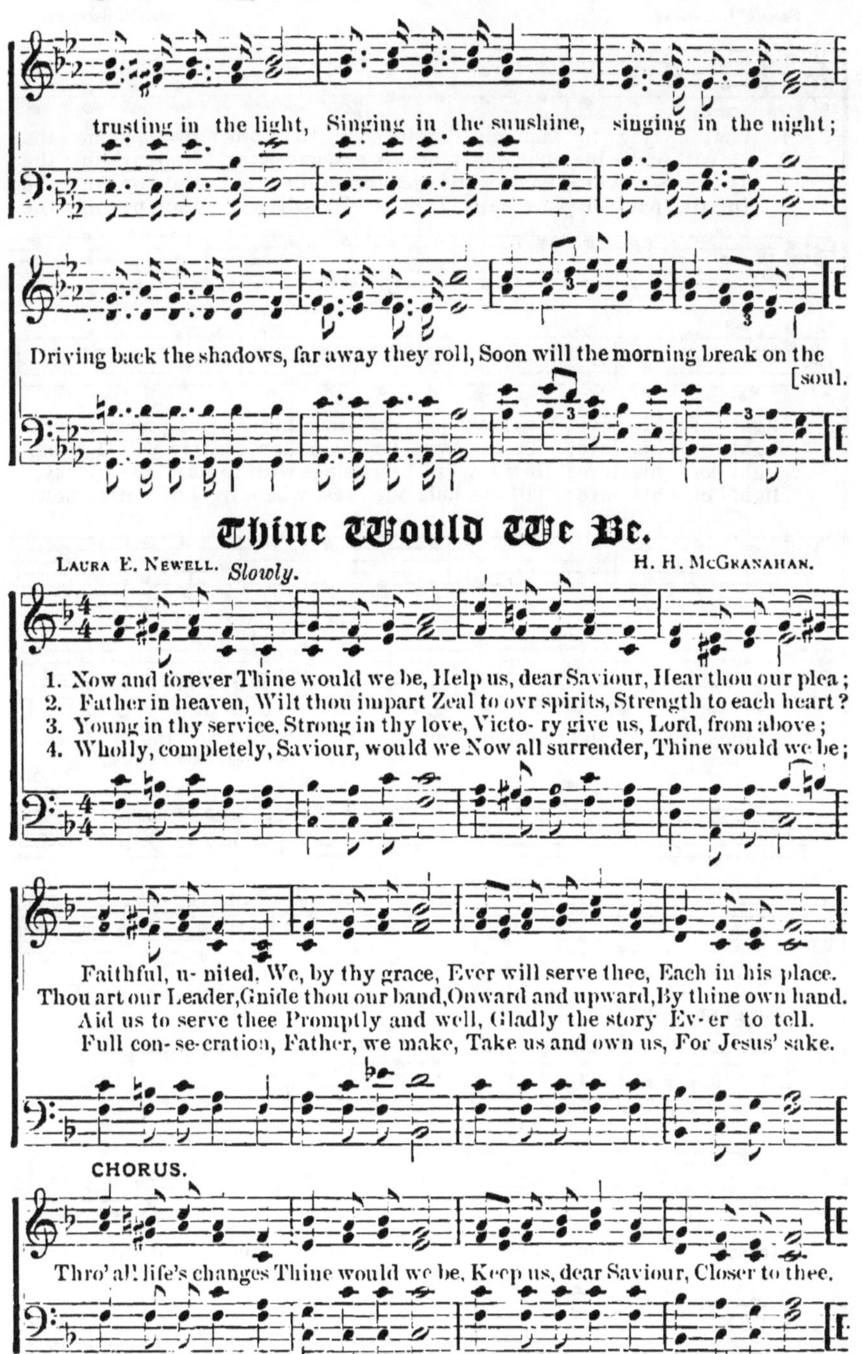
trusting in the light, Singing in the sunshine, singing in the night;
Driving back the shadows, far away they roll, Soon will the morning break on the [soul.
Thine Would We Be.
Laura E. Newell.
Slowly.
H. H. McGranahan.
1. Now and forever Thine would we be, Help us, dear Saviour, Hear thou our plea;
2. Father in heaven, Wilt thou impart Zeal to ovr spirits, Strength to each heart?
3. Young in thy service, Strong in thy love, Victo- ry give us, Lord, from above;
4. Wholly, completely, Saviour, would we Now all surrender, Thine would we be;
Faithful, u- nited, We, by thy grace, Ever will serve thee, Each in his place.
Thou art our Leader, Guide thou our band, Onward and upward, By thine own hand.
Aid us to serve thee Promptly and well, Gladly the story Ev- er to tell.
Full con- se-cration, Father, we make, Take us and own us, For Jesus' sake.
CHORUS.
Thro' all life's changes Thine would we be, Keep us, dear Saviour, Closer to thee.

# In the Light of His Love.

Fanny J. Crosby. Jno. R. Sweney.

1. What a joy to cast my burden on the Lord, Hap-py in the light of his love; What a joy to trust his precious, precious word, Happy in the light of his love.
2. I will praise his name, my gracious, gracious King, Hap-py in the light of his love; To the cross he bore how glad-ly will I cling,
3. To the soul's dear home while pressing on the way, Hap-py in the light of his love; How my full heart sings with rapture ev-'ry day,
4. In the path of peace with Je-sus I will go, Hap-py in the light of his love; Till he bids me rest where liv-ing waters flow,
CHORUS.
I am walk - ing, I am walk - ing
walking, I am walking, walking, I am walking
In the sunshine of his love, brightly falling from above; Ever trust - ing in my Sav-iour, I am happy in the light of his love.
trusting, ever trusting

# Standing By the Cross.

ALLEN-SHIRLEY. REF. by A. J. S.
A. J. SHOWALTER. By per.
1. Sweet the moments, rich in blessing, Which before the cross I spend,
2. Here I'll rest, for - ev - er viewing Mer-cy poured in streams of blood;
3. Tru - ly bless-ed is this sta-tion, Low before his cross to lie,
4. Here I feel my sins for-giv - en, While up-on the Lamb I gaze,
5. Still in ceaseless con-tem-pla-tion Fix my heart and eyes on thee,
Life and health and peace possessing, From the sinner's dy - ing Friend.
Precious drops my soul be - dewing, Plead and claim my peace with God.
While I see di-vine compassion Beaming in his gracious eye.
And my thoughts are all in heav-en, And my lips o'er-flow with praise.
Till I taste thy full sal - va-tion, And unveiled thy glo-ries see.
REFRAIN.
Stand - ing by the cross, stand - ing by the cross,
Standing by the cross of Cal - va - ry; Looking up to Christ,
trust-ing in his love, Hop-ing in his mer - cy full and free.

# Bear the Cross for Jesus.

"Take up the cross and follow me."—Mark x. 21.

Mrs. Annie S. Hawks. R. Lowry. By per.

1. Bear the cross for Jesus, Bear it every day; Tho' the path be rugged,
2. Bear the cross for Jesus, Bear it thro' the strife, Or in pain and silence-
3. Bear the cross for Jesus; Would you know the pow'r Of his grace to save you
Bear it all the way; Bear the cross for Jesus, Whatsoe'er it be;
Whatsoe'er thy life? Bear the cross with patience Tho' you sigh for rest;
Save you hour by hour; Bear the cross for Jesus, Never mind its weight;
Bear it, and remember All his love for thee.
Just the one he gives you Is for you the best.
We shall leave our burden At the golden gate.
REFRAIN.
Bear the cross, bear the cross,
Bear it ev'ry day; Bear the cross for Jesus, Bear it all the way.

# I Know that My Redeemer Lives.

Rev. H. A. Merrill. Arranged by W. J. K.

1. I know that my Redeem - er lives, And has pre-
2. I'm trust - ing Je - sus Christ for all, I know his
3. I'm now en - raptured at the thought, I stand and
4. I know that Je - sus soon will come, I know the
D. C.—For I am on - ly wait - ing, now, To hear the
pared a place for me; That crowns of vic - to - ry he gives
blood now speaks for me; I'm list - 'ning for a welcome voice,
won - der at his love, That he from heav'n to earth was brought
time will not be long, Till I shall reach my heav'nly home,
summons, "child, come home," For I am on - ly waiting, now,
Fine.
CHORUS.
To those who would his children be. Then ask me not to
To say, "The Master waiteth thee!"
To die, that I may live a - bove.
To sing with joy the heav'nly song.
To hear the summons, "child, come home."
D. C.
lin - ger long A - mid the gay and thoughtless throng,

# The Blessed Story.

Edgar P. Stites. Jno. R. Sweney.

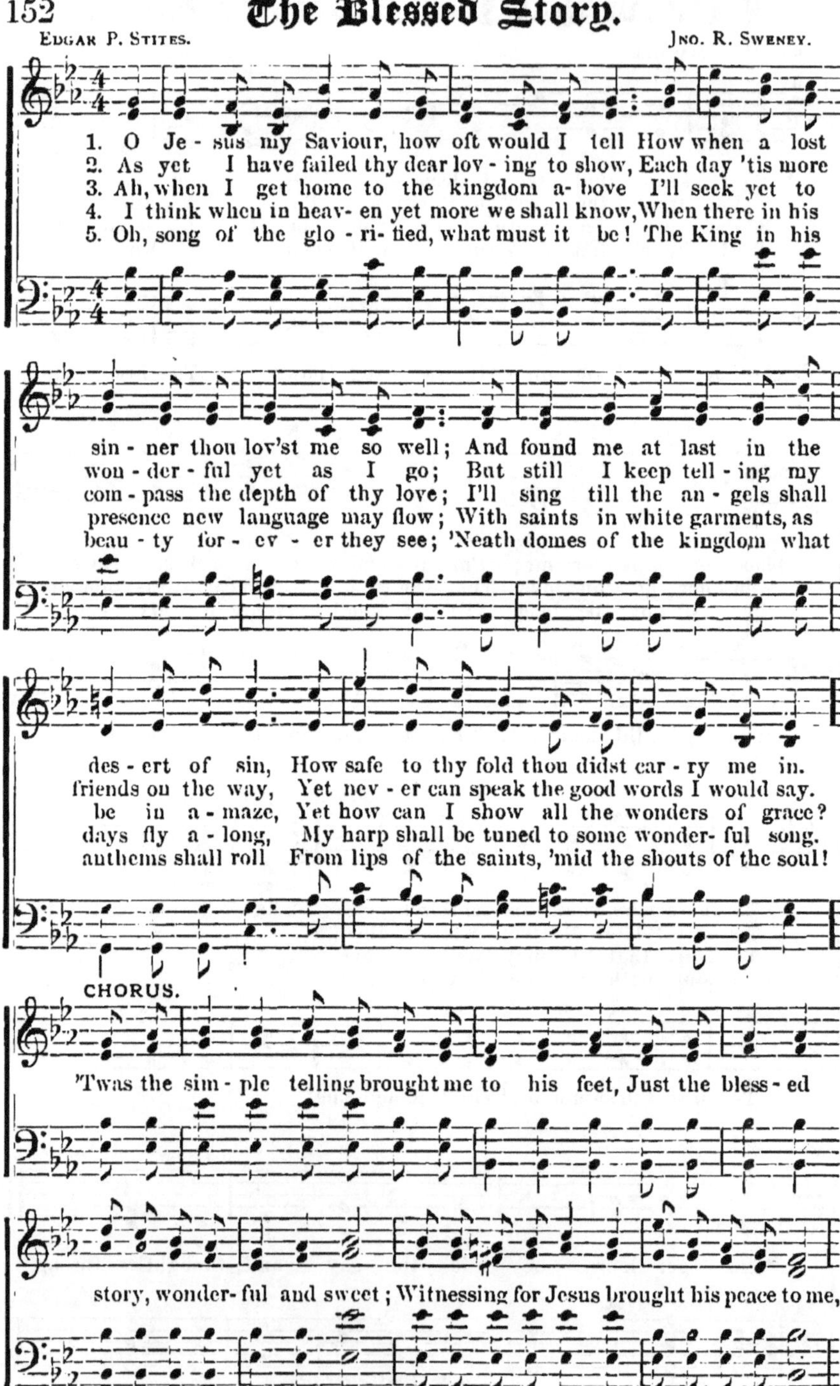
1. O Jesus my Saviour, how oft would I tell How when a lost sinner thou lov'st me so well; And found me at last in the desert of sin, How safe to thy fold thou didst carry me in.
2. As yet I have failed thy dear loving to show, Each day 'tis more wonderful yet as I go; But still I keep telling my friends on the way, Yet never can speak the good words I would say.
3. Ah, when I get home to the kingdom above I'll seek yet to compass the depth of thy love; I'll sing till the angels shall be in amaze, Yet how can I show all the wonders of grace?
4. I think when in heaven yet more we shall know, When there in his presence new language may flow; With saints in white garments, as days fly along, My harp shall be tuned to some wonderful song.
5. Oh, song of the glorified, what must it be! The King in his beauty forever they see; 'Neath domes of the kingdom what anthems shall roll From lips of the saints, 'mid the shouts of the soul!
CHORUS.
'Twas the simple telling brought me to his feet, Just the blessed story, wonderful and sweet; Witnessing for Jesus brought his peace to me,

So I tell it o - ver, pilgrim, un - to thee, Witnessing for Je - sus
brought his peace to me, So I tell it o - ver, pilgrim, un - to thee.
'Tis Best.
E. E. Hewitt.
F. E. Belden.
With feeling.
1. 'Tis best; like moonbeams tender Seem golden hopes declining; But in the
2. 'Tis best; his promise heeding, We'll trust him in our blindness; Our Shepherd
3. 'Tis best; tho' veiled the meaning Of life's oft-darkened story, We'll read the
4. 'Tis best; here, incompletely, The Master's praise we're singing, But grandly
REFRAIN.
morning splendor Immortal joys are shining. 'Tis best, and they are blest Who
gently leading In paths of loving kindness.
blessed sequel In sparkling lines of glory.
there, and sweetly, The perfect chords are ringing.
own his ways are good: When ends the night, In heaven's light 'Twill all be under-
[stood.
Copyright, 1895, by John J. Hood.

# Marching on Life's Journey.

Hope Tryaway. Wm. J. Kirkpatrick.

1. Marching, marching, marching on life's journey, Pilgrims to a better land;
2. Marching, marching, "looking unto Jesus," Trusting ever in his might;
3. Marching, marching, passing clouds may gather, Fear not! thro' the shadows dark,
4. Marching, marching, helping one another, Telling of his wondrous love;

Singing, singing of our Father's goodness, By whose grace we stand.
Singing, singing of the grace that saves us, "Walking in the light."
Brightly, brightly, see, the day is breaking, Press we t'ward the mark.
Upward, upward, step by step he leads us T'wards the home a- bove.

CHORUS.

Happy journey will it be, . . . When we're trusting, Lord, in thee;

Hark, what hal- le- lu- jahs roll From the bless - ed, shining goal.

# What Have I Done?

A young man reconciled to God on his deathbed, exclaimed, "Yes, I am saved; but oh, I have sacrificed nothing for the Man who died for me!"

F. G. Burroughs. H. L. Gilmour.

1. What have I done to show my love For him who died on Cal - va - ry?
2. Tho' rich, yet for my sake made poor, A man of sorrows he became;
3. What has God done to show his love? No greater love could ev - er be·
4. What have I sac - ri - ficed for him Who sac - rificed so much for me?
5. All that I have, all that I am, I owe to Je - sus—Cru - cified!

His blood my ransom price has paid, And I am saved by grace so free.
While all his wealth of grace and strength By simply ask - ing I may claim.
For Je - sus died to save my soul, While I was yet an en - e - my.
O Lord, can I take all thy gifts, And still give nothing up for thee?
What have I done to show my love For that dear Man who died for me?

CHORUS

He died for me, he died for me, That cru - el death on Cal - va - ry!

What have I done for God's dear Son, Who died for me, who died for me?

# I Know.

Rev. E. H. Stokes, D.D. Wm. J. Kirkpatrick.

1. I know there's a beautiful, beautiful land Beyond the realms of woe,
2. I know there are beautiful, beautiful crowns With gems all rich and rare,
3. I know there are beautiful, beautiful harps For all the pure and true,
4. I know there are beautiful, beautiful palms In ho- ly realms a- bove,
A- bove the fad- ing scenes of time, Where all the good shall go.
And these the honored vic- tor's brow E- ter- nal- ly shall wear.
Whose har- mo- nies, so soft and sweet, For ev - ermore are new.
And these im - mortal hands shall wave In vic- to- ries of love.
CHORUS.
Beau- ti- ful home, beau- ti- ful home, Home be- yond the sky;....
be - yond the sky;
Where the Lord shall gather into his fold His loved ones, by and by.
Copyright, 1896, by Wm. J. Kirkpatrick.

5 I know of these beautiful, beautiful things;
These and a thousand more;
But shall they all be mine at last,
When earthly toils are o'er?

6 Lord, grant me a beautiful, beautiful heart,
A life entirely thine;
Then home, and crown, and victor's palm,
Shall be forever mine!

# Speeding Away.

Fanny J. Crosby. | Mrs. J. G. Wilson.

1. Speeding away o'er the riv - er of time, Where the sweet bells of e- ter - ni- ty chime; Speeding away to the E- den above, Filled with the fulness of rapture and love.
2. Speeding away to the val- ley of song, Speeding a- way to a glorified throng; Sweeping the chords of their harps while they sing, Praise that to Je- sus for- ev- er shall ring.
3. Speeding away to be severed no more, Speeding a- way to the evergreen shore; There in the garment of summer arrayed, Lil- ies are blooming that nev- er shall fade.
4. Speeding away, we are speeding a- way, On to the region of in - fi- nite day; On- ly a veil to be lift- ed, and then, O what a meeting with dear ones a- gain.
CHORUS.
Beauti- ful land, beauti- ful land,
Beautiful,
In thy green pastures the wea- ry shall rest: Beau- ti - ful land,
Beautiful,
rit.
beau - ti - ful land, Home of the glo - ri - fied, home of the blest.

# I Called On the Lord.

ELTA M. LEWIS. Ps. 1: 15. WM. J. KIRKPATRICK.

1. I called on the Lord in my hour of need, The bus - y world had no time to heed, But full of faith in his changeless word, I cried to the Lord, and lo! he heard.
2. He seemed to my thought far a - way to stand, I called and found he was near at hand; So close, his heart by my own was stirred, So close that my low - est sigh was heard.
3. He hears, yes, he hears when his chil - dren call, His care un- fail - ing is o - ver all; By love en - compassed, I fear no harm, But rest on my Saviour's might - y arm.
CHORUS.
Glo - ry and praise to his ho - ly name, I called on the Lord, and de - liv - 'rance came; Glory and praise thro' my length of days, Glory to his ho - ly name.

# Send the Fire.

General Booth. Jno. R. Sweney.

1. Thou Christ of burning, cleansing flame, Send the fire, send the fire!
2. God of E - li - jah, hear our cry, Send the fire, send the fire!
3. 'Tis fire we want, for fire we plead, Send the fire, send the fire!
4. To make my weak heart strong and brave, Send the fire, send the fire!

Thy blood-bought gift to-day we claim, Send, send the fire! Look
Oh, make us fit to live or die, Send, send the fire! To
The fire will meet our ev - 'ry need, Send, send the fire! For
To live this dy - ing world to save, Send, send the fire! Oh,

down and see this waiting host, Give us the promised Ho - ly Ghost—
burn up ev - 'ry trace of sin, To bring thy light and glo - ry in,
strength to ev - er do the right, For grace to conquer in the fight,
see me on thy al - ter lay My life, my all, this ver - y day—

We want an - oth - er Pen - te - cost, Send, send the fire!
The rev - e - lu - tion now be - gin, Send, send the fire!
For power to walk the world in white, Send, send the fire!
To crown the of - f'ring now, I pray, Send, send the fire!

# Let the Saviour In.

Josephine Pollard.
Mrs. Joseph F. Knapp. By per.
Tenderly.
1. 'Tis the Saviour who would claim Entrance to your heart; Will you
2. No one like the Saviour knocks At the sin- ner's door; 'Tis no
3. Oh, how can you bid him wait 'Till an - oth - er day? When al-
send your Lord away? Will you say, "Depart?" He will all your trials share;
stranger that implores, He has knocked before, He has often sought your heart,
read- y Jesus weeps At the long de-lay; 'Twas for you that Jesus died,
CHORUS.
He will cleanse you from all sin. 'Tis your Saviour,
Shall he cleanse it now from sin?
And 'tis you he longs to win.
'tis your Saviour standing there,
pp
let him in,
Haste and let him in, let him in, . Lest he turn a- way, let him in. . .
let him in,
let him in.
pp
rit.

# Go, Work To-day.

This is the last hymn written by the author, who fell asleep April 16, 1895.—
"She, being dead, yet speaketh."

M. D. K. — May D. Kirkpatrick.

1. Go, work to-day, the Master commands, Why stand ye waiting with idle hands?
2. Go, work to-day, in the morning of youth, Go, tell the message of love and truth,
3. Go, work to-day, go forth in His might, Make some load lighter, some sad heart [bright,
There is work to do; there are hearts to win. And perishing souls to be saved from sin.
Go and seek the lost, from the fold astray, And point them to Jesus, the Life, the Way.
Comfort those who weep, help those in need, For plenteous harvest sow precious seed.
CHORUS.
Go, work to-day, go, work to-day, Time passes swiftly, no longer delay;
Hear the dear Master lovingly say—"In my vineyard, go, work to-day."

162
Banner of the Cross.
Johnson Oatman, Jr.
Jno. R. Sweney.
1. We're marching to a country whose fair shores are not in sight. And oft we're called [to
2. We're marching 'neath a banner whose red folds are o'er us all, King Jesus is our
3. We're marching, and we're asking all the world to go along, And volunteer for
4. We're marching on to glory, but the march will soon be o'er, The fight will soon be
battle here up- on the side of right; But there is one who goes before, will
Captain, we o- bey his ev- 'ry call: As we go marching onward, all our
service in this battle 'gainst the wrong; We're shouting and we're singing every
ended, and we'll meet the foe no more; But till we all shall ground our arms up-
arm us for the fight, We're marching 'neath the banner of the cross.
foes be- fore us fall, We're marching 'neath the banner of the cross.
day the vic- tor's song, We're marching 'neath the banner of the cross.
on that peaceful shore, We're marching 'neath the banner of the cross.
CHORUS.
We are march - ing, march - ing, marching 'neath the
We are marching, we are marching, marching, we are marching,
banner of the cross, We will help our great Commander to de-
'neath the banner of the cross,

Banner of the Cross.—CONCLUDED.
163
fend our flag from loss, We are marching 'neath the banner of the cross.
The Olden Story.
F. G. Burroughs.
H. L. Gilmour.
1. There is an old-en story, wafting sweet smelling odors across the sea;
2. Ages have sped that story onward, Still its glad tidings are ever new;
3. Young men and maids have sung its praises,
Old men and children have joined the song;
Fresh from the vernal Mount of Olives, O'er the blue waters of Gal - i- lee.
Prophets and priests have learned its music, Praising the Father in worship true.
And by the notes of babes and sucklings That blessed story still flows along.
CHORUS.
Sweet, sweet, old-en sto - ry, Sing, sing, in joy - ful lay;
Sweet, O sweet, the old - en sto - ry, Sing it, O sing it, in joy - ful lay;
See, see, the gold-en glo- ry, Lights the pathway to endless day.
See, O see, the

# My Cup Runneth Over.

Rev. H. J Zelley. Psalm xxiii : 5. H. L. Gilmour.

1. He gives me life, and home, and friends, My cup it runneth o - ver;
2. New goodness and new mercies rare, My cup it runneth o - ver;
3. His word reveals the way of life, My cup it runneth o - ver;
And mercies new each hour he sends, My cup it runneth o - ver.
So constant is his loving care, My cup it runneth o - ver.
And by his side I'm kept from strife, My cup it runneth o - ver.
CHORUS.
O bless- ed be my Shepherd, Friend, New pastures I dis- cov - er;
His lov- ing care will nev- er end, My cup it runneth o - ver.
Copyright, 1895, by H. L. Gilmour.

4 He guides my feet along the way,
My cup it runneth over;
And helps me onward day by day,
My cup it runneth over.

5 In pastures green my steps he leads,
My cup it runneth over;
With bread of life my spirit feeds,
My cup it runneth over.

6 He gives me drink from living streams,
My cup it runneth over;
His love exceeds my wildest dreams,
My cup it runneth over.

7 He calls me now his own, his bride,
My cup it runneth over;
And draws me closer to his side,
My cup it runneth over.

# The Morning Shore.

E. E. Hewitt. Wm. J. Kirkpatrick

1. There's a land of which we read in the book of truth divine, And within its jewelled walls everlasting glories shine; When the night has passed away, There's a fair, unclouded day On the happy, happy Morning Shore.
2. All its gates are made of pearl, and its streets of purest gold; There the Shepherd bids his flock sweetly rest within the fold; Saints, arrayed in snowy white, Sing his praise, with angels bright, On the happy, happy Morning Shore.
3. All who serve the Lord shall meet in those fields of spice and balm; On head a starry crown; in each hand a victor palm; Washed in Calv'ry's precious flow, Those eternal joys we'll know, On the happy, happy Morning Shore.
4. In the blessed book we read our Redeem-er holds the key To this City of Delight, where the evening shadows flee; Saviour, keep us in thy care, Bring, oh, bring us safely there, To that happy, happy Morning Shore.

CHORUS.

We shall meet again, we shall meet again, When this fleeting life is o'er;
We shall meet again, we shall meet again, On the happy, happy Morning Shore.

# The Ocean of God's Love.

Mrs. F. G. Burroughs. Wm. J. Kirkpatrick.

SOLO and CHORUS.
1. Have you sat beside the ocean When its waves were hushed and still, Gazing
2. O this love of God, so mighty, We can nev- er grasp it all; Yet each
3. Blessed ocean of love's fulness, Where there's always a great calm! With its
o'er its calm, blue waters? Have you felt an inward thrill Of that love which
soul can fill his ves- sel, Tho' the lim - it may be small. Ev'ry day and
perfect peace it stills us, E'en when tempests would alarm. On this faithful
passeth knowledge, In its boundlessness so free? Great enough to reach all
ev- 'ry moment We may plunge within this tide, Keeping where its living
bosom resting Joy un- spoken we may know; For there is no fear, no
nations, Yet so nigh to you and me!
wa- ters Can for aye in us a - bide.
sorrow, In love's peaceful, cleansing flow.
CHORUS.
Oh, what rapture! oh, what
grandeur, In the thought of God's great love! Deeper than the deepest o- cean,

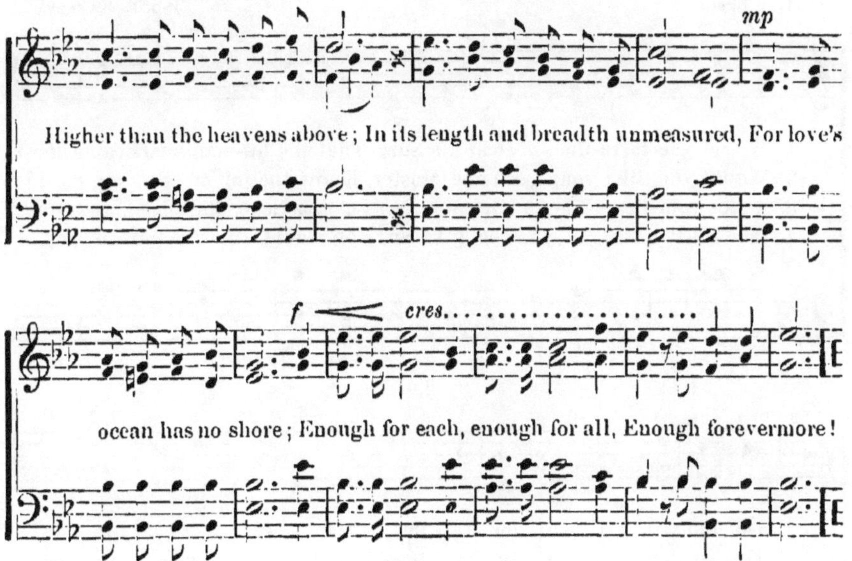
mp
Higher than the heavens above; In its length and breadth unmeasured, For love's
f
cres.
ocean has no shore; Enough for each, enough for all, Enough forevermore!

# The Gospel Call to Arms.

TOM CARDER, Jr. HERBERT C. ROWELL.

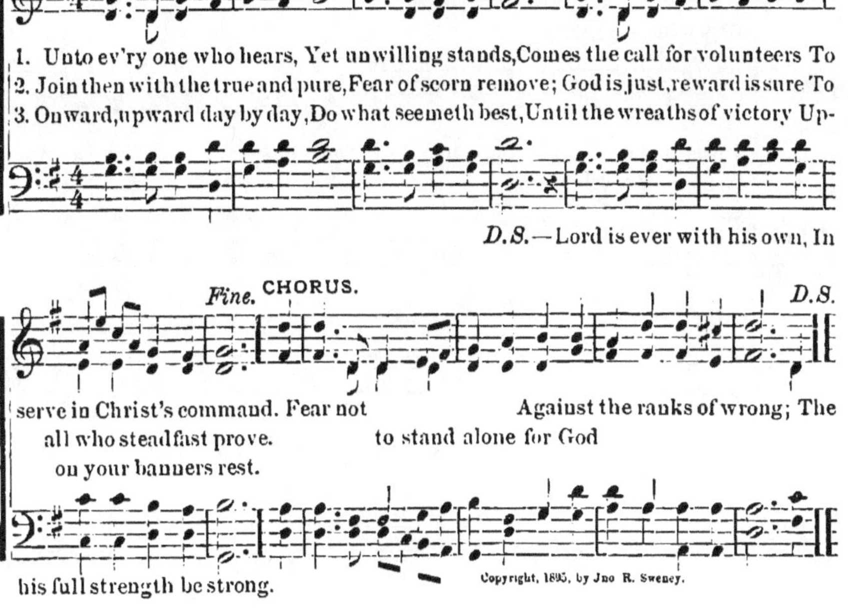
1. Unto ev'ry one who hears, Yet unwilling stands, Comes the call for volunteers To
2. Join then with the true and pure, Fear of scorn remove; God is just, reward is sure To
3. Onward, upward day by day, Do what seemeth best, Until the wreaths of victory Up-
D.S.—Lord is ever with his own, In
Fine.
CHORUS.
D.S.
serve in Christ's command. Fear not Against the ranks of wrong; The
all who steadfast prove. to stand alone for God
on your banners rest.

his full strength be strong.

# The Joy of Doing Good.

H. B. Beegle. Jno. R. Sweney

1. Would you taste the sweetest pleasure That the hu-man heart can know? Go and win a soul for Je - sus, This will set your heart a- glow.
2. Would you, like your Lord and Master, Know the joy of do - ing good? Hasten then to ho - ly la - bor, Win a sin - ner back to God.
3. Set your heart up- on the sin- ner, Love, believe, and plead, and pray; La- bor hard to be the win - ner, Wea - ry not at some de- lay.
4. Should success to you be giv - en, You would know as pure a joy As the an - gels know in heav - en, In their pure and loved employ.
CHORUS.
It would make . . an angel hap - py, Souls to save . . from endless woe;
It would make
Souls to save
Go and win . . . a soul for Je - sus, This will set your heart a- glow.
Go and win

# Come into the Sunshine.

F. G. BURROUGHS. H. L. GILMOUR.

1. Come into the sunshine, why linger in shade? Come into love's freedom,
2. Come into the sunshine, O walk in the light! Heirs of this salvation
3. Come into the sunshine, faith's portion so blest; Doubts chill and distress you,
cres.................
O be not afraid! Come, take of God's bounties, for all things are yours;
are not of the night: Tho' trials o'ertake you, yet, be of good cheer!
come into this rest! Cast now your soul's anchor in this haven fair.
CHORUS.
Faith's claim will be honored, the promise assures. Come into the sunshine,
The dawn of redemption from suff'ring is near.
For peace as a riv - er flows blissfully there.
Beautiful, beautiful sunshine; Come into the sunshine, The beautiful light of God.
Copyright, 1895, by H. L. Gilmour.

# Wonderful Salvation.

F. S. Shepard.
Wm. J. Kirkpatrick.
1. Have you ev- er heard of this wonderful sal- vation That hath been re-
2. Have you ev- er drank of this wonderful sal- vation That from Calv'ry's
3. Have you ev- er told of this wonderful sal- vation. Purchased by the
4. Je- sus saves to-day with this wonderful sal- vation, Sing a- loud his
vealed to the ru- ined-ones of earth? Free- ly it is giv - en to
cross as a healing fountain flows? Yield your heart to-day to the
Lord in his death up- on the tree? Je- sus' love proclaim, that the
praise and his mighty love proclaim; Send the joy- ful news un - to
those of ev- 'ry nation, Willing to receive this great boon of priceless worth.
Spirit's supplication, Taste the heav'nly joys that his gracious love bestows.
world in ad - o - ra- tion May before him bow and from pow'r of sin be free.
ev'ry tribe and nation, That they may rejoice in the blessed Saviour's name.
CHORUS.
Won - derful salvation, Won - derful sal- va- tion, Freely it is
Wonderful, wonderful sal- va - tion, Wonderful, wonderful sal - va - tion,
given to ev'ry tribe and nation, Wonderful, wonderful, wonderful salvation.
Copyright, 1895, by Wm. J. Kirkpatrick.

# In Fellowship Sweet.

L. H. Edmunds. Francis Burgette Short.

1. Walking with Jesus in fel - lowship sweet, He will defend us when
2. Walking with Jesus how bright is the way, Thro' earthly clouds breaks the
3. Working with Jesus, his service is joy, No gift too humble for
4. Walking and working with him whom we love, Feeding on manna that
dangers we meet; Leaning by faith on the arms of his love,
heaven - ly day; Why should we wander a - lone in the night,
him to em - ploy; Wisdom and strength he will dai - ly pro - vide,
drops from a - bove; Life in its fulness shall flow to the soul,
Learning the songs that are ringing above.
When by his side we may keep in the light.
Ask, and his blessing is nev - er denied.
Ev - 'ry step near - er the fair, shining goal.
CHORUS.
All glo - - ry and
All glory and praise, all
praise.... we'll joy - ful - ly raise; So close to the Master our
glory and praise We'll joyfully raise, we'll joyfully raise,
footsteps he'll guide To that hap - py country where pleasures a - bide.

# White-Winged Angels.

E. E. Hewitt.
Jno. R. Sweney.
1. Speed thee, Christian, sweetly cheer thee, Speed thee to the "secret place;"
2. Hide thee, Christian, safely hide thee, 'Neath his tender, brooding love;
3. Praise him, Christian, gladly praise him, Lift thy soul in joy- ful song;
Call to God and he will hear you, Trust his promise and his grace;
Let thy Father keep and guide thee, Lead thee to his home a - bove.
Ev- 'ry wind that blows o- beys him, Heaven shall thy notes pro- long.
Sore- ly baffled, wea- ry-heart - ed, Like a bird far out at sea;
Thou hast made the Lord thy refuge; Whereso - ev- er thou shalt be,
Radiant fa- ces, gleaming pin - ions, Mor- tal eyes not now may see;
God shall give his white-winged angels Tender charge concerning thee.
God shall give his white-winged angels Tender charge concerning thee.
Yet he gives his white-winged angels Tender charge concerning thee.
CHORUS.
Till the day . . . . of wondrous glory, When the clouds forev- er flee;
Copyright, 1896, by Jno. R. Sweney.

God shall give . . his white-winged angels Tender charge concerning thee.

# I Come.

Rev. F. D. Sanford. Fanny H. Smith.

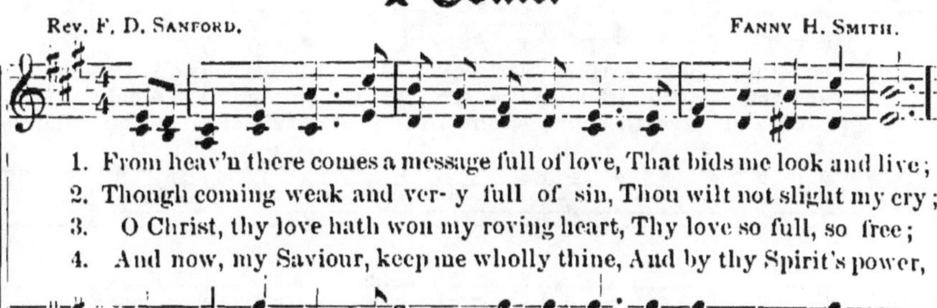
1. From heav'n there comes a message full of love, That bids me look and live;
2. Though coming weak and ver- y full of sin, Thou wilt not slight my cry;
3. O Christ, thy love hath won my roving heart, Thy love so full, so free;
4. And now, my Saviour, keep me wholly thine, And by thy Spirit's power,

Fine.
'Tis Christ, the Saviour, speaking from above, O come, I will for- give.
I know thy wondrous grace will take me in, I'll on that grace re - ly.
Oh, give me grace with all of earth to part, And give thyself to me.
Let life and tongue proclaim thy grace divine, In ev - 'ry passing hour.

D.S.—On Calv'ry's cross thy precious blood was shed, From sin to set me free.

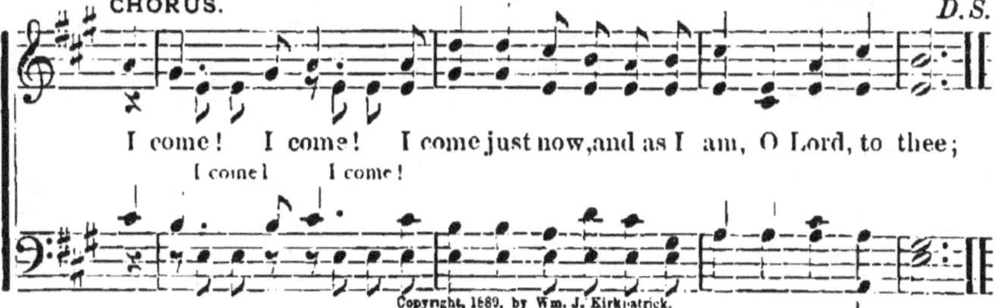
CHORUS.
D.S.
I come! I come! I come just now, and as I am, O Lord, to thee;
I come! I come!

# Are You Drifting?

MARY D. JAMES. WM. J. KIRKPATRICK.

1. Are you drifting down life's current, Drift- ing on a dang'rous tide?
2. Down the stream of worldly pleasure Drift- ing, drifting ev - er- more
3. Heed, oh, heed the kind moni - tion! Give your aimless wand'rings o'er;

Near the rapids' fearful per - il All unconscious do ye glide?
T'ward the great unfathomed o - cean, Bound for yon e - ter- nal shore?
Cease to seek in earth your pleasure, Head your bark for heav'n's bright shore,

Down the stream of sin and fol - ly,—Heed- ing not the danger near,
Drift - ing, drifting,—going,—whither? Aim - less, purposeless;—how vain!
Take on board the skillful pi - lot, Use the oars of faith and prayer;

Drift - ing on in self-com- pla - cence, Feel - ing no remorse or fear?
To the dark and dread forev - er! What, oh, what have ye to gain?
Then you'll make the port of glo - ry, God will guide you safely there.

CHORUS.

Hark the voice . . of yonder pilot: Cease your drifting, seize the oar;
Hark the voice, the warning voice of yonder pilot: seize the oar;

Make the blest, celestial harbor, Steer your bark for Canaan's shore.
Make the blest, celestial harbor, make the harbor,
Wonderful Peace.
L. H. E.
"My peace I give unto you."—John xiv: 27.
L. H. Edmunds.
1. Je - sus gives his peace to me, Wonderful peace, wonderful peace;
2. Surface feel- ings ebb and flow, Wonderful peace, wonderful peace;
3. Not my charge his gift to hold, Wonderful peace, wonderful peace;
4. This my part—to trust in him, Wonderful peace, wonderful peace;
5. Praying, watching, serv- ing still, Wonderful peace, wonderful peace;
Fine.
Like his love, a boundless sea, Won- der- ful, wonder - ful peace.
Sweet, a - bid - ing calm be- low, Won- der- ful, wonder - ful peace.
Je - sus keeps it—grace untold—Won- der- ful, wonder - ful peace.
Whether skies be bright or dim, Won- der- ful, wonder - ful peace.
Let me learn, and do his will, Won- der- ful, wonder - ful peace.
D. S.—Je - sus gives his peace to me, Won- der- ful, wonder - ful peace.
REFRAIN.
D.S.
Peace, peace, won - der - ful peace, Peace, peace, won - der- ful peace;
Copyright, 1895, by John J. Hood.

The Best Friend is Jesus.
P. B.
P. Bilhorn.
1. Oh, the best friend to have is Je - sus, When the cares of life up- on you roll; He will heal the wounded heart, He will strength and grace impart; Oh, the best friend to have is Je - sus.
2. What a friend I have found in Je - sus! Peace and comfort to my soul he brings; Leaning on his mighty arm, I will fear no ill or harm; Oh, the best friend to have is Je - sus.
3. Tho' I pass thro' the night of sor - row, And the chilly waves of Jor - dan roll, Nev - er need I shrink or fear, For my Sav- iour is so near; Oh, the best friend to have is Je - sus.
4. When at last to our home we gath - er, With the loved ones who have gone be - fore, We will sing up - on the shore, Praising him for ev - ermore; Oh, the best friend to have is Je - sus.
CHORUS. Spirited.
The best friend to have is Je - sus, The best friend to have is
Je - sus ev-'ry day,

Je - sus, He will help you when you fall, He will
Je- sus all the way;
hear you when you call; Oh, the best friend to have is Je - sus.
He Came to Rescue Me.
JOHNSON OATMAN, JR.
JNO. R. SWENEY.
1. When Christ was born, the hosts on high Were filled with mystery; But I can
2. In paths of sin my feet did roam, No day-star could I see; But when so
3. The storm was gath'ring dark and wild, I had no place to flee; 'Twas then to
4. When I have reached that port of love, Safe for eter- ni - ty; I'll tell the
CHORUS.
tell the reason why, He came to rescue me. He came to rescue me, He
far away from home, He came to rescue me.
save his wand'ring child, He came to rescue me.
shining hosts above, He came to rescue me.
came to rescue me; When Jesus left his home on high, He came to rescue me.
He came
Copyright, 1895, by Jno. R. Sweney.

# Shall We Meet Again in Heaven.

JOHNSON OATMAN, Jr. — JNO. R. SWENEY.

1. As we part to-day in sadness, As we part to-day in sadness, Shall we meet again with gladness Where we'll know no parting pain? When all earthly ties are riv- en, When all earthly ties are riven, Shall we meet again in heaven? Meet to nev- er part again?

2. Shall we walk the streets together? Shall we walk the streets together? There to part no more for-ev- er, While e- ter- nal ages roll. Shall we rest down by the river? Shall we rest down by the river? Where no tearful eye will quiver, In that home-land of the soul.

3. Shall we join in that sweet singing? Shall we join in that sweet singing? Where the angel-harps are ringing, On the blessed streets of gold. Shall we join with ev'ry nation? Shall we join with ev'ry nation, In the sto - ry of sal- vation, And the woundrous tale unfold?

CHORUS.

Shall we meet again in heaven? Shall we meet a- gain in heav- en? That blest house that God has given, When our

pilgrimage is o'er; There we'll never leave each other, There we'll never leave each
other, But we'll dwell with Christ our Brother, Safe forever on that shore.
By and By.
Fanny J. Crosby.
Wm. J. Kirkpatrick.
1. O'er the cold and chilly blast, By and by, by and by; We shall gather
2. We shall see our Saviour's face, By and by, by and by; We shall sing re-
3. In the golden fields above, By and by, by and by; We shall meet the
home at last, By and by, by and by. Far beyond the stormy gale, Anchored
deeming grace, By and by, by and by. Where the rose and lily grow, Where our
friends we love, By and by, by and by. On that pure and fragrant shore All our
safe within the vale, We shall furl our shattered sail, By and by, by and by.
tears shall cease to flow, Oh, the joy that we shall know, By and by, by and by.
trials will be o'er, We shall say farewell no more, By and by, by and by.
Copyright, 1895, by Wm. J. Kirkpatrick.

# A Promise of Dawn.

A. Rosalthe Carey.
Wm. J Kirkpatrick.
1. Oh, speak not the bitter thoughts burning, They will harm wheresoever they fall;
2. Oh, wound not the hearts all around thee,
With the thorns that may lurk in thine own;
3. Shrink not from the pathway of duty, Tho' 'tis rough with temptation and ill;
Pour forth all thy spirit's pure yearning, Unmingled with wormwood and gall.
Unshared tho' the cares that have bound thee, Remember there's help at the throne.
No gems can compare in their beauty With souls that are doing God's will.
If thy life on a desert seems flinging Wasted showers from its fountains of love,
If thy earth-hopes in darkness are shrouded, And the frost on each joy-blossom lies,
Keep thy hands from oppression and folly, Let thy lips speak the truth of the Lord,
Thou canst turn with a closer heart-clinging To the friendship undying above.
Thou canst cherish the hopes all unclouded Of a bliss ne'er to fade in the skies.
And thy life-work, tho' fameless and lowly, Will be crowned with eternal reward.
CHORUS.
Then watch thro' the shade for the sunlight, And smile when the cold-hearted frown;
Copyright, 1895, by Wm. J. Kirkpatrick.

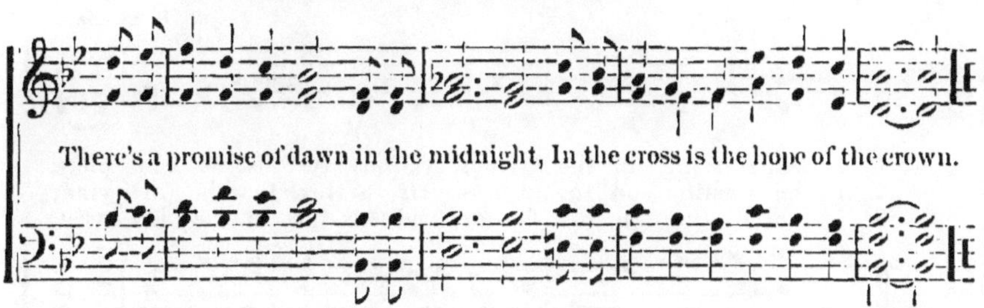
There's a promise of dawn in the midnight, In the cross is the hope of the crown.

# At Thy Door.

"Behold, I stand at the door and knock."—JESUS.

IDA L. REED. H. L GILMOUR

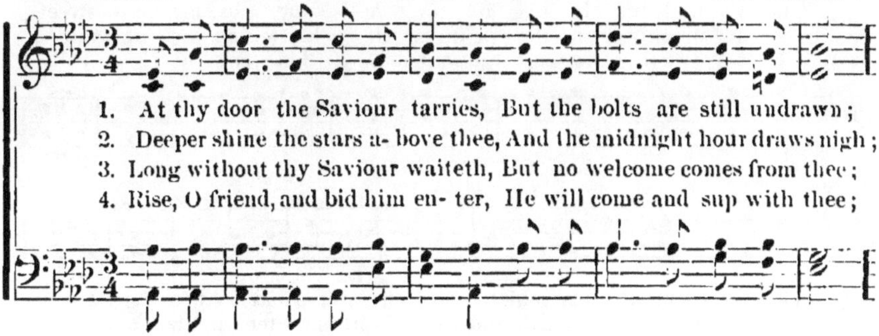

1. At thy door the Saviour tarries, But the bolts are still undrawn;
2. Deeper shine the stars a- bove thee, And the midnight hour draws nigh;
3. Long without thy Saviour waiteth, But no welcome comes from thee;
4. Rise, O friend, and bid him en- ter, He will come and sup with thee;

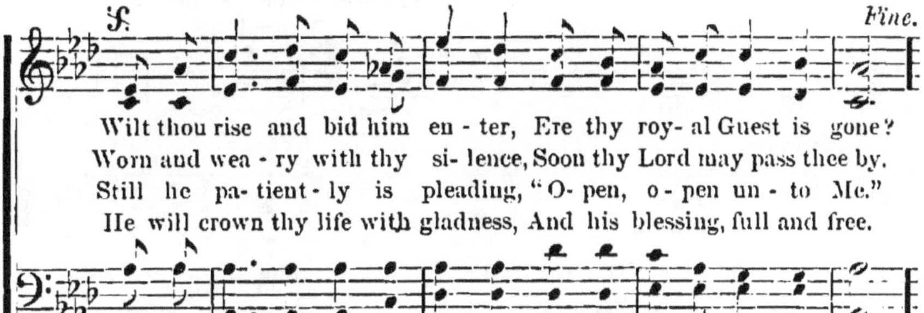

Wilt thou rise and bid him en - ter, Ere thy roy- al Guest is gone? *Fine.*
Worn and wea - ry with thy si- lence, Soon thy Lord may pass thee by.
Still he pa- tient - ly is pleading, "O- pen, o - pen un - to Me."
He will crown thy life with gladness, And his blessing, full and free.

*D.S.*—At thy threshold he is standing, O - pen, ere it be too late.

CHORUS.

Haste, O haste, and bid him en - ter, Long without he may not wait; *D.S.*

# Finding All in Jesus.

Rev. W. J. Stuart, A. M. Jno. R. Sweney.

1. I am rest- ing in the Saviour, And my rest is so com- plete,
2. I am feasting on the fulness Of the love that is di - vine;
3. I am liv- ing in his fav- or, And this life to me is sweet;
That I'm find- ing in his fav - or A joy to me more sweet
I am drinking in the richness Of know- ing he is mine;
I am trusting in my Saviour, A - bid - ing at his feet,
Than ever filled my soul, be- fore I entered at his o- pen door.
This love to me, so full and free, Is life's e - ter - nal leg- a - cy.
And here my soul shall ev- er stay, Till ushered in - to perfect day.
CHORUS.
I am rest - ing in the Saviour, And I know that he is mine;
ad lib.
I am dwelling in the ful- ness Of the love that is di- vine.

# This is Rest.



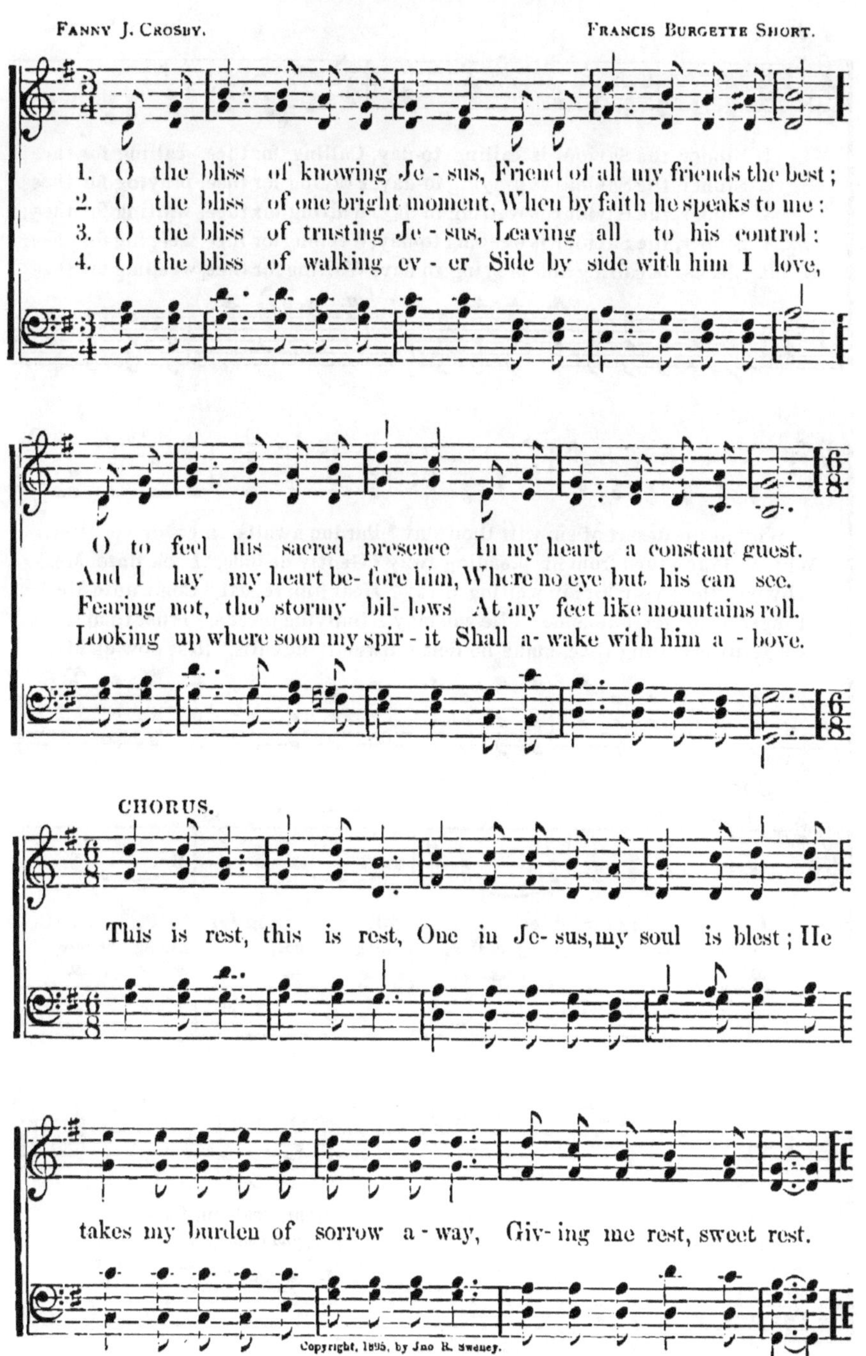

Fanny J. Crosby.
Francis Burgette Short.
1. O the bliss of knowing Je - sus, Friend of all my friends the best;
2. O the bliss of one bright moment, When by faith he speaks to me:
3. O the bliss of trusting Je - sus, Leaving all to his control:
4. O the bliss of walking ev - er Side by side with him I love,
O to feel his sacred presence In my heart a constant guest.
And I lay my heart be- fore him, Where no eye but his can see.
Fearing not, tho' stormy bil- lows At my feet like mountains roll.
Looking up where soon my spir - it Shall a- wake with him a - bove.
CHORUS.
This is rest, this is rest, One in Je- sus, my soul is blest; He
takes my burden of sorrow a - way, Giv- ing me rest, sweet rest.

# The Saviour is Calling.

JOSHUA GILL. JNO. R. SWENEY.

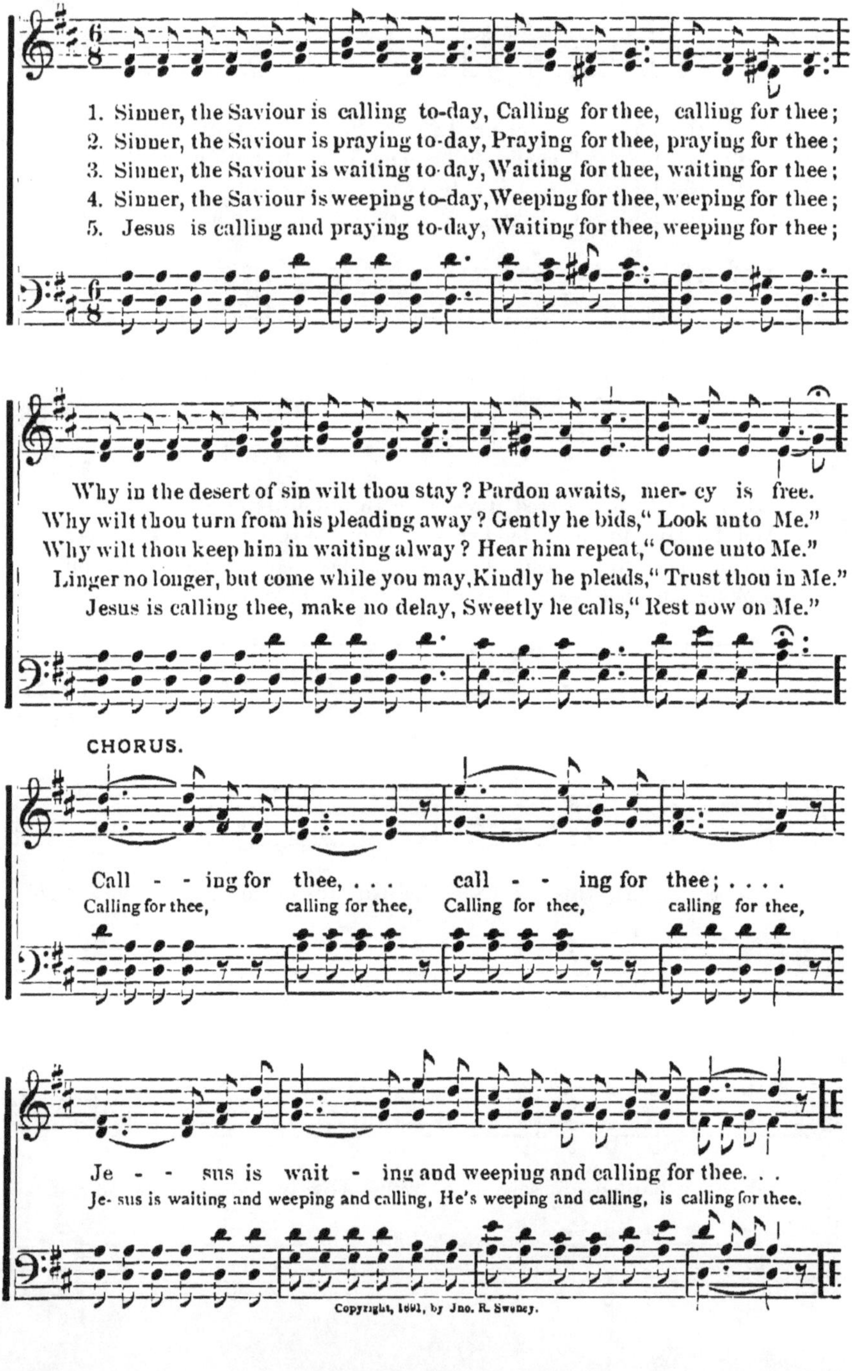

1. Sinner, the Saviour is calling to-day, Calling for thee, calling for thee;
2. Sinner, the Saviour is praying to-day, Praying for thee, praying for thee;
3. Sinner, the Saviour is waiting to-day, Waiting for thee, waiting for thee;
4. Sinner, the Saviour is weeping to-day, Weeping for thee, weeping for thee;
5. Jesus is calling and praying to-day, Waiting for thee, weeping for thee;

Why in the desert of sin wilt thou stay? Pardon awaits, mer- cy is free.
Why wilt thou turn from his pleading away? Gently he bids, "Look unto Me."
Why wilt thou keep him in waiting alway? Hear him repeat, "Come unto Me."
Linger no longer, but come while you may, Kindly he pleads, "Trust thou in Me."
Jesus is calling thee, make no delay, Sweetly he calls, "Rest now on Me."

CHORUS.

Call - - ing for thee, . . . call - - ing for thee; . . . .
Calling for thee, calling for thee, Calling for thee, calling for thee,

Je - - sus is wait - ing and weeping and calling for thee. . .
Je- sus is waiting and weeping and calling, He's weeping and calling, is calling for thee.

# Jesus Waits to Come In.

E. E. Hewitt. Mrs. W. V. Baker.

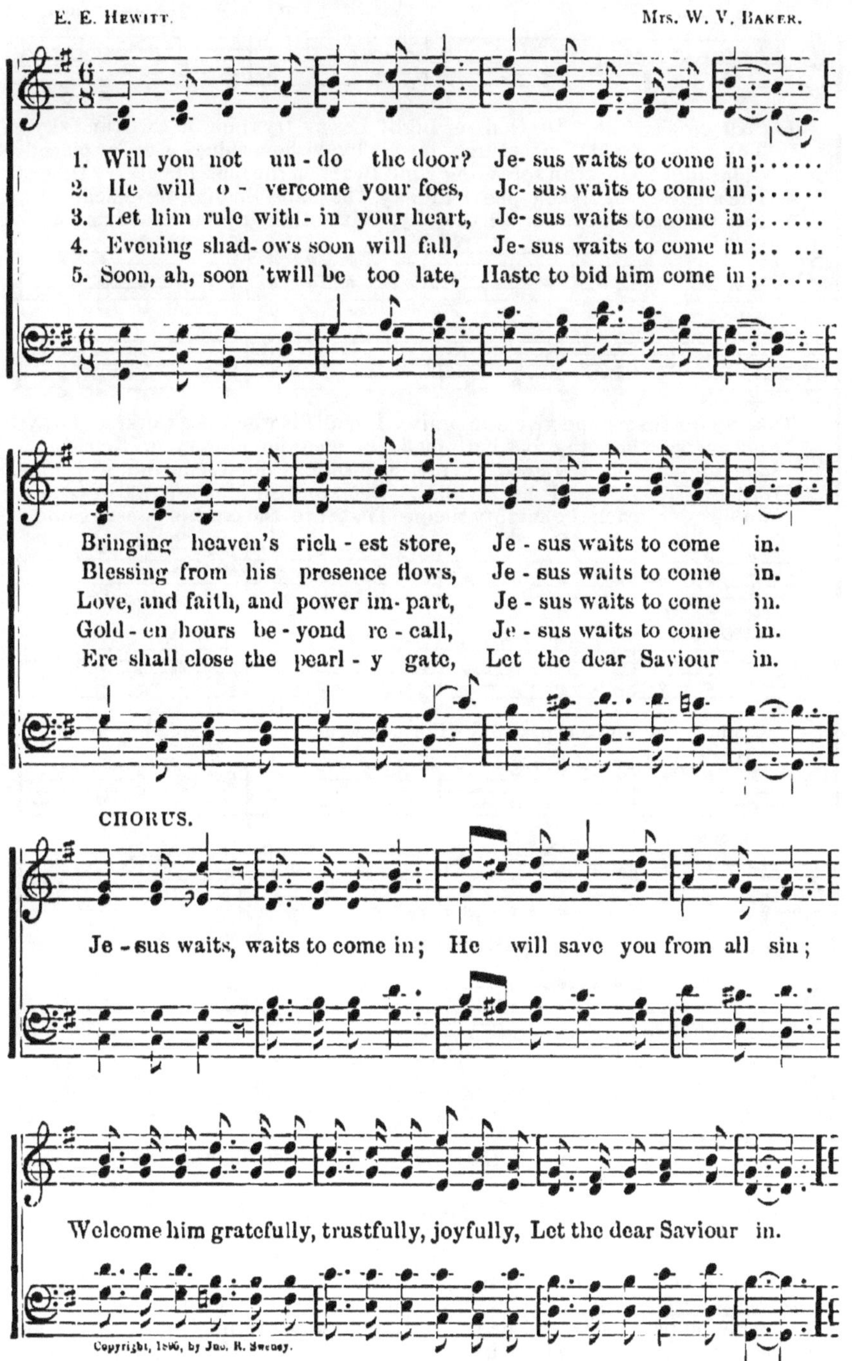
1. Will you not un - do the door? Je- sus waits to come in;......
2. He will o - vercome your foes, Je- sus waits to come in;......
3. Let him rule with - in your heart, Je- sus waits to come in;......
4. Evening shad- ows soon will fall, Je- sus waits to come in;.. ...
5. Soon, ah, soon 'twill be too late, Haste to bid him come in;......
Bringing heaven's rich - est store, Je - sus waits to come in.
Blessing from his presence flows, Je - sus waits to come in.
Love, and faith, and power im- part, Je - sus waits to come in.
Gold - en hours be - yond re - call, Je - sus waits to come in.
Ere shall close the pearl - y gate, Let the dear Saviour in.
CHORUS.
Je - sus waits, waits to come in; He will save you from all sin;
Welcome him gratefully, trustfully, joyfully, Let the dear Saviour in.

# All Glory Be to God.

Rev M. M. Brabham
Wm. J. Kirkpatrick.
1. All glo- ry be to God on high! Let ev-'ry thing in earth and sky
2. Thy name is writ on nature's face, Thy wisdom shines in ev-'ry place;
3. The mighty o- cean spreading wide Bears on the face of ev- 'ry tide
4. The highest mounts that pierce the sky, The plains that far, out-reaching lie,
5. But earth and sea, and all the sky, With all their praises loud and high,
Take up the theme, and give him praise, For all his wondrous works and ways.
And ev- 'ry where thy foot hath trod Is seen the glo - ry of our God.
Some to- ken of thy good divine, And sounds aloud some praise of thine.
With ev - 'ry vale and ev- 'ry hill, Declare their Maker's praises still.
Can nev - er reach the mighty theme That thro' the cross of Jesus came.
CHORUS.
O praise the Lord, O praise the Lord, Let ev- 'ry creature sing a- loud!
Let man and beast, in earth and sea, Loud anthems bring, our Lord, to thee;
Yea, let the mu - sic of the spheres Thy praises ring thro' all the years.
Copyright, 1895, by Wm. J Kirkpatrick.

6 'Tis by the wonders of his cross
That men may count all things but loss,
And triumph over death and hell,
And sing aloud his praise to tell.

7 And by and by, beyond the tide,
When heaven's joys reach far and wide,
We'll join the mighty blood-washed throng,
And sing the everlasting song.

# He is Coming.

JAMES L. BLACK. "Behold, he cometh with clouds."—REV. i: 7. JNO. R. SWENEY

1. O hail, blessed morn, when the Lord as he promised, With pow'r and great glo- ry, in clouds shall de- scend; When loud- ly the voice of the mighty arch- an- gel Shall summon the nations their King to at- tend.
2. O hail, blessed morn, for thy dawn is approaching, Thy sig - nal of beauty looks forth like a star; It gleams thro' the mist and the dew on the mountain, The watchmen of Zi - on have seen it a - far.
3. O hail, blessed morn, when the children of Ju- dah Shall render to Je- sus their trib - ute of praise; Shall own and con - fess him their promised Mes - si - ah, And bow at his foot- stool the ancient of days.
4. O watch, for the hour of his coming we know not; O watch, with our lamps ev - er burning and bright, And then if he come at the dawn or the nightfall, We'll greet him with anthems of ho- ly de - light.
CHORUS.
He is coming to claim his own, He is coming to gather them home;
Home to mansions of bliss a- bove, Never, no, never in sorrow to roam.

# Joy and Light.

FANNY J. CROSBY. J. BARNBY.

1. Joy and light, joy and light, O- ver the crys- tal sea; Come, come, soft and bright, O- ver the crys- tal sea. Come on your snow - y pin- ions white, Come in the si - lent calm of night, Watch when the pale stars keep, Bring the troubled one, bring the weary one sleep. . . .
2. Love and rest, love and rest, Car- ol in sil - ver tone; Glad songs, pure and blest, Car- ol in sil - ver tone. Come from the fade- less flow'rs that grow, Come from the sparkling streams that flow, Come in the midnight deep, Bring the troubled one, bring the weary one sleep. . . .
3. Voice di- vine, voice di- vine, Speak and our souls shall hear; Sweet, sweet words are thine, Speak and our souls shall hear. Tell of a cloudless re - gion fair, Tell of the ma - ny mansions there. Speak to the hearts that weep, Bring the troubled one, bring the weary one sleep. . . .
sf
p
mf
pp
f
rall. e dim.

# Ask and Receive.

Willie E. Smith.
Jno. R. Sweney.
1. Ask and receive, that your joy may be full, Words ever welcome to all;
2. Ask and receive, that our joy may be full, Ask in the Saviour's dear name;
3. Ask and receive, that our joy may be full, Ask that our joy may remain;
4. Ask and receive, that our joy may be full, Ask, it will surely be given;
Softly they come when the heart is oppressed, Sweeter than music they fall.
We who are children and heirs of a King, Riches unbounded may claim.
Then we are read- y for all that may come, Sorrow, af - fliction or pain.
Joy that is perfect, a - biding and sure, Born of our Father in heaven.
CHORUS.
Ask and receive, trust and believe, Je- sus has taught us to ask and receive;
Ask and receive, trust and believe, Oh, blessed promise, ask and receive.
Copyright, 1891, by Jno. R. Sweney.

# One Thing I Know.

E. E. Hewitt. Wm. J. Kirkpatrick.

SOLO OR QUARTET.
1. One thing I know; . . oh, bless his name, . . To me the Lord . . of mercy
2. One thing I know; . . he heard my cries, . With mighty power he touched my
3. One thing I know; . . he died for me, . . In him my hope, . my trust shall
4. One thing I know; . . the Saviour's mine, . Oh, boundless grace, . . oh, joy di-
5. One thing I know; . . oh, help me sing . . Such happy praise . . to Christ our
One thing I know; oh, bless his name, To me, the Lord
came, . . . He filled my heart . . with love's bright flame, . . . This I
eyes, . . . To see the light . . . that never dies, . . . . This I
be, . . . My Saviour lives . . . . e - ternal- ly, . . . . This I
vine! . . . And heavenly beams . . around me shine, . . . This I
King, . . . While smiling faith . . . and love upspring, . . . This I
of mercy came, He filled my heart with love's bright flame,
CHORUS.
know, . . . this I know. I know, I know, . . . . he loved me
This I know, I know, I know,
so, . . . . He saved my soul . . . . from sin and woe, . . Now peace and
He loved me so, He saved my soul from sin and woe,

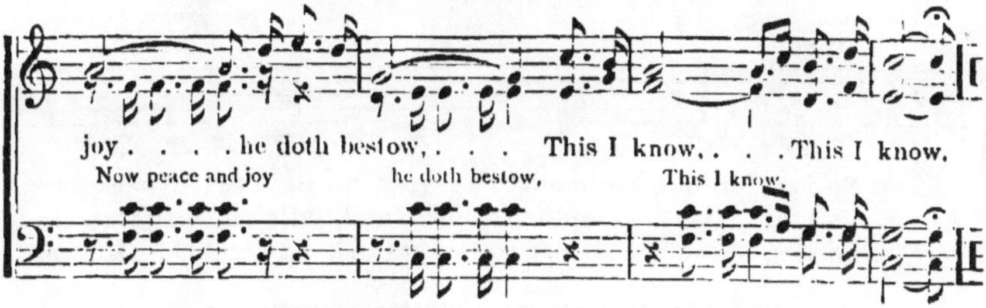

## One Thing I Know.—CONCLUDED.

joy . . . . . he doth bestow, . . . . This I know, . . . . This I know.
Now peace and joy he doth bestow, This I know.

# Why not To-night?

J. S. H.

Oh! do not let the Word depart, Nor close thine eyes against the Light,

Poor sinner, harden not your heart, Thou would'st be saved, why not to-night?

REFRAIN.
Rit.
Why not to-night? why not to-night? Thou would'st be saved, why not to-night?

2 To-morrow's sun may never rise
  To bless thy long-deluded sight,
This is the time, oh, then, be wise!
  Thou would'st be saved, why not to-night?

3 Our God in pity lingers still,
  And wilt thou thus his love requite?
Renounce at length thy stubborn will,
  Thou would'st be saved, why not to-night?

4 The world has nothing left to give,
  It has no new, no pure delight;
Oh, try the life which Christians live,
  Thou would'st be saved, why not to night?

5 Our blessed Lord refuses none
  Who would to him their souls unite,
Then be the work of grace begun,
  Thou would'st be saved, why not to-night?

# No Longer Wait.

F. N. Riggs.
Jno. R. Sweney.
DUET.
1. No long - er wait, my brother, e - ven now God's Spir- it seeks an entrance to your heart; Come to the cross, and to the Saviour bow, Un- bar the door, make haste lest he de- part.
2. No long - er wait, O sad and troubled soul, His pard'ning grace he of- fers free to all; O wea - ry one, that grace will make you whole, Oh, why not hear the loving Saviour's call?
3. No long - er wait, the Lord your God has said, I will not strive for- ev- er with your heart; Oh, come ere yet the spark of life has fled, And thou hast failed to choose the better part.
CHORUS.
O sin- ner, come to Christ the living Way, Still he is plead - ing, why not come to- day?

# Will You Come to Jesus.

Mrs. Frank A. Breck.
H. L. Gilmour.
1. Will you come to the Saviour? he invites you to-day, Will you come, come to Jesus, will you come? Come, oh, come to the fountain that will wash guilt away,
2. You are sad, you are weary with the wrong, bitter past, Will you come, come to Jesus, will you come? On his heart of compassion you shall know peace at last,
3. Take his blest yoke upon you, it will ease the oppressed, Will you come, come to Jesus, will you come? Will you learn of the lowly One who giveth you rest?
4. Are you longing for pardon? Jesus waits to forgive, Will you come, come to Jesus, will you come? To the cross of redemption will you look, will you live?
Will you come, come to Jesus, will you come?
Fine.
CHORUS.
Will you come to Jesus? will you come to Je-sus? Lowly at his bleeding feet to bow?
come
come
Will you let him take your sin, Let him make you pure within?
D.S.
D. S.—Will you come, will you come to Jesus now?

# Made Whole.

Jno. W. Beebe. Wm. J. Kirkpatrick.

1. The press was great, the throng was wild, And I, a sin- ner all defiled, How
2. Who touch'd me? hear the dear Lord say!
The throng was awed, the mass gave way, And
3. "Thou seest all these people, Lord, And yet thou seekest by thy word To
4. Go thou in peace, oh, hear him say! From all thy plague be healed this day; Oh,
could I reach my Saviour? Reach him I must, without de- lay; And
I stood near my Saviour. Who touch'd me? came the gracious word; New
find who touch'd thee, Saviour?" 'Twas thus that his dis - ci - ples said, But
what a bless - ed Saviour! To heal the bod - y, save the soul. The
in the press, with fear, dismay, I, trembling, sought my Saviour. 1, 2, 3. His
life-blood thro' my being stirred, For I had touch'd my Saviour.
I be - fore him bowed my head, I knelt be- fore my Saviour.
vil - est of the vile make whole, Oh, how I love my Saviour. 4. His
CHORUS.
words were full of comfort. They cheer'd my weary soul. For I had touch'd his gar-[ment,
words are full of comfort. Oh, how they cheer my soul! By faith I touch his garment,
ritard.
His grace had made me whole, For I had touch'd his garment, His grace had made me whole.
He makes me clean and whole. By faith I touch his garment, He makes me clean and [whole.

# Another Day Closes.

WM. H. GARDNER. H. L. GILMOUR.

1. Guide us, dear Jesus, thro' sunshine and sorrow, Safe till we en-ter thy mansions a-bove; May we with faith view the coming to-morrow, Cir-cle us, Lord, with the arms of thy love.
2. Guide us, dear Jesus, thro' thorns and thro' roses, Strength'ning our tired and wea-risome feet; Here, while up-on us an-oth-er day clos-es, Pour out, O Sav-iour, a blessing most meet.
3. Guide us, dear Jesus, across death's dark river, Show us the way to the fountains of rest; From sin's do-minion O grant to de-liv-er, Give us a place in thy mansions so blest.
CHORUS.
Help us and guide us, O Jesus, our Saviour, O-ver us angels in watchfulness keep; And till the morning, beneath thy protection, May we secure-ly and peacefully sleep.

# Your Mother is Praying for You.

Mrs. Frank A. Breck. H. L. Gilmour.

*With feeling.*

1. Tho' far you may stray, tho' you cir- cle the earth, The pleasures of
2. How gent- ly she pillowed your head on her breast. When you were an
3. How oft she has prayed for the child of her care, With love that for-
4. Oh, come to her Saviour and know of his love, His grace will your
5. It may not be long you will have her to pray, The days of her

life to pursue; Tho' you weep in your sadness, or sing in your mirth,
in - nocent child; How she tenderly soothed you and hushed you to rest,
ev - er is new; Will you let her to- day know an answer to prayer?
spir - it re- new; Will you fly to his heart like a worn, weary dove?
life may be few; Will you choose then the God of your mother to-day,

Your moth- er is pray - ing for you.
And sweetly your sor - rows beguiled.
Your moth- er is pray - ing for you.
Your moth- er is pray - ing for you.
Just while she is pray - ing for you?

CHORUS.

Your mother is pray- ing, *pp* pray - ing. With love that is ten - der and true; You may wander a-

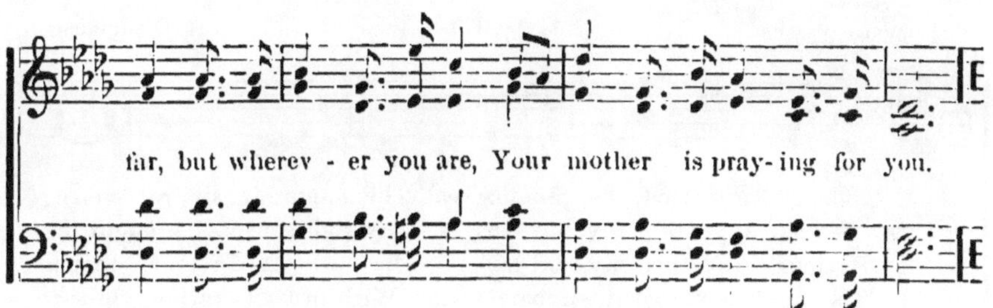
far, but wherev - er you are, Your mother is pray- ing for you.

# Weeping will not Save Me.

"For by grace are ye saved through faith."—Eph. ii: 8.

R. L. R. Lowry.

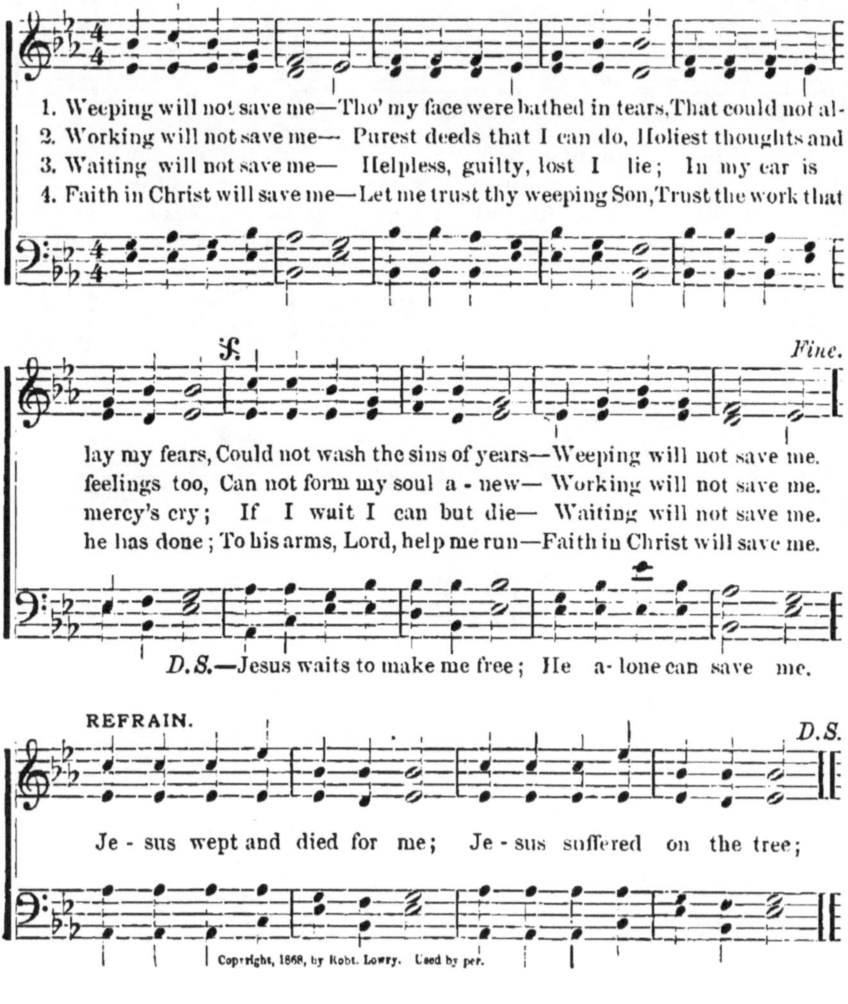

1. Weeping will not save me—Tho' my face were bathed in tears, That could not allay my fears, Could not wash the sins of years—Weeping will not save me.
2. Working will not save me— Purest deeds that I can do, Holiest thoughts and feelings too, Can not form my soul a - new— Working will not save me.
3. Waiting will not save me— Helpless, guilty, lost I lie; In my ear is mercy's cry; If I wait I can but die— Waiting will not save me.
4. Faith in Christ will save me—Let me trust thy weeping Son, Trust the work that he has done; To his arms, Lord, help me run—Faith in Christ will save me.

*Fine.*

*D.S.*—Jesus waits to make me free; He a- lone can save me.

REFRAIN.

Je - sus wept and died for me; Je - sus suffered on the tree;

*D.S.*

# The Victory of Faith.

Charles Wesley. (Cho. by H. L. G.) H. L. Gilmour.

1. Come, O my God, the promise seal, This mountain, sin, re - move;
2. I want thy life, thy pur - i - ty, Thy righteousness, brought in:
3. Saviour, to thee my soul looks up, My present Saviour thou!
4. 'Tis done! thou dost this moment save, With full sal - vation bless;

Now in my waiting soul re- veal The vir - tue of thy love.
I ask, de - sire, and trust in thee To be redeemed from sin.
In all the con - fi- dence of hope, I claim the blessing now.
Re- demption thro' thy blood I have, And spotless love and peace.

CHORUS.

'Tis done! 'tis done! I do believe, The blood now cleanseth me;
My pen - te- cost has ful- ly come, By trusting, Lord, in thee.

Pressing Toward the Mark.
199
E. E. Hewitt.
Jno R. Sweney.
1. Let us press toward the mark, tho' it shines far above, With the ar- dor of faith and the courage of love, Leaning hard on the arms that will fail not nor tire, And our spirits aglow with the heavenly fire.
2. Let us not be content with the progress we've made, Looking up un- to Jesus, we'll not be dismayed, For his hand ever helps us in running the race; And he shows in our weakness the triumph of grace.
3. They who wait on the Lord shall their strength still renew, Then we'll prove the [sweet promise is evermore true; Lord, we yield up our lives to thy wonderful power; Helps us press toward the mark thro' the sunshine and show'r.
CHORUS.
Pressing on, toward the mark, pressing on, toward the mark, When the day is sunny, when the sky is dark; Pressing on, toward the mark, pressing on, toward the mark, Till we reach the prize before us, and the crown is won.
Copyright, 1896, by Jno. R. Sweney.

# Will Jesus Find us Watching?

Fanny J. Crosby. W. H. Doane.

1. When Je - sus comes to re - ward his servants, Whether it be
2. If at the dawn of the ear - ly morning, He shall call us
3. Have we been true to the trust he left us? Do we seek to
4. Bles - sed are those whom the Lord finds watching, In his glo - ry
noon or night, Faith - ful to him will he find us watching,
one by one, When to the Lord we re - store our tal - ents,
do our best? If in our hearts there is naught condemns us,
they shall share; If he shall come at the dawn or midnight,
rit.
REFRAIN.
With our lamps all trimm'd and bright. Oh, can we say we are
Will he ans - wer thee—Well done?
We shall have a glo - rious rest.
Will he find us watch - ing there?
rea - dy, brother? Rea - dy for the soul's bright home? Say, will he
find you and me still watching, Waiting, waiting when the Lord shall come?

# Zerah. C. M.

Dr. L. Mason.

**201** **Come, ye that love.**

1 Come, ye that love the Saviour's name,
And joy to make it known,
The Sovereign of your hearts proclaim,
And bow before his throne.

2 Behold your Lord, your Master crowned
With glories all divine;
And tell the wondering nations round
How bright those glories shine.

3 When, in his earthly courts, we view
The glories of our King,
We long to love as angels do,
And wish like them to sing.

4 And shall we long and wish in vain?
Lord, teach our songs to rise:
Thy love can animate the strain,
And bid it reach the skies.

**202** **What glory gilds.**

1 What glory gilds the sacred page!
Majestic, like the sun,
It gives a light to every age;
It gives, but borrows none.

2 The power that gave it still supplies
The gracious light and heat;
Its truths upon the nations rise;
They rise, but never set.

3 Lord, everlasting thanks be thine
For such a bright display,
As makes a world of darkness shine
With beams of heavenly day.

4 My soul rejoices to pursue
The steps of him I love,
Till glory breaks upon my view
In brighter worlds above.

**203** **The Prince of Peace.**

1 To us a Child of hope is born,
To us a Son is given;
Him shall the tribes of earth obey,
Him, all the hosts of heaven.

2 His name shall be the Prince of Peace,
Forevermore adored;
The Wonderful, the Counselor,
The great and mighty Lord.

3 His power, increasing, still shall spread;
His reign no end shall know;
Justice shall guard his throne above,
And peace abound below.

4 To us a Child of hope is born,
To us a Son is given;
The Wonderful, the Counselor,
The mighty Lord of heaven.

**204** **The joyful sound.**

1 Salvation! O the joyful sound
What pleasure to our ears!
A sovereign balm for every wound,
A cordial for our fears.

2 Salvation! let the echo fly
The spacious earth around,
While all the armies of the sky
Conspire to raise the sound.

3 Salvation! O thou bleeding Lamb!
To thee the praise belongs:
Salvation shall inspire our hearts,
And dwell upon our tongues.

**205** **Doxology. C. M.**

To Father, Son, and Holy Ghost,
The God whom we adore,
Be glory, as it was, is now,
And shall be evermore.

# 206 Jesus, the Name.

C. Wesley. Tune, CORONATION. C. M.

1. Je - sus! the name high o - ver all, In hell, or earth, or sky;
2. Je - sus! the name to sin- ners dear, The name to sin-ners given;

An - gels and men be - fore it fall, And dev - ils fear and fly.
It scat - ters all their guilt - y fear; It turns their hell to heaven.

An- gels and men be - fore it fall, And dev - ils fear and fly.
It scat-ters all their guilt - y fear; It turns their hell to heaven.

3 Jesus the prisoner's fetters breaks,
And bruises Satan's head;
Power into strengthless souls he speaks,
And life into the dead.

4 O that the world might taste and see
The riches of his grace!
The arms of love that compass me
Would all mankind embrace.

5 His only righteousness I show
His saving truth procla m:
'Tis all my business here below,
To cry, "Behold the Lamb!"

6 Happy, if with my latest breath
I may but gasp his name;
Preach him to all, and cry in death,
"Behold, behold the Lamb!"

## 207 Crown Him Lord of All. C. M.

1 All hail the power of Jesus' name!
Let angels prostrate fall;
Bring forth the royal diadem,
And crown him Lord of all.

2 Crown him, ye morning stars of light,
Who fixed this earthly ball;
Now hail the strength of Israel's might,
And crown him Lord of all.

3 Ye chosen seed of Israel's race,
Ye ransomed from the fall,
Hail him who saves you by his grace,
And crown him Lord of all.

4 Sinners, whose love can ne'er forget
The wormwood and the gall,
Go, spread your trophies at his feet,
And crown him Lord of all.

5 Let every kindred, every tribe,
On this terrestrial ball,
To him all majesty ascribe,
And crown him Lord of all.

6 O that with yonder sacred throng
We at his feet may fall!
We'll join the everlasting song,
And crown him Lord of all.

## Antioch. C. M.

208 **O for a thousand tongues**

1 O FOR a thousand tongues, to sing
My great Redeemer's praise;
The glories of my God and King,
The triumphs of his grace!

2 My gracious Master and my God,
Assist me to proclaim,
To spread through all the earth abroad,
The honors of thy name.

3 Jesus! the name that charms our fears,
That bids our sorrows cease;
'Tis music in the sinner's ears,
'Tis life, and health, and peace.

4 He breaks the power of canceled sin,
He sets the prisoner free;
His blood can make the foulest clean;
His blood availed for me.

5 He speaks, and, listening to his voice,
New life the dead receive;
The mournful, broken hearts rejoice;
The humble poor believe.

6 Hear him, ye deaf; his praise, ye dumb,
Your loosened tongues employ;
Ye blind, behold your Saviour come;
And leap, ye lame, for joy.

209 **Joy to the world!**

1 JOY to the world! the Lord is come;
Let earth receive her King;
Let every heart prepare him room,
And heaven and nature sing.

2 Joy to the world! the Saviour reigns;
Let men their songs employ;
While fields and floods, rocks, hills and plains,
Repeat the sounding joy.

3 No more let sin and sorrow grow,
Nor thorns infest the ground;
He comes to make his blessings flow
Far as the curse is found.

4 He rules the world with truth and grace,
And makes the nations prove
The glories of his righteousness,
And wonders of his love.

210

## The Lord's Prayer.

*Reverently.*

1. Our Father which art in heaven, hallowed | be thy | name, || Thy kingdom come, thy will be done in | earth, as-it | is in | heaven.

2. Give us this day our | daily | bread, || And forgive us our trespasses, as we forgive | them that | trespass a- | gainst us.

3. And lead us not into temptation, but deliver | us from | evil; || For thine is the kingdom, and the power and the | glory for- | ever and | ever. || A- | men.

## 211 The Morning Light.

SAMUEL F. SMITH. Tune, WEBB. 7, 6.

1 The morning light is breaking,
The darkness disappears;
The sons of earth are waking
To penitential tears;
Each breeze that sweeps the ocean
Brings tidings from afar,
Of nations in commotion,
Prepared for Zion's war.

2 See heathen nations bending
Before the God we love,
And thousand hearts ascending
In gratitude above;
While sinners, now confessing,
The gospel call obey,
And seek the Saviour's blessing,
A nation in a day.

3 Blest river of salvation,
Pursue thine onward way;
Flow thou to every nation,
Nor in thy richness stay:
Stay not till all the lowly
Triumphant reach their home:
Stay not till all the holy
Proclaim, "The Lord is come!"

## 212 GEO. DUFFIELD, Jr. Stand up, stand up for Jesus. Tune above.

1 STAND up, stand up for Jesus,
Ye soldiers of the cross;
Lift high his royal banner,
It must not suffer loss;
From victory unto victory
His army shall he lead
Till every foe is vanquished
And Christ is Lord indeed.

2 Stand up, stand up for Jesus,
The trumpet call obey:
Forth to the mighty conflict,
In this his glorious day:
"Ye that are men, now serve him,"
Against unnumbered foes:
Your courage rise with danger,
And strength to strength oppose.

3 Stand up, stand up for Jesus,
Stand in his strength alone;
The arm of flesh will fail you;
Ye dare not trust your own:
Put on the gospel armor,
Each piece put on with prayer;
Where duty calls, or danger,
Be never wanting there.

4 Stand up, stand up for Jesus,
The strife will not be long;
This day the noise of battle,
The next the victor's song:
To him that overcometh,
A crown of life shall be;
He with the King of glory
Shall reign eternally.

## 213 Work, for the Night is Coming.

WORK, for the night is coming,
Work through the morning hours;
Work, while the dew is sparkling,
Work 'mid springing flowers;
Work, when the days grow brighter,
Work in the glowing sun;
Work, for the night is coming,
When man's work is done.

2 Work, for the night is coming,
Work through the sunny noon;
Fill brightest hours witn labor,
Rest comes sure and soon,
Give every flying minute
Something to keep in store:
Work, for the night is coming,
When man works no more.

3 Work, for the night is coming,
Under the sunset skies;
While their bright tints are glowing.
Work, for daylight flies.
Work till the last beam fadeth,
Fadeth to shine no more;
Work while the night is darkening,
When man's work is o'er.

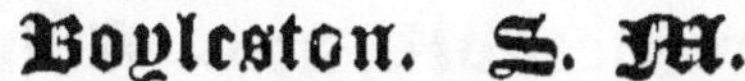

# Boylston. S. M.

Lowell Mason

## 214 And can I yet Delay?

And can I yet delay
My little all to give?
To tear my soul from earth away
For Jesus to receive?

2 Nay, but I yield, I yield;
I can hold out no more:
I sink, by dying love compelled,
And own thee conquerer.

3 Though late, I all forsake;
My friends, my all resign:
Gracious Redeemer, take, oh, take
And seal me ever thine.

4 Come, and possess me whole,
Nor hence again remove;
Settle and fix my wavering soul
With all thy weight of love.

## 215 A Charge to Keep I Have.

A charge to keep I have,
A God to glorify;
A never-dying soul to save,
And fit it for the sky.

2 To serve the present age,
My calling to fulfill,—
Oh, may it all my powers engage
To do my Master's will.

3 Arm me with jealous care,
As in thy sight to live;
And oh, thy servant, Lord, prepare,
A strict account to give.

4 Help me to watch and pray,
And on thyself rely,
Assured, if I my trust betray,
I shall forever die.

# Laban. S. M.

## 216 Come, Ye that Love the Lord.

Come, ye that love the Lord,
And let your joys be known;
Join in a song with sweet accord,
While ye surround his throne.

2 Let those refuse to sing
Who never knew our God,
But servants of the heavenly King
May speak their joys abroad.

3 The men of grace have found
Glory begun below;
Celestial fruit on earthly ground
From faith and hope may grow:

4 Then let our songs abound,
And every tear be dry;
We're marching through Immanuel's [ground,
To fairer worlds on high.

## 217 My Soul, be on Thy Guard.

My soul, be on thy guard,
Ten thousand foes arise,
And hosts of sin are pressing hard
To draw thee from the skies.

2 Oh, watch, and fight, and pray,
The battle ne'er give o'er,
Renew it boldly every day,
And help divine implore.

3 Ne'er think the victory won,
Nor once at ease sit down;
Thine arduous work will not be done
Till thou hast got the crown.

4 Fight on, my soul, till death
Shall bring thee to thy God:
He'll take thee, at thy parting breath,
Up to his blest abode.

## 218 My Beloved and Friend.

"This is my Beloved, and this is my Friend."—Canticles v: 16.

VIRGINIA W. MOYER. H. L. GILMOUR.

1. The world may sing its siren song, May lure where love and laughter blend;
2. Though I may suffer loss and death, No human arm its strength may lend;
3. The judgment has no fears for me, I safe shall be when mountains rend;

It has no charm to win my soul, For Christ my Lover is, and Friend.
The bruised reed he will not break, For Christ my Lover is, and Friend.
My Lord is my suf - fi - ciency, And he my Lov- er is, and Friend.

*D. S.*—Fairest to my inward gaze, My soul's enraptured with the sight.

Oh, Christ is my Beloved and Friend; I lean on him with such delight, The

## 219 Rich are the Gifts.

"Freely ye have received, freely give."—Matt. x: 8.

MAY MAURICE. WM. J. KIRKPATRICK.

1. Rich are the gifts that our Father in heav'n Scattered so lavishly here;
2. Speaketh the Saviour in accents of love, "Ye who my word have believed,
3. "Give to the needy and never withhold, So have ye done it to me,

# Rich are the Gifts.—CONCLUDED.

Countless the blessings his bounty has given To brighten each passing year.
Freely bestow, lest ungrateful ye prove, For freely have ye re- ceived."
Give of your talent, your strength and your gold, Christ giveth his life for thee."
CHORUS.
Praise ye the Lord for the Gift of his grace, The wonderful Gift of his love;
With grateful hearts raise a tribute of praise To him who reigneth a-bove.
220
Tell it to Jesus.
Fanny J. Crosby.
W. H. Doane.
1. Broken in spirit And laden with care, Sweet is thy refuge, Find it in pray'r.
2. Art thou neglected And sighing to know Joys that in friendship Tenderly flow?
3. Art thou recalling The years that have fled, Weeping in sorrow, Mourning the dead?
4. Bear thy affliction, Whatever it be, Jesus, thy Saviour, Bore it for thee.
CHORUS.
Tell it to Je-sus, Tell it to Jesus, Tell it to Jesus, He'll give relief.
Copyright, 1889, by W. H. Doane. Used by per.

221 Tell Me of Jesus.
H. L. G.
H. L. Gilmour.
1. Tell me, O tell me of Je - sus, I'm weary and worn to - night;
2. Tell me, O tell me of Je - sus, As his foot-prints marked the way;
The day tho' gone leaves a shadow, But mem'ries of him bring light;
Thro' olive glen up the mountain, When seeking repose to pray.
Fine.
D. S.—Longing for glad de- liv'rance, Still hoping for rest, sweet rest.
D. S.—Rippling in soft rythmic accent, To the step of the Naz-a - rene.
D. S.
Speak of his lov- ing compassion, As the suff'ring a- bout him pressed,
Tell how by Kedron's dark wa-ter, So tinged, by a thousand lambs slain,
Copyright, 1895, by H. L. Gilmour.
3 Tell me, O tell me of Jesus,
In gloomy Gethsemane's shade;
So woven by intertwined olives
The secret place, where he prayed.
Tell of the cross, and the thorn-crown
Deridingly placed on his brow;
Tell of his solid-rock casket;
O tell, he's ascended now.
222 Give Your Heart to Jesus.
L. E. J.
L. E. Jones.
1. Wander- er in ways of sin, Give your heart to Je- sus; To his
2. Come to him, he is the door, Give your heart to Je- sus; Come, re-
3. Come in faith, his word believe, Give your heart to Je- sus; Pardon
Copyright, 1895, by H. L. Gilmour.

Give Your Heart to Jesus.—CONCLUDED.
CHORUS.
rest come, enter in, Give your heart to Jesus. He is calling you to-day,
pent, and sin no more, Give your heart to Jesus.
thro' the blood receive, Give your heart to Jesus.
Why in paths of evil stray? Leave, oh, leave the barren way, Give your heart to Jesus
223 There Shall I Be Satisfied.
E. E. Hewitt.
Wm. J. Kirkpatrick.
Solo, if preferred.
1. In the land of peace and gladness, Just beyond the silent tide, Where the heart for-
2. Sat-is-fied to be like Jesus, And his blessed face behold, Satisfied to
3. How it sweetens every duty, Looking forward with delight, To the home of
4. Comfort then the broken-hearted With the promise of the day, When the shadows
5. We will sing love's tender story In those Eden-bowers so fair, But the best of
gets its sadness, There shall I be sat-isfied, There shall I be sat-isfied.
sing his praises, In the city paved with gold, In the city paved with gold.
joy and beauty, With immortal radiance bright, With immortal radiance bright!
have departed, Every tear-drop wiped away, Every tear-drop wiped away.
heaven's glo-ry Is, to be like Jesus there, Is, to be like Jesus there.
Copyright, 1895, by Wm. J. Kirkpatrick.

224 H. L. Gilmour. Jesus, the Light. Arr. by H. L. G.
1 2 Fine.
1. { Let my gaze be fixed on thee, Jesus, the light of the world;
As I look, new beauties see, Jesus, the light . . . . of the world.
D.C.—Falling around us by day and by night,—Jesus, the light . . . of the world.
CHORUS. D.C.
Walk in the light, beautiful light, Come where the dew-drops of mercy are bright,
Copyright, 1893, by H. L. Gilmour
2 Let my hands be strong for thee,
Jesus, the light of the world;
And my feet be swift and free,
Jesus, the light of the world.
3 When the tempter would alarm,
Jesus, the light of the world;
Bare, oh, bare thy mighty arm,
Jesus, the light of the world.
4 Walk the waves, across life's sea,
Jesus, the light of the world;
Nearer come, O Lord, to me,
Jesus, the light of the world.
5 Be a shelter in the storm,
Jesus, the light of the world;
Keep, oh, keep thy child from harm,
Jesus, the light of the world.
225 E. E. Hewitt. A Song of Praise. Arr. by W. J. K.
1. My heart uplifts a happy song, While tender rec-ollections throng;
2. Have sparkling sunbeams cheered the day, And roses bloomed along the way?
3. Or have the clouds o'erspread the sky, While at my feet the roses die?
4. Bright angels, sweep your harps of gold, But half his praise hath not been told;
And above the rest this note shall swell, This note shall swell, this note shall swell,
As sweet as bells that ring above, The strains that breathe my Saviour's love.
Let mem'ry each fair scene recall, And bless the Lord who sent them all.
Since Je-sus bore the cross for me, I'll trust him tho' I cannot see.
Come, all who my Redeem-er know, Still let the joy-ful mu-sic flow.
Copyright, 1894, by Wm. J. Kirkpatrick.
And above the rest this note shall swell, My Jesus hath done all things well.

226 **Leaning on the Everlasting Arms.**

Rev. E. A. Hoffman. A. J. Showalter.

1. What a fel-lowship, what a joy divine, Leaning on the ev-er-
2. Oh, how sweet to walk in this pilgrim way, Leaning on the ev-er-
3. What have I to dread, what have I to fear, Leaning on the ev-er-
last-ing arms; What a bless-ed-ness, What a peace is mine,
last-ing arms; Oh, how bright the path grows from day to day,
last-ing arms? I have bless-ed peace with my Lord so near,
REFRAIN.
Lean-ing on the ev-er-last-ing arms. Lean - ing,
Lean-ing on the ev-er-last-ing arms.
Lean-ing on the ev-er-last-ing arms. Lean-ing on Je-sus,
lean - ing, Safe and se-cure from all a-larms;
Lean-ing on Je-sus,
Lean - ing, lean - ing, Leaning on the ev-er-lasting arms.
Lean-ing on Je-sus, lean-ing on Je-sus,

By per. A. J. Showalter.

# 227 Wayside Communion.

"And they said one to another, did not our heart burn within us, while he talked with us by the way."—Luke xxiv: 32.

H. L. Gilmour. Arr. and har. by H. L. G.

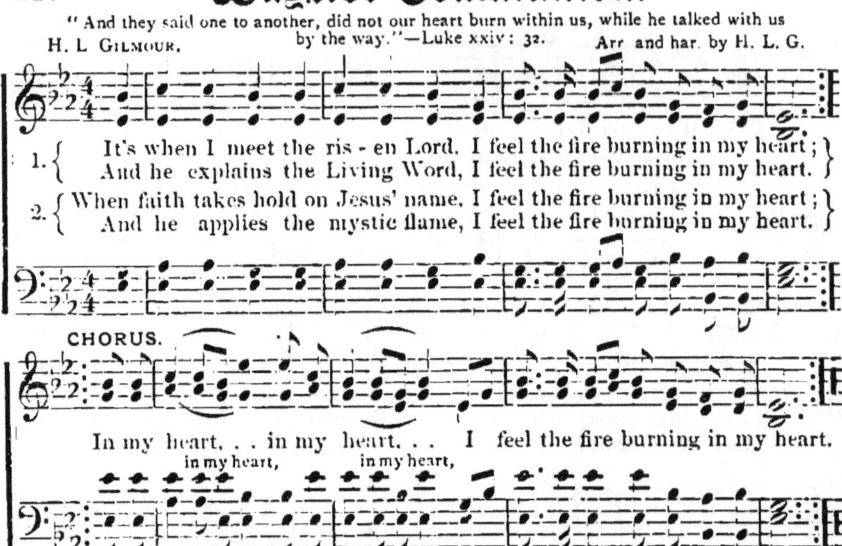

1. It's when I meet the ris - en Lord, I feel the fire burning in my heart;
And he explains the Living Word, I feel the fire burning in my heart.
2. When faith takes hold on Jesus' name, I feel the fire burning in my heart;
And he applies the mystic flame, I feel the fire burning in my heart.
CHORUS.
In my heart, . . in my heart, . . I feel the fire burning in my heart.
in my heart,
in my heart,

3 It's when anointed from above,
I feel the fire burning in my heart;
And witnessing for perfect love,
I feel the fire burning in my heart.

4 It's when glad vict'ry comes to greet,
I feel the fire burning in my heart;
A captive freed, at Jesus' feet,
I feel the fire burning in my heart.

*Music 130 in "Love and Praise No. 1."*

## 228 Brother, Will You Go? (*Copyr't.*)

AWAY beyond the stars which the midnight sky unfolds, [aces of gold;
There are scenes of rarest beauty, and pal-
And o'er that lovely prospect there falls no winter's snow,
:There warblers sing in endless spring,
O brother, will you go?:

2 There are cities rich in grandeur inviting you to come, [city home?
And who can tell the wealth of a heavenly
Its rural scenes, its mansions, its crystal streams that flow, [er, will you go?:
:All, all are free for you and me, O broth-

3 There leap the lame for joy, there the blind receive their sight;
There ears long closed to sound will be ravished with delight;
There tongues that never uttered a sentence here below, [er, will you go?:
:Burst into song thro' ages long, O broth-

4 But, one will meet us there who has been our heart's delight,
Whose praises we have sung through the sleepless hours of night:
How sweet the thought that Jesus we then shall see and know,
:Who by his grace prepared that place,
O brother, will you go?:

—W. Woodward.

*Music 252 in "Living Hymns."*

## 229 My Country.

My country! 'tis of thee,
Sweet land of liberty,
Of thee I sing:
Land where my fathers died!
Land of the pilgrims' pride!
From every mountain side
Let freedom ring!

2 My native country, thee,
Land of the noble, free,
Thy name I love:
I love thy rocks and rills,
Thy woods and templed hills:
My heart with rapture thrills
Like that above.

3 Let music swell the breeze,
And ring from all the trees
Sweet freedom's song:
Let mortal tongues awake;
Let all that breathe partake;
Let rocks their silence break,
The sound prolong.

4 Our fathers' God! to thee,
Author of liberty,
To thee we sing:
Long may our land be bright
With freedom's holy light;
Protect us by thy might,
Great God, our King!

# Save Thou Me.

Fanny J. Crosby. W. H. Doane.

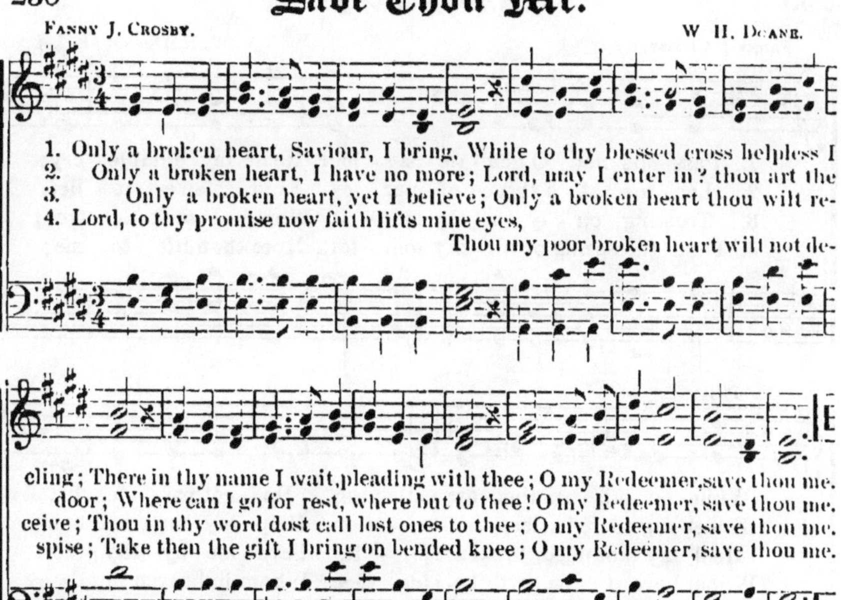
1. Only a broken heart, Saviour, I bring, While to thy blessed cross helpless I
2. Only a broken heart, I have no more; Lord, may I enter in? thou art the
3. Only a broken heart, yet I believe; Only a broken heart thou wilt re-
4. Lord, to thy promise now faith lifts mine eyes,
Thou my poor broken heart wilt not de-
cling; There in thy name I wait, pleading with thee; O my Redeemer, save thou me.
door; Where can I go for rest, where but to thee! O my Redeemer, save thou me.
ceive; Thou in thy word dost call lost ones to thee; O my Redeemer, save thou me.
spise; Take then the gift I bring on bended knee; O my Redeemer, save thou me.
Copyright, 1881, by W. H. Doane, used by per.

*Music No. 189 in "Love and Praise No. 1."*

## 231 Lord, I'm Coming Home. (*Copyr't.*)

I'VE wandered far away from God,
Now I'm coming home;
The paths of sin too long I've trod,
Lord, I'm coming home.

CHO.—Coming home, coming home,
Never more to roam;
Open wide thine arms of love,
Lord, I'm coming home.

2 I've wasted many precious years,
Now I'm coming home;
I now repent with bitter tears,
Lord, I'm coming home.

3 I'm tired of sin and straying, Lord,
Now I'm coming home;
I'll trust thy love, believe thy word,
Lord, I'm coming home.

4 My soul is sick, my heart is sore,
Now I'm coming home;
My strength renew, my hope restore,
Lord, I'm coming home.

5 My only hope, my only plea,
Now I'm coming home;
That Jesus died, and died for me,
Lord, I'm coming home.

6 I need his cleansing blood I know,
Now I'm coming home;
Oh, wash me whiter than the snow,
Lord, I'm coming home.—W. J. K.

*Music No. 218 in "Love and Praise No. 1."*

## 232 The Gospel Feast. (*Copyr't.*)

COME, sinners, to the gospel feast;
It is for you, it is for me;
Let every soul be Jesus' guest;
It is for you, it is for me.

CHO.—Salvation full, salvation free,
The price was paid on Calvary;
O weary wand'rer, come and see,
It is for you, it is for me.

2 Ye need not one be left behind,
For God hath bidden all mankind.

3 Sent by my Lord, on you I call;
The invitation is to all:

4 Come, all the world! come, sinner thou!
All things in Christ are ready now.

5 Come, all ye souls by sin oppressed,
Ye restless wanderers after rest;

6 Ye poor, and maimed, and halt and blind
In Christ a hearty welcome find.

7 My message as from God receive;
Ye all may come to Christ and live:

8 O let this love your hearts constrain,
Nor suffer him to die in vain.

9 See him set forth before your eyes,
That precious, bleeding sacrifice:

10 His offered benefits embrace,
And freely now be saved by grace.

## 233 Pass Me Not.

FANNY J. CROSBY. W. H. DOANE. By per.

1. Pass me not, O gen - tle Sav - iour, Hear my humble cry;
2. Let me at a throne of mer - cy Find a sweet re - lief;
3. Trusting on - ly in thy mer - it, Would I seek thy face;
4. Thou the spring of all my com - fort, More than life to me;
Fine.
While on oth - ers thou art call - ing, Do not pass me by.
Kneel- ing there in deep con- tri - tion, Help my un - be lief.
Heal my wounded, broken spir - it, Save me by thy grace.
Whom have I on earth be- side thee? Whom in heaven but thee?
D. S.—While on oth - ers thou art call - ing, Do not pass me by.
CHORUS.
D.S.
Sav - iour, Sav - iour, Hear my hum - ble cry,

*Music to in "Love and Praise No. 1."*

## 234 Salvation's River. *(Copyr't.)*

DOWN at the cross, on Calvary's mountain,
Where mercies flow,
I plunged in the redeeming fountain,
Washed whiter than the snow.
When nothing in the whole creation
Could purchase peace,
My Saviour brought his free salvation,
Gave me complete release.

CHO.—Brothers, won't you hear the story?
See the fountain flow!
Oh, glory in the highest, glory!
Jesus saves me, this I know

2 When lost in sin, my all I squandered,
Far from the fold:
My Saviour sought me where I wandered,
Gave me his wealth untold.
All bonds of sin and Satan rending,
Christ made me whole:
I'll ne'er forget that joy transcending,
When Jesus saved my soul.

3 All round my way the sun is shining,
Darkness has fled:
On Jesus' breast I am reclining,
Daily by him I'm fed.
My Lord has cast his robe around me,
No more I'll roam;
The Shepherd of the sheep has found me,
Jesus has brought me home.
—R. K. Carter.

*Music No. 75 in "Love and Praise No. 1."*

**235 Shall I Turn Back?** (*Copyr't.*)

LOST, lost on the mountain of sin and despair, [there,
Till Jesus in love, sought and rescued me
He saved me from wand'ring, he gave me release, [peace.
And led me to pathways of blessing and

CHO.—And shall I turn back into the
Oh, no! not I! not I! [world?
And shall I turn back into the world?
No, no, not I!

2 My days, swiftly passing, have brought from above
So many bright tokens of mercy and love;
"More grace" he has given, and burdens removed, [proved
Yes, over and over, his goodness I've

3 How well I remember, in sorrow's dark night, [light,
The lamp of his word shed its beautiful
And sweet was the voice of the Comforter then,
Awaking new praises again and again.

4 Before me the tow'rs of Jerusalem rise,
Each day I am nearing my home in the skies;
My Saviour a mansion of joy will prepare,
And loved ones are waiting to welcome me there. —E. E. Hewitt.

*Music No. 104 in "Love and Praise No. 1."*

**236 Thy Holy Spirit.** (*Copyr't.*)

THY Holy Spirit, Lord, alone
Can turn our hearts from sin,
His power alone can sanctify
And keep us pure within.

CHO.—O Spirit of Faith and Love,
Come in our midst, we pray,
And purify each waiting heart;
Baptize us with power to-day.

2 Thy Holy Spirit, Lord, alone
Can deeper love inspire,
His power alone within our souls
Can light the sacred fire.

3 Thy Holy Spirit, Lord, can bring
The gifts we seek in prayer,
His voice can words of comfort speak,
And still each wave of care.

4 Thy Holy Spirit, Lord, can give
The grace we need this hour,
And while we wait, O Spirit, come
In sanctifying power.

O Spirit of Love, descend,
[illegible] midst we pray,
[illegible] wind

*Music No. 90 in "Love and Praise No. 1."*

**237 He is Mine, I am His** (*Copyr't.*)

BLESSED Lily of the Valley, oh, how fair
He is mine, I am his; [is he!
Sweeter than the angel's music is his voice
He is mine, I am his. [to me,
Where the lilies fair are blooming by the waters calm,
There he leads me, and upholds me by his strong right arm;
All the air is love around me, I can feel no
He is mine, I am his. [harm,

CHO.—Lily of the valley, he is mine!
Lily of the valley, I am his! [to me.
Sweeter than the angel's music is his voice
He is mine, I am his.

2 Let me sing of all his mercies, of his
He is mine, I am his; [kindness true,
Fresh at morn, and in the evening, comes
He is mine, I am his! [a blessing new,
With the deep'ning shadows comes a whisper, "safely rest!
Sleep in peace, for I am near thee, naught shall thee molest;
I will linger till the morning, keeper, friend
He is mine, I am his. [and guest."

3 Tho' he lead me thro' the valley of the
He is mine, I am his; [shade of death,
Should I fear, when, oh, so tenderly he
He is mine, I am his! [whispereth,
For the sunshine of his presence doth illume the night,
And he leads me thro' the valley to the mountain height;
Out of bondage into freedom, into cloud-
He is mine, I am his. [less light.
—Grace Elizabeth Cobb.

*Music No. 108 in "Love and Praise No. 1."*

**238 Since I Found My Saviour.** (*Cop't.*)

LIFE wears a different face to me,
Since I found my Saviour;
Rich mercy at the cross I see,
My dying, living Saviour.

CHO.—Golden sunbeams 'round me play,
Jesus turns my night to day,
Heaven seems not far away,
Since I found my Saviour.

2 He sought me in his wondrous love,
So I found my Saviour,
He brought salvation from above,
My dear, almighty Saviour.

3 The passing clouds may intervene,
Since I found my Saviour,
But he is with me, though unseen,
My ever-present Saviour.

4 A strong hand kindly holds my own,
Since I found my Saviour,
It leads me onward to the throne,
Oh, there I'll see my Saviour!
—E. E. Hewitt.

*Music No. 31 in "Unfading Treasures."*

**239 It Just Suits Me.** (*Copyright.*)

WHAT a wonderful salvation!
For its length and breadth and height
Far excel the grandest knowledge
Of the seraphim in light;
I can never, never fathom
Half its holy mystery,
But I know it is for sinners,
And it just suits me.

CHO.—‖: It just suits me.:‖
This wonderful salvation,
It just suits me.

2 Oh, this blessed "whosoever,"
Calling every one who will,
To the sparkling, living waters,
Flowing fully, freely still;
No, I know not why he loves me,
But his blood is all my plea;
I can trust his "whosoever,"
For it just suits me.

3 Precious promises of Jesus,
Sweeping every human need!
For the grace of our Redeemer
Must our highest thought exceed;
To the mighty, royal storehouse
Let me use the golden key,
Find the special, tender promise
That will just suit me.

4 What a perfect, present Saviour!
What a true and loving friend!
Can we ever praise him lightly?
Tell how grace and glory blend?
Now the Prince of Peace is reigning,
Over-ruling all I see;
So, whatever lot he orders,
May it just suit me.—E. E. Hewitt.

*Music No. 106 in "Unfading Treasures."*

**240 Sunshine in the Soul.** (*Copyr't.*)

THERE's sunshine in my soul to-day,
More glorious and bright
Than glows in any earthly sky,
For Jesus is my light.

CHO.—Oh, there's sunshine, blesed sunshine, [roll;
When the peaceful happy moments
When Jesus shows his smiling face
There is sunshine in the soul.

2 There's music in my soul to-day,
A carol to my King,
And Jesus, listening can hear
The songs I cannot sing.

3 There's springtime in my soul to-day,
For when the Lord is near
The dove of peace sings in my heart,
The flowers of grace appear.

4 There's gladness in my soul to-day,
And hope, and praise, and love,
For blessings which he gives me now,
For joys "laid up" above.—E. E. [illegible]

*Music No. 93 in "Unfading Treasures."*

**241 Is my Name Written There.** (*Cop.*)

LORD, I care not for riches,
Neither silver nor gold;
I would make sure of heaven,
I would enter the fold.
In the book of thy kingdom,
With its pages so fair,
Tell me, Jesus, my Saviour,
Is my name written there?

CHO.—Is my name written there,
On the page white and fair?
In the book of thy kingdom,
Is my name written there?

2 Lord, my sins they are many,
Like the sands of the sea,
But thy blood, oh, my Saviour!
Is sufficient for me;
For thy promise is written,
In bright letters that glow,
"Though your sins be as scarlet,
I will make them like snow."

3 Oh! that beautiful city,
With its mansions of light,
With its glorified beings,
In pure garments of white;
Where no evil thing cometh,
To despoil what is fair;
Where the angels are watching—
Is my name written there?—M. A. K.

*Music No. 51 in "Unfading Treasures."*

**242 Stepping in the Light.** (*Copyr't.*)

TRYING to walk in the steps of the Saviour,
Trying to follow our Saviour and King;
Shaping our lives by his blessed example,
Happy, how happy, the songs that we bring.

CHO.—How beautiful to walk in the steps of the Saviour,
‖: Stepping in the light; :‖ [Saviour,
How beautiful to walk in the steps of the
Led in paths of light.

2 Pressing more closely to him who is leading. [way,
When we are tempted to turn from the
Trusting the arm that is strong to defend us
Happy how happy, our praises each day.

3 Walking in footsteps of gentle forbearance, [love,
Footsteps of faithfulness, mercy and
Looking to him for the grace freely promised,
Happy, how happy, our journey above.

4 Trying to walk in the steps of the Saviour, [Guide,
Upward, still upward we'll follow [illegible]
When we shall see him, "th[illegible]
beauty."
Hap[illegible]

*Music No. 195 in "Unfading Treasures."*

## 243 I Do Believe.

FATHER, I stretch my hands to thee;
No other help I know:
If thou withdraw thyself from me,
Ah! whither shall I go?

CHO.—I do believe, I now believe,
That Jesus died for me; [blood,
And thro' his blood, his precious
I shall from sin be free.

2 What did thine only Son endure,
Before I drew my breath!
What pain, what labor, to secure
My soul from endless death!

3 O Jesus, could I this believe,
I now should feel thy power;
And all my wants thou wouldst relieve,
In this accepted hour.

4 Author of faith! to thee I lift
My weary, longing eyes:
Oh, let me now receive that gift;
My soul without it dies.

5 Surely thou canst not let me die;
Oh, speak, and I shall live;
And here I will unwearied lie,
Till thou thy Spirit give.

6 How would my fainting soul rejoice
Could I but see thy face!
Now let me hear thy quickening voice,
And taste thy pardoning grace.
—Chas. Wesley.

*Music No. 69 in "Unfading Treasures."*

## 244 Glorious Fountain.

THERE is a fountain ‖: filled with blood, :‖
Drawn from Immanuel's veins,
And sinners, plunged ‖: beneath that
Lose all their guilty stains. [flood, :‖

CHO.—Oh, glorious fountain!
Here will I stay,
And in thee ever
Wash my sins away.

2 The dying thief ‖: rejoiced to see :‖
That fountain in his day,
And there may I, ‖: though vile as he, :‖
Wash all my sins away.

3 Thou dying Lamb, ‖: thy precious
Shall never lose its power, [blood: ‖
Till all the ransomed ‖: Church of God :‖
Are saved to sin no more.

4 E'er since by faith ‖: I saw the stream :‖
Thy flowing wounds supply,
Redeeming love ‖: has been my theme, :‖
And shall be till I die. —Cowper

*Music No. 109 in "Unfading Treasures."*

## 245 Even Me.

LORD, I hear of showers of blessing,
Thou art scatt'ring full and free—
Showers, the thirsty land refreshing;
Let some droppings fall on me.—
Even me, even me,
Showers the thirsty land refreshing;
Let some droppings fall on me.

2 Pass me not, O gracious Father!
Sinful though my heart may be;
Thou might'st leave me, but the rather
Let thy mercy fall on me.—
Even me, even me, etc.

3 Pass me not, O tender Saviour!
Let me live and cling to thee;
I am longing for thy favor;
Whilst thou'rt calling oh, call me.—
Even me, even me, etc.

4 Pass me not, O mighty Spirit!
Thou can'st make the blind to see;
Witnesser of Jesus' merit,
Speak the word of power to me,—
Even me, even me, etc.

5 Love of God, so pure and changeless;
Blood of Christ, so rich and free;
Grace of God, so strong and boundless,
Magnify them all in me.—
Even me, even me, etc.
—Mrs. E. Codner.

*Music No. 169 in "Unfading Treasures."*

## 246 The Beautiful Light. (*Copyr't.*)

JESUS is the light, the way,
‖: We are walking in the light; :‖
Shining brighter day by day,
We are walking in the beautiful
light of God.

CHO.—‖: We are walking in the light, :‖
We are walking in the light,
We are walking in the beautiful
light of God.

2 We who know our sins forgiven,
‖: We are walking in the light; :‖
Find on earth the joy of heaven,
We are walking in the beautiful
light of God.

3 As we journey here below,
‖: We are walking in the light; :‖
Oh, what joy and peace we know,
We are walking in the beautiful
light of God.

4 We will sing his power to save,
‖: We are walking in the light; :‖
We will triumph o'er the grave,
We are walking in the beautiful
light of God. —R. Kelso Carter.

*Music No. 149 in "Unfading Treasures."*

## 247 The Haven of Rest. (*Copyr't.*)

My soul in sad exile was out on life's sea,
So burdened with sin, and distrest,
Till I heard a sweet voice saying, make me your choice;
And I entered the "Haven of Rest!"

CHO.—I've anchored my soul in the haven
I'll sail the wide seas no more; [of rest,
The tempest may sweep o'er the wild, stormy deep,
In Jesus I'm safe evermore.

2 I yielded myself to his tender embrace,
And faith taking hold of the word,
My fetters fell off and I anchored my soul;
The haven of rest is my Lord.

3 The song of my soul, since the Lord made me whole,
Has been the OLD STORY so blest
Of Jesus, who'll save whosoever will have
A home in the "Haven of Rest!"

4 How precious the thought that we all may recline,
Like John the beloved and blest,
On Jesus' strong arm, where no tempest can harm,—
Secure in the "Haven of Rest!"

5 Oh, come to the Saviour, he patiently
To save by his power divine; [waits
Come, anchor your soul in the haven of
And say, "my Beloved is mine." [rest.

—H. L. Gilmour.

*Music No. 271 in "Unfading Treasures."*

## 248 Keep Close to Jesus. (*Copyr't.*)

WHEN you start for the land of heavenly
Keep close to Jesus all the way; [rest,
For he is the Guide and he knows the way
Keep close to Jesus all the way. [best,

CHO —‖: Keep close to Jesus. :‖
Keep close to Jesus all the way; [right,
By day or by night never turn from the
Keep close to Jesus all the way.

2 Never mind the storms or trials as you
Keep close to Jesus all the way; [go,
'Tis a comfort and joy his favor to know.
Keep close to Jesus all the way.

3 To be safe from the darts of the evil
Keep close to Jesus all the way; [one,
Take the shield of faith till the victory is
Keep close to Jesus all the way. [won.

4 We shall reach our home in heaven by and bye,
Keep close to Jesus all the way;
Where to those we love we'll never say good-bye,
Keep close to Jesus all the way.

—John Lane.

*Music No. 122 in "Unfading Treasures."*

## 249 At the Cross. (*Copyright.*)

ALAS! and did my Saviour bleed,
And did my Sovereign die?
Would he devote that sacred head
For such a worm as I?

CHO.—At the cross, at the cross,
Where I first saw the light, [way,
And the burden of my heart rolled a
It was there by faith
I received my sight,
And now I am happy all the day.

2 Was it for crimes that I had done,
He groaned upon the tree?
Amazing pity, grace unknown,
And love beyond degree!

3 But drops of grief can ne'er repay
The debt of love I owe;
Here, Lord, I give myself away,
'Tis all that I can do!

—I. Watts.

*Music No. 127 in "Unfading Treasures."*

## 250 Jesus Saves. (*Copyright.*)

WE have heard a joyful sound,
Jesus saves, Jesus saves;
Spread the gladness all around,
Jesus saves, Jesus saves;
Bear the news to ev'ry land, [waves,
Climb the steeps and cross the
Onward, 'tis our Lord's command,
Jesus saves, Jesus saves.

2 Waft it on the rolling tide,
Jesus saves, Jesus saves;
Tell to sinners, far and wide,
Jesus saves, Jesus saves;
Sing, ye islands of the sea,
Echo back, ye ocean caves,
Earth shall keep her jubilee,
Jesus saves, Jesus saves

3 Sing above the battle's strife,
Jesus saves, Jesus saves;
By his death and endless life,
Jesus saves, Jesus saves;
Sing it softly thro' the gloom,
When the heart for mercy craves,
Sing in triumph o'er the tomb,
Jesus saves, Jesus saves.

4 Give the winds a mighty voice,
Jesus saves, Jesus saves;
Let the nations now rejoice,
Jesus saves, Jesus saves;
Shout salvation full and free,
Highest hills and deepest caves,
This our song of victory,
Jesus saves, Jesus saves.

—Priscilla J. Owens.

*Music No. 248 in "Unfading Treasures."*

## 251 Fill Me Now. (*Copyright.*)

HOVER o'er me, Holy Spirit;
Bathe my trembling heart and brow;
Fill me with thy hallow'd presence,
Come, oh, come and fill me now.

CHO.—Fill me now, fill me now,
Jesus, come, and fill me now;
Fill me with thy hallow'd presence,—
Come, oh, come and fill me now.

2 Thou canst fill me, gracious Spirit,
Though I cannot tell thee how;
But I need thee, greatly need thee,
Come, oh, come and fill me now.

3 I am weakness, full of weakness;
At thy sacred feet I bow;
Blest, divine, eternal Spirit,
Fill with power, and fill me now.

4 Cleanse and comfort; bless and save me;
Bathe, oh, bathe my heart and brow!
Thou art comforting and saving,
Thou art sweetly filling now.

—Rev. E. H. Stokes, D. D.

*Music No. 350 in "Living Hymns."*

## 252 Love Divine.

LOVE divine, all love excelling,
Joy of heaven, to earth come down!
Fix in us thy humble dwelling!
All thy faithful mercies crown.
Jesus, thou art all compassion,
Pure, unbounded love thou art;
Visit us with thy salvation;
Enter ev'ry trembling heart.

2 Breathe, oh, breathe thy loving Spirit
Into every troubled breast!
Let us all in thee inherit,
Let us find that second rest.
Take away our bent to sinning;
Alpha and Omega be;
End of faith as its beginning,
Set our hearts at liberty.

3 Come, almighty to deliver,
Let us all thy life receive;
Suddenly return, and never,
Never more thy temples leave;
Thee we would be always blessing,
Serve thee as thy hosts above,
Pray, and praise thee without ceasing,
Glory in thy perfect love.

4 Finish then thy new creation;
Pure and spotless let us be;
Let us see thy great salvation,
Perfectly restored in thee:
Changed from glory into glory,
Till in heaven we take our place,
Till we cast our crowns before thee,
Lost in wonder, love, and praise.

—Charles Wesley.

## 253 A Little Talk.

THO' dark the night and clouds look black
And stormy overhead,
And trials of almost ev'ry kind
Across my path are spread;
How soon I conquer all,
As to the Lord I call—
A little talk with Jesus makes it right, all right.

CHO.—‖: A little talk with Jesus makes it right, all right, :‖
In trials of ev'ry kind,
Praise God, I always find,—
A little talk with Jesus makes it right, all right.

2 When those who once were dearest friends
Begin to persecute,
And those who once professed to love
Have silent grown and mute;
I tell him all my grief,
He quickly sends relief,—
A little talk with Jesus makes it right, all right.

3 And thus, by frequent little talks,
I gain the victory,
And march along with cheerful song,
Enjoying liberty;
With Jesus as my friend,
I'll prove until the end,
A little talk with Jesus makes it right, all right.

*Music No. 184 in "Love and Praise No. 1."*

## 254 Jesus for Me (*Copyr't.*)

JESUS, my Saviour, is all things to me,
Oh, what a wonderful Saviour is he:
Guiding, protecting, o'er life's rolling sea,
Mighty Deliv'rer—Jesus for me.

CHO.—‖: Jesus for me, :‖
All the time, everywhere,
Jesus for me.

2 Jesus in sickness, and Jesus in health,
Jesus in poverty, comfort or wealth,
Sunshine or tempest, whatever it be,
He is my safety:—Jesus for me.

3 He is my Refuge, my Rock, and my Tower,
He is my Fortress, my Strength and my Power;
Life Everlasting, my Day'sman is he,
Blessed Redeemer—Jesus for me.

4 He is my Prophet my Priest and my King,
He is my Bread of Life, Fountain and Spring;
Bright Sun of Righteousness, Day-star is he,
Horn of Salvation—Jesus for me.

5 Jesus in sorrow, in joy, or in pain,
Jesus my Treasure in loss or in gain;
Constant Companion, where'er I may be,
Living or dying—Jesus for me!

—Wm. J. Kirkpatrick.

# TOPICAL INDEX.

# INDEX.

Titles in CAPITALS; First lines in Roman type.

www.ingramcontent.com/pod-product-compliance
Lightning Source LLC
Chambersburg PA
CBHW030323270326
41926CB00010B/1487